The Illustrated Book of
Signs &
Symbols

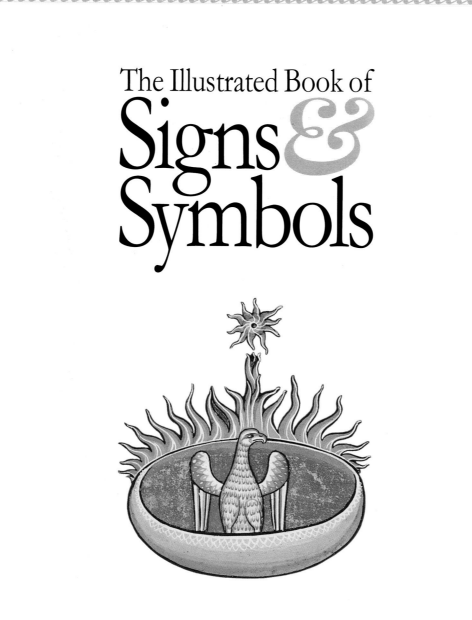

VISHNU, EMBODIMENT
OF LOVE, TRUTH,
AND MERCY

DIAMOND
CADUCEUS
BROOCH

RED ROSE OF
LOVE AND BEAUTY

MEDUSA, WITH HAIR
OF SNAKES

RAVEN TOTEM

The Illustrated Book of
Signs &
Symbols

Miranda Bruce-Mitford

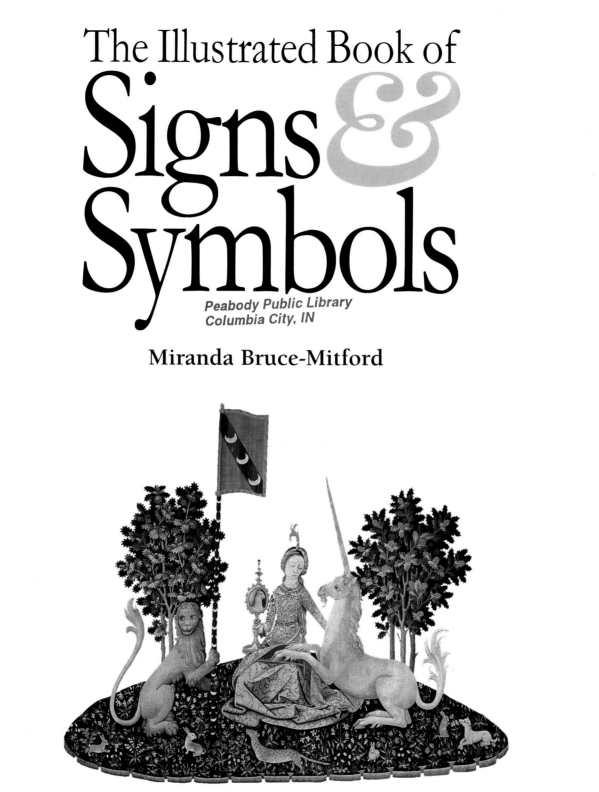

THE LION AND THE UNICORN TAPESTRY, C.1500

IVY, SACRED TO DIONYSUS

EGYPTIAN FUNERARY STELA (DETAIL)

ISLAMIC EYE OF WISDOM

A DK PUBLISHING BOOK

SENIOR EDITOR *Emma Foa*
US EDITOR *Camela Decaire*
SENIOR ART EDITOR *Sarah Ponder*
MANAGING EDITOR *Anna Kruger*
MANAGING ART EDITOR *Peter Bailey*
ART EDITORS *Joanna Pocock, Martin Wilson*
EDITOR *Shirin Patel*
ASSISTANT DESIGNER *Ali Cobb*
DTP DESIGNER *Nicola Studdart*
PICTURE RESEARCH *Sharon Southren*
PRODUCTION *Katy Holmes*
INDEX & GLOSSARY *Joanna Lane*

First American Edition, 1996
4 6 8 10 9 7 5
Published in the United States
by DK Publishing, Inc.,
95 Madison Avenue, New York, New York 10016
Visit us on the World Wide Web http://www.dk.com
Copyright © 1996 Dorling Kindersley Limited, London

A CIP catalog record for this book is available from the Library of
Congress.

ISBN 0-7894-1000-1

Colour reproduction by Colourscan, Singapore
Printed and bound in Spain by Artes Gráficas Toledo, S.A.
D.L. TO: 1192 - 1999

SHAMROCK

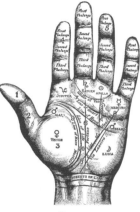

PALMISTRY

SHIVA, LORD OF THE DANCE

DANCE OF DEATH

CONTENTS

UROBOROS

INTRODUCTION

IT IS A FUNDAMENTAL PART OF HUMAN NATURE not only to survive and reproduce, but also to seek explanations for the mysteries of life. Because these mysteries are in fact beyond explanation, we use the language of symbolism to represent them. Whether we live in commercialized societies or communities relatively unchanged by time, we are surrounded by signs, images, and ideas that are often highly symbolic.

Signs in a familiar context

Most of us are largely unaware of the meaning and significance – even the presence – of much of this symbolism, and an area of great richness is closed to us. This book sets out to examine the nature of symbolism and to present, in simple terms, both familiar and unfamiliar symbols.

Alchemical symbol showing the serpent of Arabia, the triple sun, and the moon

SIGNS OR SYMBOLS?

A sign is an object or idea that represents or points to something else in a fairly straightforward way. An advertisement, for example, reminds us of the product it is promoting; a road sign indicates conditions ahead; and a gesture expresses a mood. As the modern world challenges our sense of identity, we often adopt signs to define ourselves, for example by donning badges or brand-name clothing.

A symbol is clearly linked in function to a sign, and the two words are often used interchangeably, but symbol generally has a deeper meaning. A symbol is something that through its nature or appearance reflects or represents another thing more profound than itself. A fire, for instance, may symbolize the flames of the sun, which itself has qualities of warmth, light, and creative power, and is thus equated with life force and masculine creative strength. The creator gods of mythology, who possess these very qualities, are usually linked to the sun. On a small scale, objects such as the candle or lamp can be also related to the imagery of the sun. A symbolic image is thus linked to many interpretations.

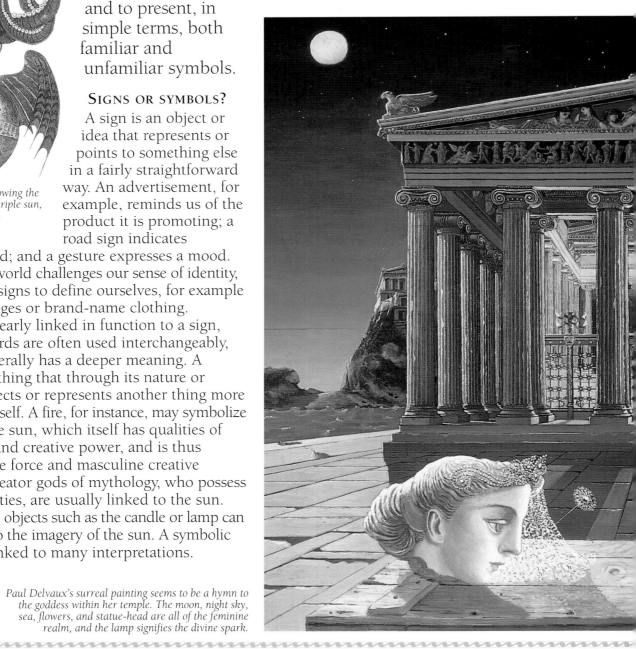

Paul Delvaux's surreal painting seems to be a hymn to the goddess within her temple. The moon, night sky, sea, flowers, and statue-head are all of the feminine realm, and the lamp signifies the divine spark.

ANCIENT SYMBOLS

Symbols grow in meaning and complexity over hundreds of years, changing according to their cultural context. But the subjects that have preoccupied mankind from the earliest times have remained relatively constant: fertility, both of the soil and of the human race, birth, life, and death.

Like the sun, the symbol of the moon has also always been recognized as significant because of qualities it possesses that relate in some way to deeper truths. The moon controls the tidal waters and passes through stages from new moon to full moon. It is thus symbolic of water, pregnancy, and the cycle of death and birth. Women, sea creatures, the dark, and things of the night all belong to the

Christ's sacrifice bears fruit of redemption for the faithful

sphere of the moon. *The Temple*, by Delvaux, combines much of this lunar imagery, with the full moon shining down on a mysterious goddess figure.

Animals, birds, and trees all have their individual associations, as well. A tree may represent life and growth, for example, and the Tree of Life is a symbol the world over. In the 16th-century engraving above, Christ is seen crucified on the Tree of Life, and his crucifixion can be viewed as a symbol of sacrifice. The death or sacrifice of a god or king is a common theme – the shedding of divine blood ensures the well-being of mankind.

Egyptian carving of bird in combat with snake

LOCKED IN COMBAT

Images of two creatures used to represent opposing forces are widespread. One form, found almost universally, shows a bird of prey doing battle with a serpent, perhaps the most symbolic of all creatures. Here the bird represents the sun and the heavens, while the serpent, which writhes on the ground and in the water, symbolizes the earth and

In Henri Pierre Picou's Homage to Nature, *summer revelers take their pleasures at the feet of the goddess*

Fate, or Fortuna, presides over the random turning of the wheel

the life-giving waters. The two together represent creation and fertility and the precariously balanced forces of nature.

UNIVERSAL SYMBOLS

The theme of the Goddess, or Earth Mother, permeates world mythology and dates back thousands of years. Clay figurines depicting large-breasted women in their nurturing, procreative role have been found dating from as early as 20,000 BC. All human life sprang from this symbolic mother figure and depended on her. The earth itself is regarded as feminine and nurturing because it is fertilized by rain, and life springs from its soil.

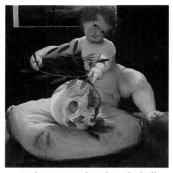

15th-century cherub with skull

Perplexed by the random, often cruel, nature of fate, some cultures chose to personify fate in the form of a woman. She is sometimes shown blindfolded to symbolize the arbitrary nature of her decisions.

Along with the randomness of life, the inevitability of death turns up in common symbolic images. These take many forms, from paintings showing a cherub juxtaposed with a human skull, to the more familiar image of sand ebbing out of an hourglass – all stark reminders of the fate that must befall us all.

However, although certain images are recognized as symbolic by many societies, the symbolism of a particular image may vary from place to place and over time. The forest, for example, is symbolic of retreat and meditation to many Indians, a place in which the soul may draw nearer to Brahman, the one true totality. However, in the West, the forest tends to be a sinister place, harboring dangerous animals and robbers, its shadows representing the dark places of the unconscious.

In The Cat that Walked by Himself, *the cat is "neither a friend nor a servant" to humankind*

CATS IN MYTHOLOGY AND THE IMAGINATION

The cat has captured our imaginations from ancient Egyptian times to the present day, although, like the forest, its symbolism has varied enormously. In farming communities the cat has always been a working animal, used to kill rats and mice, and there has been little mystique surrounding it; however something in the cat's nature and appearance has given it associations with the night, mystery,

Ancient Egyptian cat goddess Bastet

Tuesday, *by Leonora Carrington, combines bizarre, cat-like creatures in a personal dream sequence*

and aloofness. Black cats, now considered lucky in many places, were once associated with witchcraft, and cats feature prominently in children's stories. Both the Cheshire cat from *Alice's Adventures in Wonderland* and Kipling's *Cat that Walked by Himself* emanate mockery and enigma.

In ancient Egypt cats were worshiped and the cult of Bastet centered around a cat goddess. Images of cats were revered, and domestic cats were mummified at death so that, like people, they could enter an afterlife.

Lewis Carroll's Alice meets the enigmatic Cheshire cat

THE SYMBOLISM OF DREAMS

In many parts of the world dream symbolism is treated with respect. Wise men interpret dream images, often thought to be sent by the gods, and people act on these interpretations. In the West however, dreams are nowadays thought to be relatively unimportant, and the urgings of the unconscious mind go largely ignored by most people. The psychologist Sigmund Freud studied the symbolism of dreams and found

Goya's The Sleep of Reason Produces Monsters *shows how daytime fears can produce night-time terrors*

In this Indian miniature, men grapple with a giant trapped in a well, representing "the shadow," or base desires we try to bury in the unconscious.

much of it to be related to wish-fulfillment. He believed that dreams reflected our deepest desires, often rooted in infancy, and thought many had sexual or erotic overtones. His pupil Carl Jung believed that the symbolism went deeper than the purely sexual to include a spiritual dimension.

Jung was fascinated by the way in which ordinary objects or people appear in strange, often distressing, contexts in people's dreams and sought to understand why. Many images, he believed, appear in our dreams as a direct product of the individual unconscious, which is a highly personal amalgam of memories and emotions buried deep within us. Often we are not conscious of these impulses and they can only surface in dreams. A hairbrush, for instance, might trigger memories of one's hair being brushed by one's mother in childhood, so symbolizing a caring mother; however another individual might have been struck with a hairbrush in childhood, triggering very different associations. In Magritte's painting *The Restless Sleeper*, a figure dreams about a series of mundane and apparently unrelated objects, but they are all somehow linked meaningfully in his unconscious.

UNIVERSAL SUBCONSCIOUS

After analyzing the dreams of many patients, Jung concluded that certain images appear as symbols universally and are therefore part of what he called the collective unconscious, built on the cultural experiences and memories of our ancestors. Images of being pursued by a huge monster, of yearning for safety, or of dangers lurking in the dark, are very commonly experienced in dreams in all parts of the world.

Jung termed these universal images "archetypes." There is the "anima," or female principle, which can manifest as the goddess, queen, princess, or witch; and an "animus," or male principle, which could be a god, king, prince, wizard, or demon character. These figures symbolize for us our image of male and female and could represent either an aspect of ourselves, a parent, or a loved one.

Other archetypes include the shadow, embodiment of feelings of guilt or fear, particularly about our hidden and unacknowledged feelings or desires.

MODERN SYMBOLISM

In today's world, symbols retain their power to affect us, although we are perhaps less aware of their effects

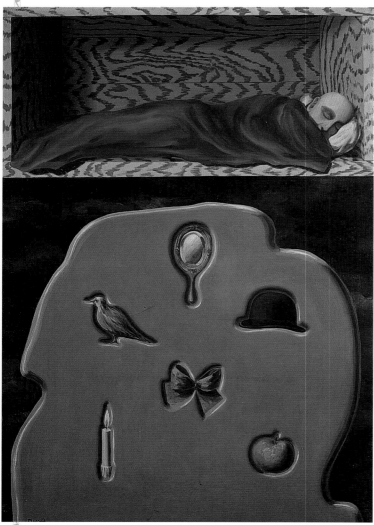

The images in Magritte's Restless Sleeper *seem disconcertingly simple*

Neil Armstrong makes "a giant leap for mankind"

The film star is often literally larger than life

than in the past. Some symbols have remained constant for centuries, some have evolved new meanings, and yet others are entirely new. One dramatic symbol to have emerged during the course of the twentieth century is the mushrooming cloud of the atomic bomb. This surely is the ultimate image of the great shadow of destruction that humankind has brought upon itself by opening the Pandora's box of knowledge.

A more positive image is the American moon landing from 1969. Witnessed by 600 million people throughout the world, it has become the ultimate symbol of man's indomitable spirit and urge for conquest.

TODAY'S GODS, GODDESSES, AND SUPERHEROES

Some modern fictitious characters assume semi-godlike status similar to that of the ancient Greek heroes. Creations such as Superman are not thought of as real, yet they embody the classic male archetype of the powerful and heroic force for good. In righting the wrongs of the world, such figures appeal to an innate need in all of us.

Superman is today's superhero – embodying all that is good and powerful

Also appealing to this need are the pop, sports, and film stars who, for some, have largely supplanted the gods of old. Since the death of "the King" Elvis Presley, for example, his home, Graceland, has become a shrine and place of pilgrimage for millions of devoted followers.

Sports heroes, too, attract a huge following, especially among men. The sense of group identity – and passion – they inspire is evident at any football stadium as hordes of fans cheer their heroes on in moments of shared admiration. Similar instinctual urges can be seen at rock concerts when members of the audience strike matches, light lighters, and hold up candles to express their devotion to their idols. The resultant sea of flickering flames harks back to the symbolism of fire in religions and cultures throughout history.

Audiences at rock concerts show their admiration and reverence by holding flames up to their heroes

MYTHOLOGIES & RELIGIONS

*O*ur search to explain what lies beyond our understanding is expressed in the many myths and religions that have evolved over the centuries. This quest has resulted in the complex web of myth, legend, and faith that is our inheritance – from nature religions and the almost human gods of ancient Greece to today's multiplicity of faiths.

ANCIENT DEITIES

THE CLASSICAL RELIGIONS of Europe and Egypt no longer exist as belief systems, but their mythology survives. Like modern-day Hinduism, these religions were centered around groups of gods who more or less controlled the lives of humans – and much of human activity involved the worship and placation of those gods. Many of these ancient gods live on in our imagination, and their symbolism has been absorbed into our language, our music, poetry, and art. It is hardly unusual to hear songwriters pay tribute to Venus, symbol of feminine beauty, or to Cupid's arrow piercing a lover's heart.

EGYPTIAN

Egyptian gods developed from the merging of two earlier cultures, one with gods in human form, and one with animal-shaped gods. Gradually a remarkable religion evolved that centered around the cult of the dead.

ISIS AND HORUS
Isis was the mother goddess, a queen, and the sister of Osiris. She is shown here suckling her son, Horus. Her crown is in the form of a throne, suggesting that she was originally a personification of the throne of the pharaohs.

THOTH
Depicted variously as an ibis-headed man and a baboon (the two animals sacred to him), Thoth is lord of the moon, lord of time, and reckoner of the years. He is the helper of the dead and protector of Osiris, ruler of the underworld.

OSIRIS
Originally a powerful fertility god, Osiris was drowned in the Nile River. His body was dismembered and scattered over the Nile valley, ensuring the growth of crops, which sprang from his flesh. He was later restored to life and became a symbol of resurrection, as well as the god of the underworld. He is often depicted in a mummylike posture.

AMUN-RE
The creator god, Amun, was merged with Re, the sun god, to form Amun-Re. Known as "the hidden one," Amun-Re was the power of the invisible wind and the soul of all things. Even the other gods were unable to penetrate his mysterious nature.

ANUBIS
Originally the jackal-headed god of the dead, Anubis was supplanted by Osiris. He was nevertheless the protector of the dead, and was often carved on rock tombs.

SKY GODDESS, NUT
Nut was the sky goddess of Egyptian mythology and she is often depicted touching the earth with her toes and fingers. The arch of her body represents the arc of heaven. The stars on her body denote the Milky Way, and she is sometimes surrounded by astrological signs.

GREEK

In the second millennium BC, Aegean religion revolved around the cult of the mother goddess, but later the center of civilization moved to the mainland, where the Greeks worshiped divinities who fought, squabbled, and loved, just like humans.

Zeus's thunderbolt, symbol of his power

ZEUS
Zeus was king of the gods and god of the skies. His well-known amorous conquests reflect the Greek conquest of many outlying regions, and the absorption of their mother goddess cults.

APOLLO
Apollo, twin brother of Artemis and son of Zeus, was the sun god, and caused the fruits of the earth to ripen. His arrows were the sun's rays. He was also god of shepherds and music.

ATHENA
The daughter of Zeus, Athena was the goddess of wisdom and learning, but also of warfare (hence her helmet). Often depicted with an owl, she was the patron of Athens – her owl is the emblem of that city.

EROS
Known to the Romans as Cupid, Eros was a symbol of earthly love. He was the son of Aphrodite, and carried a bow and arrows with which he pierced the hearts of his victims, causing them to fall passionately in love.

POSEIDON
Brother of Zeus and god of the sea, Poseidon (the Roman Neptune) was symbolic of the power of the waters. He carried a trident, symbol of creation, and could protect those at sea.

ROMAN

The Romans absorbed elements of all the cultures they came into contact with. They adopted the Greek gods as well as those of other peoples they conquered, and had hundreds of different gods, goddesses, demigods, and spirits – each of which related to virtually every aspect of life. They honored and worshiped the gods in order to safeguard themselves – in this life and the next.

MINERVA
The warlike Minerva often wears armor. Like her Greek counterpart Athena, she represents the arts, wisdom, and learning.

MARS
The son of Jupiter and Juno, Mars was the much-respected god of war. He is usually depicted with a spear in one hand and a shield in the other. The month of March comes from his name.

MERCURY, JUPITER, JUNO, APOLLO
Mercury was the god of commerce. He appeared late in the pantheon, at a time when trade flourished. He is sometimes equated with the Greek god Hermes, messenger of the gods. Here he weighs Trojan against Greek to decide the victor of the Trojan War. With him are: Jupiter (the Greek Zeus); Juno, wife of Jupiter and goddess of light, marriage, and childbirth; and Apollo, son of Jupiter.

FLORA
Flora was the goddess of spring, the vine, fruit, flowers, and grain, and she symbolized fertility. Festivals in her honor were often wild events.

BACCHUS
Usually depicted as a beautiful youth, Bacchus was the god of wine, and his worship featured much drunken revelry.

CELTIC

Although the pre-Roman Celts of Europe and the British Isles adopted some of the gods of the conquering Romans, they had their own beliefs in a creator god, a mother goddess, and nature gods. A trio of mother or fertility goddesses are sometimes presented together.

Antler-headed god

CERNUNNOS
The horned god Cernunnos is found throughout the Celtic lands. Here he is shown with antlers, surrounded by animals. In his left hand he holds a ram-headed serpent, symbol of fertility.

NORSE

The Nordic people, who lived in a harsh climate, worshiped gods of the elements and nature. By respecting and honoring the gods, they hoped to exert some control over the fierceness of the weather.

THE BIRTH OF APHRODITE/VENUS

The name Aphrodite means "born from the foam," and in Greek myth the goddess was said to have appeared from the sea, emerging from a scallop shell. The image captured the imagination of poets and painters through the ages: English poet Alfred Lord Tennyson wrote of "Aphrodite beautiful, fresh as the foam." Then, as now, Aphrodite symbolized love and beauty. Her Roman equivalent, Venus, is equally famous. Below, in Botticelli's painting, the god of the West Wind is gently blowing the beautiful Venus toward the shore, where a nymph awaits ready to cloak her.

GREEK SCULPTURE OF APHRODITE

ROMAN BRONZE
STATUE OF VENUS

The nymph wears a garland of myrtle, the tree of Venus

THE BIRTH OF VENUS, SANDRO BOTTICELLI, C.1482

ODIN, THOR, FREY
This 12th-century tapestry depicts three Norse deities. Odin, god of war and intelligence, could transform himself into whatever shape he wanted. Thor was feared as the god of thunder, whose hammer, when thrown, caused lightning. Frey was a god of fertility and birth.

JUDAISM

JUDAISM EMERGED IN ABOUT THE 14TH CENTURY BC and has evolved into a strongly monotheistic religion based on a dialogue between God, or Yahweh, and his chosen people, the Jews. The patriarchs of Judaism are the ancient leaders Abraham, his son Isaac, and grandson Jacob, whose deeds are recorded in Genesis, the first book of the Bible. Today Jews are scattered throughout the world, but all are linked by a culture centered on Jewish history, law, and family life.

The two triangles symbolize the balance of the universe

STAR OF DAVID
Allied to Jewish mysticism, the star of David is made up of two triangles, the upward-pointing being the sun, fire, and masculine energy; the downward-pointing the moon, water, and female energy.

"Servant candle," used to light the others

HANUKKAH
This 8-armed menorah is used to celebrate Hanukkah, the festival of lights. Candles are lit on 8 consecutive nights to mark the miracle of a day's supply of sacramental oil lasting 8 days, when the eternal light in the temple of Jerusalem was relit in 164 BC.

JERUSALEM
Holy to Judaism, Islam, and Christianity, Jerusalem was the capital of the ancient Jewish kingdom and site of the second temple, built 3,000 years ago. To Jews the city has come to symbolize the Jewish nation.

MEDIEVAL VIEW OF JERUSALEM

MEZUZAH
Traditionally the mezuzah is positioned by the front door. It contains a tiny scroll, or *shema*, with words from the Bible. This calls on God's people to love him totally, and sums up the heart of the Jewish faith.

SHOFAR
The shofar horn signals Rosh Hashanah, the Jewish New Year, and calls on the Jews to repent their sins before the Day of Atonement. The shofar is made of a ram's horn as a reminder of the animal God gave to Abraham to sacrifice in place of Isaac.

SHOFAR

ASPECTS OF PRAYER
Prayer plays an important part in Judaism, both in the synagogue and at home. More fervent Jews pray three times a day, and all Jews say prayers on the sabbath, their holy day, which starts at sunset on Friday. The sabbath marks the Israelites' liberation from slavery and the forming of a Jewish nation.

SILVER PRAYER BOOK

PRAYER BOOK
This silver prayer book was probably a Bar Mitzvah gift, celebrating a boy's official coming of age at thirteen.

WESTERN WALL
This is the only wall that survives from the Temple of Jerusalem, destroyed by the Romans in AD 70. It is a symbol both of the temple itself and of the Jewish nation, and is the most holy place of pilgrimage and worship.

KIPPAH

TEFIILLIN

KIPPAH & TEFILLIN
Male Jews wear a skull-cap, or *kippah*, as a sign of respect for God. The small leather boxes, or *tefillin*, contain passages from the Torah and are also worn while praying.

BOY AT PRAYER
This boy has the ritual tefillin strapped around his arm and on his forehead. The wearing of "God's words" in this way is thought to foster humility. The boy also wears a *tallit*, or prayer shawl, which has a tassel at each corner, symbolizing the four corners of the earth.

TORAH
The Torah is the Jewish law, and contains 613 commandments – God's instructions to the people of Israel. Because the Torah scrolls represent the word of God, they are considered so sacred that no one may touch them. They may be unrolled only by means of the handles.

Woven leaves of palm, myrtle, and willow, representing the spine, the eyes, and the mouth

TORAH SCROLL

YAD, OR POINTER

The crown is a symbol of the Torah because the Torah is the crowning glory of Jewish life

TORAH MANTLE
Torah scrolls are often traditionally covered in an embroidered mantle, which both protects them and reinforces their aura of preciousness.

Lulav is carried around the temple seven times at Sukkot

CITRUS FRUIT (ETROG OR CITRON), SYMBOL OF THE HEART

MOSES DESCENDING FROM MOUNT SINAI, AFTER DORE, 1865

THE BIRTH OF JEWISH LAW
During the Jewish people's long journey from Egypt, where they had been slaves, God spoke to Moses, their leader, and made a pact, or covenant, with them. His Ten Commandments to the Jews were written in fire on tablets of stone and set out a moral and religious code of conduct for his chosen people.

SUKKOT
The festival of sukkot commemorates the way God provided for the Jews as they wandered in the wilderness on their way to the Promised Land. Festive huts are built, and leaves of palms, myrtle, and willow are woven into a lulav to symbolize the tents that gave them shelter.

PASSOVER
The Passover festival commemorates the Exodus of the Jews from Egypt, when the angel of death "passed over" the Israelites, sparing their lives. At the Passover seder, or ritual meal, all the foods are symbolic of that journey.

Egg is the symbol of sacrifice

Fresh lettuce for frugal meals eaten in slavery

Shank of lamb recalls lambs killed at the first Passover

SALTWATER
A dish of saltwater represents the tears shed by the Jews during their long years in captivity.

Bitter herbs represent the bitterness of slavery

Nut and fruit paste represent bricks and mortar used to build cities in Egypt

"Pesach," Hebrew for Passover

MATZAH
The flat, unleavened matzah bread is eaten as a reminder of the haste with which the Israelites fled from Egypt.

MATZAH

PASSOVER PLATE
The seder plate forms the centerpiece of the table in a Passover meal. It contains portions of all the ceremonial foods that play a part in the story of the Exodus of the Jews from Egypt.

HOLY ARK
The Ark of the Covenant was a portable wooden chest overlaid with gold that contained the original Torah. The Jews carried it from the desert to the Temple in Jerusalem. Today, Torah scrolls are housed in a symbolic "holy ark" behind a curtain in the wall of the synagogue that faces Jerusalem.

CHRISTIANITY

CHRISTIANITY HAS ITS ROOTS in the Jewish faith and its belief of the Bible prophecies of a Messiah (savior). Christians believe these prophecies were fulfilled in the life of Jesus, who they believe is the Son of God. His teachings, recorded in the gospels of the New Testament, stress brotherly love and compassion, and are rich in symbolic meaning. Since its birth 2,000 years ago the Christian church has split into many denominations, but all Christians are united in the central belief that Christ died to redeem the sins of the world and that his resurrection offers salvation.

SACRED LAMB
The sacrificial lamb is a symbol of Christ. John the Baptist described him as "the lamb of God that taketh away the·sins of the world." In this crozier (bishop's crook) the lamb stands for the salvation of the faithful.

JESUS CHRIST
This modern Russian icon shows Christ blessing in the manner of the Eastern church. The thumb forms a circle with the fourth finger and the middle and index fingers are crossed. This represents Chi and Rho, the first two Greek letters of his name. Icons are seen as embodying spiritual truths.

THE VIRGIN MARY
In the Eastern and Roman Catholic churches Mary, Jesus' mother, is worshiped in her own right. She intercedes between man and God, and is often called Mother of God. The cult of Mary is similar to some mother goddess cults, and arose out of the need for a mother figure.

FISH
The fish is a symbol of Christ because in Greek the first letters of the five words Jesus Christ, Son of God, Savior, spell Ichthus, or fish. Three fishes together represent the Trinity: the Father, the Son, and the Holy Spirit.

ROSARY
The rosary is both the repetition of the prayer "Hail Mary" and also the string of beads used to count each incantation. It takes its name from the rose, symbol of Mary.

DOVE
John the Baptist saw the Holy Spirit enter Jesus in the form of a dove.

CROWN OF THORNS
The crown of thorns Christ was made to wear has become a symbol of his crucifixion.

THE CROSS

The cross has many forms: St. Peter was crucified upside down; Constantine's combines the first two letters for Christ in Greek; an anchor combines the cross with a crescent, symbol of Mary; and the Russian cross includes the inscription and the footrest of the crucifix.

DANISH CRUCIFIX, GILDED COPPER OVER CARVED OAK

CRUCIFIX
The image of Christ on the cross, the crucifix, is an object of Christian devotion. It is the most powerful symbol of Christianity, a reminder that although Jesus died on the cross, he rose again, triumphing over death.

ST. PETER'S CROSS

CONSTANTINE'S CROSS

ANCHOR CROSS

RUSSIAN CROSS

Circle of sun and eternity

CELTIC CROSS
The ring on a Celtic cross, symbol of Irish Christianity, stands for the sun and eternity.

Spire, God's finger pointing to heaven

CHURCH
The church refers both to Christian believers and also to a place of worship. The central part of a church, the nave, is named after the Latin for ship, symbol of the church itself.

SAINTS

Christian saints were particularly devout people who lived – and often died – for the Christian cause and have since been canonized by the church. There are thousands of saints, and many of them are depicted in sculpture and paintings carrying attributes related to their life or manner of death. St. Francis, for instance, is seen with birds or animals, and St. Catherine sometimes carries a wheel. St. John the Baptist carries his severed head on a platter.

SERBIAN ICON PAINTING, 1645

MARY MAGDALENE
A former prostitute, St. Mary Magdalene represents the penitent sinner.

PERUVIAN NATIVITY SCENE

NATIVITY
Jesus was born in a stable, and his whole life was lived in simplicity. Such humble beginnings emphasize the spiritual nature of his teachings as opposed to material richness.

JOHN THE BAPTIST
John the Baptist was the last of the Old Testament prophets and Jesus' first disciple. He foretold the coming of Christ and baptized him. He was beheaded at the wish of Herod's wife and her daughter, Salome, and his head was presented to them on a plate.

ST. CHRISTOPHER
St. Christopher carried a child across a river – the child was Christ, or the world itself. St. Christopher is the patron of travelers.

COMMUNION

At his last supper with his disciples, Jesus broke bread and poured wine, which he blessed and shared among them, saying that they were his body and blood. By imitating his actions at the communion service, Christians partake ritually of the body and blood of Christ.

BREAD
Bread symbolizes the body of Christ. In communion it takes the form of a wafer.

WINE
The wine drunk at communion is the blood of Christ, shed for mankind.

CATHERINE'S WHEEL
St. Catherine died for her Christian beliefs, crucified on four flaming wheels – hence her symbol is the wheel.

THE FOUR APOSTLES, ALBRECHT DÜRER, 1523-26

FRANCIS OF ASSISI
St. Francis embodies purity and simplicity. He is said to have preached to the birds.

MEDIEVAL BOOK OF HOURS

RELIGIOUS BOOKS
The Bible consists of the Old and the New Testaments, the latter dealing with the life and teachings of Jesus and his apostles. For some, the Bible is the direct word of God. Books of Hours were meditations, often on religious themes, for different times of the day.

FOUR APOSTLES
The Apostles were sent out by Christ to preach the Gospel. St. John (left), one of the writers of the Gospel, carries his book. Next to him, Peter holds the keys to the kingdom of Heaven. Paul holds a sword and a letter, symbolizing his manner of martyrdom and letters to the churches he founded. On the right Mark, like John, holds the Gospel.

SEE ALSO

JESUS CHRIST ☞
UNICORN 28; PHOENIX 31; WHEAT 46; SEA CREATURES 54; ANCHOR 97

THE VIRGIN MARY ☞
THE LANGUAGE OF THE ROSE 51; THE LILY AND CHRISTIANITY 53, 106; STARFISH 55; BEES IN CHRISTIANITY 56

HINDUISM

HINDUISM IS THE MAJOR RELIGION OF INDIA. It has evolved over millennia and encompasses a complex range of traditions, religious beliefs, philosophy, and mythology. The roots of Hinduism can be traced to the Aryans, who arrived in India with a pantheon of male gods in the second millennium BC. The indigenous Indus valley peoples already had strong religious beliefs centered on fertility cults and a Mother Goddess. The Aryans adopted many of their beliefs, including the Goddess. All the gods and goddesses of Hinduism, including Brahma (creator), Vishnu (preserver), Shiva (destroyer), and the Goddess are aspects of Brahman, the one eternal principle.

Brahma's four heads face the four points of the compass

The conch, symbolizing creation and transience

The chakra, wheel of existence

KRISHNA
An incarnation of Vishnu, Krishna embodies divine love. His adventures are recorded in the *Bhagvat Purana*. Here he is a naughty child stealing butter.

BRAHMA
The four heads of Brahma, the creator, symbolize the four quarters, the four Vedas, or religious texts, and the four castes of Hinduism. Brahma has become less important than Vishnu, Shiva, and the Goddess.

The many hands symbolize the many aspects of the deity

HANUMAN
Hanuman, the mighty monkey general of the epic *Ramayana*, represents loyalty, religious devotion, and courage.

SHIVA
Originally a mountain god, Shiva, meaning auspicious, is the god of destruction. But, in a world of endless rebirths, destruction precedes creation. He may be worshiped as a *linga*, or phallic symbol, as an ascetic, as a teacher, or in his form as dancer in the great dance of creation and destruction.

Lotus, symbol of creation and purity

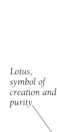

Many signs represent the universe, contained within the god

Club, symbol of authority

DURGA
Durga is the ferocious form of the Mother Goddess and wields various weapons in her ten hands. She stands for the more active, destructive aspects of feminine nature.

GANESHA
Ganesha overcomes all obstacles and is the god of new ventures. He has the head of an elephant, and so can forge through the thickest jungle. In myth Shiva mistakenly beheaded the god, and only an elephant's head could be found as a replacement.

VISHNU
Originally connected with the sun, Vishnu is the preserver of the universe and the embodiment of love, truth, and mercy. To his worshipers he is the supreme being from whom everything emanates. He rides on Garuda, the fabulous bird, or rests on Ananta, the cosmic serpent. Vishnu has been incarnated on earth in nine *avatars*, or incarnations, some human, some animal. The tenth incarnation, the horse avatar, is yet to come.

OM

This is a sacred syllable thought to be the "seed" of all *mantras*, divine and powerful words or sounds. The sound, pronounced A-U-M, is thought to be the one eternal syllable, in which the past, present, and future exist.

SWASTIKA

In India the swastika is an auspicious mark worn as jewelry or marked on objects as a symbol of well-being. Counterclockwise swastikas are sometimes considered inauspicious. The symbol, which predates Hinduism, is associated with the sun and the wheel of birth and rebirth, and is an emblem of Vishnu.

HOLY MAN

This *sadhu*, or ascetic, is a follower of Shiva, as indicated by the horizontal lines on his forehead and the buffalo horns on his staff. A Hindu ideal in later life is to live like a holy man.

SACRED COW

The cow is sacred to Hindus, and even the lowliest specimen must not be harmed. Valued for its milk and its dung, which is used as fuel, the cow probably represents Mother Earth.

SHRINE

The household shrine is an important focus of daily *puja*, or worship. This is where the gods are invited, welcomed, and worshiped. Offerings of fresh flowers, fruit, and cooked food are placed before an image of the god, and incense may be burned.

APSARAS

Sensuous nymphs like this are found on temple walls. They personify rain clouds and mists and are associated with fertility and growth.

DIVALI

The fall festival of Divali, the festival of light, is celebrated in honor of Lakshmi, consort of Vishnu and goddess of abundance and good fortune. It also celebrates the return from exile of the hero Rama, an avatar of Vishnu, when lamps were relit all over the kingdom.

OBJECTS OF WORSHIP

In Hindu worship, or *puja*, offerings representing and involving the various elements and senses are made in the form of fire, water, sweet-scented air, and clarified butter. Ritual objects are used for sprinkling rose water and scent, burning incense, or for other religious purposes.

SCENT SHAKER
This ivory scent shaker is shaped like the headily perfumed lotus, symbol of creation.

INCENSE BURNER
The incense burner is waved back and forth in the shrine. Wafting the aroma around welcomes the gods with sweet smells.

ROSE-WATER SPRINKLER
The water sprinkler, shaped like a flower, is used to sprinkle rose-water around a shrine in a symbolic purification.

TEMPLE

The architecture of a Hindu temple is symbolic. The central tower represents a mountaintop, because mountains are the sacred abodes of the gods. The image of the god is in the cavelike inner sanctum, the *garbhagrah*, or womb chamber, which has maternal symbolism.

Wheels show that this is the sky-chariot of the sun god

SUN TEMPLE, KONARAK, INDIA

GANGES

The holiest of the rivers of India, the Ganges rises in the Himalayas, home of the gods. It is personified by the goddess Ganga. Pilgrims come to the Ganges to visit holy sites, such as Benares, birthplace of Shiva. To die on the banks of the Ganges and to have one's ashes float away on its current is the best of deaths for a Hindu.

The Purana being extracted

VYASA MILKING THE PURANA OUT OF KAMADHENU, DURGARATNA BETHA, 1836

ANCIENT TEXT

The Puranas, literally old stories, contain traditional Hindu lore told in popular verse. Here the sage Vyasa is milking the Puranas out of Kamadhenu, the cow that grants wishes. The Puranas tell of the popular beliefs of Hinduism.

SEE ALSO

BRAHMA ☞ LOTUS 52
GANESHA ☞ ELEPHANT 63
KRISHNA ☞ KRISHNA'S LOVE 82; BLUE GOD 107
SHIVA ☞ LINGA AND YONI 70; LORD OF THE DANCE 76
SWASTIKA ☞ SWASTIKA 105
VISHNU ☞ GARUDA 31; MILK 49; FEET 75

BUDDHISM

BUDDHISM IS BASED ON NONVIOLENCE, compassion, and charity. Its goal is Enlightenment, which ends the cycle of birth and rebirth and leads to *Nirvana*, literally, blowing out, or absorption into the cosmos. Buddhism developed from the teachings of Gautama Buddha, born Prince Siddhartha in northeastern India in the mid-6th century BC. He renounced his worldly life in search of an existence free of suffering. When Siddhartha achieved this goal, through meditation and asceticism, he was called the Buddha, or the Enlightened.

BUDDHA, CONFUCIUS, AND LAO TZU, WANG SHU-KU, 18TH CENTURY

Vase holds wisdom

FOOTPRINT
The Footprint of the Buddha is marked with 108 auspicious signs. These include the swastika; the mace, symbol of the force that breaks lust; fish, for freedom from all restraint; the flower vase, for supreme intelligence; the conch, for the voice of the Buddha; the wheel of law or life; and the crown of Brahma, for Buddha's supremacy.

Bodhi tree — *Mara on elephant* — *Rays of enlightenment* — *Mara and troops defeated*

FOLDING BOOK
In Burma books that fold up, called *parabaiks*, tell the story of the Buddha with words and pictures. From left to right, this parabaik depicts the Buddha on his way to the Bodhi tree where he attained enlightenment; the Buddha meditating and worshiped by the gods; the approach of Mara, the evil spirit, on an elephant, and his defeat; the Buddha radiating enlightenment and being worshiped by gods and creatures.

THREE GREAT TRUTHS
The great Chinese sages Confucius and Lao Tzu, founder of Taoism, welcome in their midst the infant Buddha, symbolically representing the acceptance of Buddhism in China during the 4th century. Confucianism, Taoism, and Buddhism are known as the Three Great Truths, and together have molded Chinese thought over thousands of years.

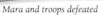

WHEEL OF LAW
With his first sermon, the Buddha is said to have set the wheel of *dharma*, or law, in motion. The wheel, therefore, represents the teachings of Buddha, and the eight spokes the Eightfold Path that leads to enlightenment.

ASPECTS OF BUDDHA

Buddhists do not worship the Buddha but pay homage to his teachings and example in front of his effigies. These portray various postures, or *asanas*, with a number of *mudras*, or hand gestures. They all have a particular significance, appropriate for teaching, meditation, or blessing.

The great snake Muchalinda protecting the Buddha

Dhyana mudra, the gesture of meditation

RECLINING BUDDHA
After a lifetime of teaching, the Buddha died and entered Nirvana, never to be reborn. This is usually symbolized by the *parinirvana asana*, in which the Buddha is shown reclining on his right side.

LAUGHING BUDDHA
Mi Lo Fo is a form of Maitreya, the future Buddha. The name means Friendly One who laughs at fate and whose obesity contains the wisdom of the universe.

MARBLE RECLINING BUDDHÁ, BURMESE, 19TH CENTURY

BUDDHA MUCHALINDA
While the Buddha was engaged in deep meditation there was a violent storm and torrential rain. The great serpent Muchalinda raised the Holy One onto his coils and protected him from the rain with his many hoods.

SHRINE
This Buddhist shrine shows Buddha images surrounded by candles and incense, both part of the act of devotion in Buddhism, as in other religions. The light produced is the light of the doctrine and the smoke from the incense wafts the truth of the doctrine toward the devotees, carrying their devotions into the heavens.

SHRINE AT BUDDHIST TEMPLE, WIMBLEDON, LONDON

Pagoda finial represents enlightenment

Terraces symbolize stages of spiritual development

Shrines contain Buddha images

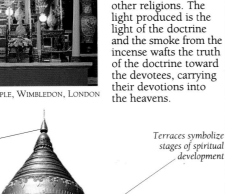

SHWE ZIGON PAGODA, PAGAN, BURMA, 11TH CENTURY

BURMESE PAGODA
Pagodas are *stupas*, which were originally burial mounds erected over the remains of important men in India. After the Buddha's death his ashes were divided and placed within stupas, and later his few possessions were similarly enshrined. Stupas act as a symbol of the Buddha's entry into Nirvana and a reminder to all of the possibility of enlightenment. In Burma, as in China, the stupa is known as a pagoda.

SACRED SYMBOLS
This architectural motif combines sacred symbols that stand for the Eightfold Path and also figure on the Footprint of the Buddha.

CHORTEN
A miniature shrine, this Tibetan silver box with mystic symbols is worn to keep evil spirits at bay. It holds a a tablet molded from the ashes of a lama.

BODHISATTVA OF COMPASSION

Many heads to look in all directions

Thousand arms with attributes of the Buddha

Lotus stalk emerging from the swirling waters

Avalokiteshvara stands on the lotus, sacred flower of Buddhism

BODHISATTVA
According to one school of Buddhism, Bodhisattvas are enlightened beings who put off Nirvana to assist others to enlightenment – the ultimate act of compassion. Avalokiteshvara, the Bodhisattva of compassion, is shown here with eleven heads and a thousand arms, so he can reach out to all conscious beings. Each hand holds an object that symbolizes an attribute of the Buddha.

BUDDHIST MONKS
The Buddha established the *sangha*, or monastic order, so that people could devote themselves to his teachings. The majority of Buddhists think that enlightenment can only be attained by following the monastic, meditative life – free from distractions – on the path to complete awareness.

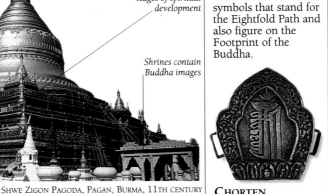

KOYASAN MONK
This monk from Japan holds the traditional alms bowl in which people place food as an act of merit. The bowl is thus a symbolic receptacle for gathering good deeds.

THAI MONK
A Thai monk sits in the window of a monastic building. He is probably studying *sutras*, Buddhist texts that young monks have to master.

PRAYER WHEEL
Mantras, or sacred verses, are inscribed on prayer wheels. Each rotation of the cylinder stands for one recitation of the mantra. Some large wheels are powered by windmills.

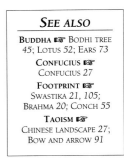

SEE ALSO
BUDDHA ☞ BODHI TREE 45; LOTUS 52; EARS 73
CONFUCIUS ☞ CONFUCIUS 27
FOOTPRINT ☞ SWASTIKA 21, 105; BRAHMA 20; CONCH 55
TAOISM ☞ CHINESE LANDSCAPE 27; BOW AND ARROW 91

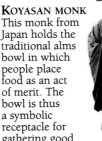

THE GREAT DEPARTURE
Prince Siddhartha, the future Buddha, leaves the palace (left), having renounced worldly life and determined on a life of meditation and asceticism. This Burmese boy (right) symbolically reenacts the momentous scene before donning monk's robes and entering a monastery as a novice monk.

STONE CARVING, ANANDA TEMPLE, PAGAN, BURMA, 11TH CENTURY

TIBETAN PRAYER WHEEL

ISLAM

ISLAM IS THE FAITH of about one-fifth of the world's population. It is based on the revelations uttered by the Prophet Mohammed who lived in Arabia (*c.* AD 570-632). These were later recorded in the volume called the Koran. Followers of Islam are Muslims. Like Jews and Christians, they worship one god, whom they call Allah, and they see their faith as an act of surrender to the will of Allah. Actions of devout Muslims are dictated by the Five Pillars, which call upon the faithful to declare their faith publicly, pray five times a day, give alms, fast during the month of Ramadan, and make a pilgrimage to Mecca.

PRAYER RUG
A Muslim usually performs *salat*, or prays, on a prayer rug. This 16th-century Ottoman example has Islamic pillars woven into the design.

STAR & CRESCENT
Thought originally to have signified the waxing moon, and once associated with the goddess Diana, the crescent was adopted as a symbol of Islam in the 14th century. The star, a symbol of sovereignty and divinity, was added later.

ASCENT OF PROPHET MOHAMMED TO HEAVEN, AGA MIRAK, 16TH CENTURY

MUSLIMS AT PRAYER
Adult males pray side by side in the mosque. As they kneel, facing Mecca, they touch their foreheads to the ground and intone the words "Allah is great," their actions symbolically mirroring their spiritual submission to God.

HAND OF GOD
Known as the Hand of Fatima, after Mohammed's daughter, this represents the Five Pillars of Islam.

THE NIGHT JOURNEY
In a dream Mohammed was led to heaven by the Archangel Gabriel. His face is veiled, according to Muslim convention, and he rides the half-human steed Al Borak, symbol of light and truth.

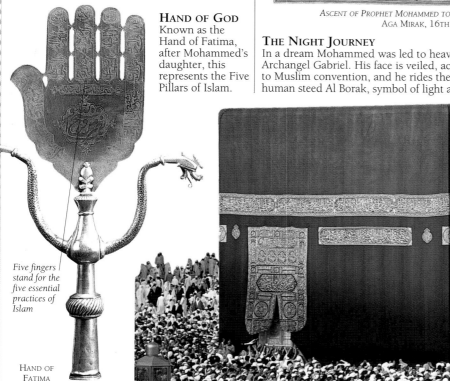

Five fingers stand for the five essential practices of Islam

HAND OF FATIMA

The cubelike shrine built around the sacred stone, probably a meteorite

KA'BAH
The Ka'bah in Mecca is the central shrine of Islam, to which the faithful must turn in prayer wherever they are in the world. Thus it acts as a point of communion between God and man. Muslims are enjoined to make the pilgrimage here at least once in a lifetime if they are able, and symbolically circle the shrine seven times, each circuit signifying an attribute of God.

THE KA'BAH, MECCA

COMPASS
Since Muslims need to face Mecca when they pray, they often use a *qiblah*, or special compass, to find the direction. Many modern prayer mats have integral compasses, with an image of the Ka'bah at the center.

MOSQUE LAMP
The interior of a mosque is lit up by lamps. The light of the lamps indicates the presence of the divine within the mosque. It is wisdom and truth and lightens the darkness of ignorance.

Verses from the Koran

Ornamental border to decorate verses

PRAYER BEADS
An Islamic rosary is made up of 99 beads. This is because they stand for 99 of the Divine Names. The hundredth, the Name of the Essence, can only be found in Paradise.

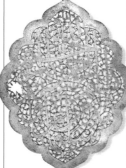

CALLIGRAPHY
Beautifully inscribed Koranic verses are used to decorate any number of objects – a symbolic and constant reminder of the word of God, as in this steel plaque.

KORAN
Some Islamic countries reject the portrayal of living creatures in art because it is thought to challenge the perfection of Allah. As a result, the word itself has been immortalized in art in the form of Koranic texts. Exquisite examples of calligraphy have been produced, one of Islam's greatest contributions to art. They are usually in Arabic, the language of Islam. These texts, often surrounded by beautiful borders and scrollwork, illustrate the authority and truth of the word of God.

Muezzin calls Muslims to prayer from top of the minaret

CERAMIC TILE
The star is a symbol of divinity and supremacy in Islam. Islamic decoration is characterized by the use of ornamented tiles, many of them star-shaped.

MINARET
The minaret is attached to the mosque, and from its summit the *muezzin*, or crier, calls the faithful to prayer five times a day. Muslims believe that one morning the dawn prayer will be called by the Angel of the Resurrection.

Dome stands for heaven

DOME OF THE ROCK
The Dome of the Rock was erected where the Temple of Solomon once stood in Jerusalem, making the site sacred to Jews, Christians, and Muslims. For the Muslims it enshrines the spot to which Mohammed was brought miraculously by the angel Gabriel for his ascent to heaven. Its great dome represents the arc of the heavens and by passing through the arched gateways around it, one symbolically passes into another state of being.

SEE ALSO
DOME OF THE ROCK ☞ DOME 95
KORAN ☞ CHADAR 85; DAGGER 91
MOHAMMED ☞ CAMEL 63
PARADISE ☞ GARDEN OF EDEN, GARDENS OF SPAIN 42; GRAPES 48
PRAYER RUG ☞ SACRED TREES 45; PRAYER HANGING 45; MAGIC CARPET 79
STAR AND CRESCENT ☞ PERSONIFICATION OF THE SUN AND MOON 34; STAR 78; FIVE 102; ISLAMIC GREEN 107

ANCESTOR & NATURE SPIRITS

IN EVERY PART of the world, at one time or another, there has been a belief that everything in nature possesses a soul or spirit. In such a belief, the spirits of the trees, mountains, crops, rivers, and rocks are ever present, and are honored so that man and nature can exist in harmony. Ancestral spirits, too, have been central to the faiths of many people, believing that when someone dies, they join the ancestors and watch over the community's links with the past. Some spirits have a protective character and serve to guard a community or individual in times of danger. They may appear on the prow of a boat or on a weapon, and may be very fierce looking in order to frighten away evil or an enemy in battle.

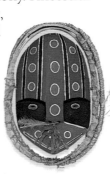

ALASKAN MASK
This Alaskan mask represents the essences of various beings. During divination rituals a shaman would wear this to assume the power of the spirits.

ZAIREAN MASK
Grass-skirted masks, such as this, represent the spirits of the ancestors among the Kuba of Zaire. During initiation ceremonies young boys symbolically meet this ancestor.

ELEPHANT SPIRIT
African masks represent sacred spirits brought to life for rituals. The sacred powers are symbolized by stylized features. This elephant spirit mask from Nigeria represents ugliness.

NATIVE AMERICAN
TOTEM POLE,
CANADA

TOTEM POLE
The totem pole symbolizes the relationship between a tribe or clan and its ancestors. Human and animal ancestor figures are carved on the pole and offerings are made to these sacred figures. This shows respect for the ancestors and solidarity with the clan, all of whom are descended from one ancestor.

THE DREAMING

Australian Aboriginals call the spiritual and natural order of all existence the Dreaming, or Dreamtime. It covers all time, and includes stories of ancestors who created human and animal life. Australian Aboriginals feel at one with nature, and ritual music and art are vital expressions of the spirit essences of the Dreamtime.

BARK PAINTING
Paintings of ancestors are filled in with markings known as *rarrk*. Australian Aboriginals believe these patterns, created by Dreamtime spirits, can release fertility.

WAIJARA SPIRIT, WALLY MANDARRK,
20TH CENTURY

ULURU
Named Ayers Rock by European settlers, Uluru is sacred to Australian Aboriginals, who imbue such sites with special powers. They perform rites to acquire this power and also to renew it.

ANCESTOR FIGURE
This male ancestor figure from Papua New Guinea, painted in sacred colors, stands for a clan father.

WAR GOD
This Hawaiian war god, with his threatening and terrifying appearance, would protect a particular group in war.

SHINTO

Shinto, which means "Way of the Kami," is the oldest religion in Japan. According to Shinto belief the world is populated by millions of Kami, spirits that inhabit any person, place, or object that possesses strange qualities. Spirits may dwell in rivers, rocks, trees, and animals, and all nature is regarded with awe and respect. In the sixth century Shinto blended with Buddhist philosophy to produce a vast pantheon of gods, including a mixture of nature spirits, guardian deities, and Buddha incarnations.

GOD OF WEALTH
A god of abundance and thus fertility, Daikoku grants a good harvest and brings prosperity.

GATEWAY
The *torii* is the gateway to a Shinto shrine. Some shrines may be approached through more than one torii. The ends of the horizontal bars reach toward heaven.

VIEW OF MOUNT FUJI, HIROSHIGE, 1853

SUN'S RAYS
Ama Terasu, goddess of the sun, is the supreme Shinto god, and Japan's emperors claim descent from her. Legend says that, angered by the Storm God, she hid in a cave. The other gods tried to lure her out with jewels and a mirror, hung on a tree outside. Fascinated by her own reflection, she emerged toward it, symbolizing the daily emergence of dawn after night.

INARI
The white fox is the messenger and symbol of Inari, the Japanese god of crops and wealth. Offerings of soybean curd, believed to be his favorite food, are made to him, and his bib signifies thanks for prayers answered.

MOUNT FUJI
The unpredictable nature of volcanoes has evoked feelings of fear and worship in many countries.The many volcanoes of Japan figure in its religion and shrines are often built on their slopes. Japan's Mount Fuji is said to be the most beautiful mountain in the world. It combines the symbolism of heaven, earth, and fire and thus inspires the feelings of awe, danger, and yet peace elicited by nature. Mount Fuji embodies the spirit of Japan and is a place of pilgrimage.

CONFUCIUS
Confucius, who lived in the 6th century BC, remains a great teacher for the Chinese. He propounded a doctrine based on loyalty and duty to parents, clan, and state. By stressing loyalty to clan, he underlined the importance of the ancestors and strengthened ancestral cults, already popular in China. Images of Confucius can be found in many traditional household shrines, especially among the overseas Chinese, reflecting the popular respect accorded to him.

17TH-CENTURY PORTRAIT OF CONFUCIUS

SACRED FIGURE FROM TIN HAU TEMPLE, HONG KONG

OCEAN MONARCH
The Chinese Monarch of the Sea personifies the spirit of the oceans. Offerings are made to him by seafarers to ensure a safe voyage, as at this temple shrine in Hong Kong.

CHINESE LANDSCAPE
The inner serenity of Taoist philosophy is expressed in landscape paintings. Such paintings portray not just the features of the land, but the very essence of nature. Often tiny human figures are placed within the landscape, stressing both the insignificance of man against nature and his place within the universe. Both Taoist philosophy and Confucianism have influenced modern Chinese thought: Taoism stresses the spiritual order within nature, and Confucianism the moral order within society.

SEE ALSO

CHINESE LANDSCAPE ☞ THREE GREAT TRUTHS *22*; BOW AND ARROW *91*; SOUTH KOREA *115*

MASKS ☞ MASKS *77*

SHINTO ☞ BUDDHISM *22-23*; CROW *65*

THE DREAMING ☞ CRYSTAL *39*; KANGAROO *63*; HAWK *67*

MYTHICAL BEASTS

MANY FABULOUS CREATURES originated in the valleys of the Tigris and the Euphrates, and from there moved both east and west. The phoenix and the many-headed serpent for example, and the image of a great bird with a serpent in its talons, are all found in the iconography of many parts of the world. Mythical beasts that are half animal and half human represent both animal instincts and human intellect. Monsters that are part bird and part land or sea creature take on the symbolic associations of both, representing perhaps the sun and the waters in addition to their own innate symbolism.

DOUBLE-HEADED SERPENT

The double-headed serpent is a common image in the Americas and is associated with life-giving rain. It was part of the rites of Tlaloc, Aztec god of the mountains, rain, and springs, to whom children were sacrificed in times of drought.

THE LION AND THE UNICORN, FRANCE, c.1500

The Virgin holds the mirror of truth

The horn can detect and counteract poison

The unicorn represents the feminine essence and the moon

The lion represents the male and the sun

UNICORN

The unicorn is pure and incorruptible. In China it represents gentleness, good will, wisdom, and longevity; in Christianity it represents Christ. According to medieval lore, a unicorn's horn was a powerful antidote to poison, but the animal was so wild that no hunter could capture it. Only a virgin could lure a unicorn to her and tame it. Here a unicorn looks into the mirror of truth, representing the wisdom of self-knowledge.

KY-LIN

This fabulous beast from China generally has the head of a dragon, the mane of a lion, the body of a stag, and the tail of an ox. It is said to appear during the reign of virtuous monarchs and to herald the birth of great people. The Ky-lin often accompanies Chinese sages and immortals. It is gentle, and symbolizes good will and kindness as well as fertility.

SLEIPNIR

The swiftest of all stallions was Sleipnir, eight-legged mount of Odin, the Teutonic magician-god of war. Sleipnir could overcome all obstacles and gallop across both land and sea. As the mount of the god, he was associated with the power of that god and also symbolized the wind.

LOCH NESS MONSTER

First sighted in the Middle Ages, the Loch Ness Monster allegedly bit a swimmer to death in AD 565. Over the years there have been numerous sightings and countless investigations, and scientists have tried to make sense of these eyewitness accounts. Originally a symbol of danger, Nessie is now a benevolent monster.

SALAMANDER

A creature of fire, the salamander is usually depicted either breathing fire or surrounded by flames. It is so cold-blooded that it remains unharmed by the flames. As a symbol it represents the righteous soul, which can emerge unscathed from the fires of temptation.

CENTAUR

With the torso and head of a man above the body of a horse, centaurs combine the instinctual nature of an animal with the judgment and virtue of a man. In Greek myth Chiron, a respected teacher, was a centaur. Centaurs are also a Christian symbol of man torn between good and evil.

Seven visible heads

HYDRA

Linked to the many-headed naga of India, the hydra was a nine-headed serpent, sometimes depicted with a doglike body. A formidable foe, if one head were cut off, two more sprang up in its place. In Greek myth it was killed by Hercules. It symbolizes the many problems that obstruct the path to truth.

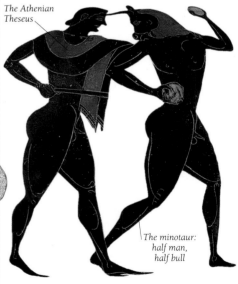

The Athenian Theseus

The minotaur: half man, half bull

MINOTAUR

This creature, with the upper half of a bull, lived in the famous labyrinth of Crete. Every year it devoured seven youths and seven maidens chosen by lot to try to appease it. The hero Theseus decided to challenge the beast and end the reign of terror. The minotaur represents the baser instincts of man.

MAKARA

In India this sea creature is the mount of the sea god Varuna and also of Ganga, goddess of the Ganges. It is part fish and part crocodile or elephant, and is symbolic of the waters of creation. It is often seen in conjunction with solar creatures, the two together representing fertility. The makara also represents the duality of good and evil.

NAGA

The naga is a many-headed serpent deity found widely in the art and legend of India and Southeast Asia. It may be depicted with human torso and serpent heads or as wholly animal. Nagas control the rains and are in constant conflict with garuda, the bird of the sun. This enmity reflects in myth the real balance between sun and rain, which are both essential for the fertility of the soil.

BISHOP FISH

This curious creature, also known as the mitered bishop, has the shaven head of a monk and a large, fishlike body. Legend has it that one of these creatures was captured in the Baltic in 1433 and presented to the King of Poland. Although the king wanted to keep it, he relented when the creature pleaded to be returned to the waters. On being released, the bishop fish made the sign of the cross.

HIPPOCAMP

In Greek legend the hippocamp is the mount of Poseidon, drawing his chariot across the oceans. It has the body of a fish and the forelegs of a horse, making it symbolic of both the waters and the earth. More familiarly known as a sea horse, it is often used in heraldry to denote a laudable action at sea. In the arms of the City of Belfast it represents overseas trade.

MERMAIDS AND SIRENS

Mermaids and sirens appear in the mythology of many countries. A mermaid has the body of a beautiful woman and the tail of a fish. She is a creature of the waters, symbolic of fertility and the unconscious. Sometimes she carries a mirror, which represents truth and the soul. Male equivalents are rarer, although the Tritons of Greek myth – embodying wantonness – were mermen. Sirens may appear in two forms: half woman, half bird, or half woman, half fish. In their fish form they can be mistaken for mermaids. They represent temptation and seduction, the luring of man from his true purpose.

19TH-CENTURY JAPANESE FIGURINE

THE LURE OF DANGEROUS WOMEN

Ulysses is forewarned that he must beware the sirens of the waters, whose voices have the power to lure men to their deaths. He orders his crew to plug their ears with wax, but to tie him firmly to the ship's mast so that he alone can hear their song in safety. The artist has represented two of the sirens in human form, but the third has the tail of a fish.

ULYSSES AND THE SIRENS,
HERBERT DRAPER, 1905

SIREN FROM FRENCH ENGRAVING, *c.*1573

TRITON JEWEL

Half man and half fish, Triton was the son of Neptune and may have been a god of seafarers. Late myths speak of a race of Tritons.

CARVED FIGUREHEAD

This mermaid graces the stern of a barge designed in 1732 for Prince Frederick, son of King George II of England.

Protective mermaid

Carved sea monster to ward off any danger

TRITON JEWEL, *c.*1590

DRAGONS

Combining characteristics of the four elements, earth, air, fire, and water, the dragon symbolizes light and dark, the sun and moon, masculine and feminine, and the unity underlying these opposing forces. The dragon possesses the wings of a bird and the scales of a snake or fish. It breathes fire and often guards a hoard of treasure in its lair. In the East and in pre-Christian Europe the dragon was seen as helpful and kind – indeed, the red dragon is the emblem of Wales – but Christianity, which saw the serpent as a symbol of evil, also viewed the dragon as a creature of ill-omen, representing destructiveness and inner chaos.

BASILISK
Usually depicted as a form of serpent, the basilisk can also have the legs and wings of a dragon. In medieval Europe its breath or gaze was believed to be fatal. It is a symbol of death.

The five claws signify that this garment belonged to the Emperor

The pearl of immortality

Head with bared teeth

WINGED DRAGON
This stylized dragon is from an Anglo-Saxon shield. In its mouth it carries what looks like a pearl – perhaps the pearl of immortality.

VIKING DRAGON
In Norse myth the "dread biter," Nidhogg, devoured corpses and gnawed ceaselessly at the roots of the ash tree Yggdrasil, the tree of life. Nidhogg symbolized evil.

Embroidered silk square, worn to denote rank

CHINESE DRAGON
A symbol of the Emperor, of male energy, and of fertility, the Chinese dragon is a benign animal and the fifth creature of the Chinese zodiac. It guards the East and represents sunrise, spring, and the rains. Indeed, torrential rain is known as "dragon rain." There are four types of dragons in Chinese legend – dragons of the air, the earth, the water, and the spirit. Dragon dances and dragon boat races are still popular in China.

ST. GEORGE AND THE DRAGON
Christians equate the dragon with the serpent, the tempter of Eve in the Garden of Eden. The dragon, too, was evil, an embodiment of man's lower nature. By slaying the dragon, the victor overcomes heresy and evil and also his own primitive drives. St. George is patron saint of England, and of all soldiers.

CLAWED FEET AND JUST TWO LEGS DENOTE THAT THE DRAGON REPRESENTS SATAN

Moth markings on batlike wings, thought to be protective

The damsel symbolizes the anima, or inner self

ST. GEORGE AND THE DRAGON, PAOLO UCCELLO, c.1460

The spiraling cloud represents divine assistance

St. George, symbol of the triumph of good over evil

Lance, symbol of masculinity

Sun symbol

Flames of fire

PHOENIX

The phoenix, sometimes known as the fire bird, sets itself on fire every one hundred years, dies in the flames, and then rises again from the ashes. It is a universal symbol of immortality, death by fire, the sun, and resurrection. It is also a symbol of gentleness because it lives only on dew, not harming any living creature. In China it represents the empress and, with the dragon, stands for inseparable fellowship. In Mexico the phoenix accompanied the great god Quetzalcoatl, and to early Christians it symbolized Christ.

GARUDA

The mount of Vishnu, Garuda is usually portrayed as part man, part eagle, and often has a golden body. It is a huge, noble creature that represents the sun and is a bird of life. The garuda is often shown doing battle with its enemies, the snakes.

KINNARA

Half human and either half bird or half horse, this heavenly musician is part of the celestial chorus surrounding the principal deities in Indian belief. It is an auspicious symbol, sometimes found on temple doorways.

QITOU

This Chinese winged figure, half human, half beast, dates from the Tang dynasty. Qitou guarded the burial chamber of a person of high rank.

SPHINX

A popular symbol originating in Egypt and Babylon, the sphinx usually has the body of a lion and a human head. The Greek sphinx was a female monster that devoured passers-by who failed to answer her riddle. In different cultures the sphinx symbolizes the ruler, wisdom, and the enigmatic.

Huge silver wings

Shakespeare described Pegasus as "pure air and fire"

PEGASUS

The great winged steed of Greek hero Bellerophon, Pegasus was born of the blood of Medusa and carried Zeus's thunderbolt. As a symbol, Pegasus is associated with speed and with storms. A similar horse exists in medieval legend – the hippogryph, symbol of innate power and the capacity to transform evil into good.

GRIFFIN

The griffin was a guardian creature with the head, wings, and talons of an eagle and the body of a lion. It was said to be greater than eight lions and stronger than a hundred eagles. Sacred to Apollo and Athena, the griffin is a symbol of vigilance, vengeance, and wisdom.

HARPY

In Greek mythology the harpy symbolized the most negative, destructive aspects of the female. Harpies had the head and breasts of a woman, and the wings and legs of a vulture. They could control the winds, causing storms and whirlpools, and were the agents of sudden death.

SIMURGH

This fabulous Persian creature, a mixture of peacock, lion, and griffin, also occurs in Russian and Caucasian mythology. With magical healing properties, the simurgh symbolizes the union of heaven and earth.

Nature

The natural world provides a vast and rich store of symbols. The sun, moon, and stars are widely seen as symbolic, affecting every aspect of our lives. Plants and flowers have diverse meanings, from flowers of love to fruits of fertility, and animals, too, have particular associations linked to their characteristics and cultural importance.

SUN & MOON

THE SUN AND MOON HAVE ALWAYS PLAYED a powerful role in imagery. For many cultures all over the world the sun is the embodiment of male energy, light, and warmth; the moon of female mystery and creation. Both are symbolic of death and rebirth: the sun because of its daily rising and setting; the moon because of its monthly waxing and waning between new moon and full moon. The sun's energy warms the land and ripens crops, while the moon's gravity influences the waters, controlling the flow of tides.

DIANA AND HER FOLLOWERS, 15TH-CENTURY MANUSCRIPT

CLOCK FACE
The moons on this 19th-century clock link time to the movements of the heavens.

MAN IN THE MOON
Although the moon is largely seen as feminine, people often speak of the man in the moon. In popular myth a man was nailed to the moon to atone for his sins.

BAYING AT THE MOON
The moon exerts its influence over creatures of the night. When wolves howl at a full moon they reflect the dark or sinister force of the moon.

ECLIPSE
An eclipse of the moon or the sun is regarded by many with fear and seen as a portent of evil. Hindu myth says that an eclipse is caused by the bodiless demon Rahu devouring the moon or sun, which then passes through his neck and back into the sky.

MOONSTRUCK MADNESS
It has long been believed that the full moon brings on or aggravates the symptoms of madness. In this painting Diana, the Roman huntress and goddess of the moon, is seated in the clouds above a group of lunatic followers. The word lunatic comes from the Latin *luna*, meaning moon, and originally meant "moonstruck."

WATER

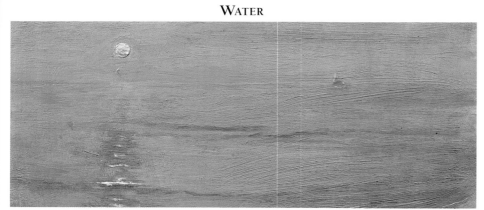

SUMMER EVENING, PETER SEVERIN KROYER, 1908

The oceans are governed by the moon, so, like the moon, water has associations with mystery and with the feminine creative principle. Water is central to many creation myths in which a "great flood" is a common theme. The sea represents the unconscious and infinity, the cosmic ocean from which all life has emerged and into which it must eventually dissolve.

Radiating power of the full moon

Diana, here as a crowned moon goddess

White cloak of purity and moonlight

Symbol of the moon

PERSONIFICATION OF SUN AND MOON
In this illustration from a 16th-century alchemical treatise, the sun and moon are personified as king and queen. The moon (Diana) wears white, in contrast to the red of her twin brother, the sun (Apollo). The flames beneath the sun's feet reflect alchemists' belief that the sun is the innate fire present in all matter. Diana's foot rests on the moon, of which she is both goddess and symbol.

Compass and square, emblems of freemasonry

Sun-head, symbol of day

The key within the triangle represents the heart as keeper of secrets

FREEMASONRY
This sun-headed freemason is made up of the materials of his lodge, with symbols relating to his order.

FLAG OF JAPAN

FLAG OF URUGUAY

FLAGS
Many countries have adopted the sun as their national emblem. Japan, known as the "land of the rising sun," has a plain red disk, while Uruguay has a more decorative sun face.

BLACK SUN
This sun adorns an 18th-century house in Prague known as the Black Sun. In alchemy the black sun, or *sol niger*, is a symbol of Saturn and stands for the dark, destructive aspect of the sun.

SCARAB
The Egyptian sacred beetle is a form of the sun god Khepri, depicted here in winged form, clasping the solar ball and representing new life.

ART DECO MOTIF
Sunbursts were popular in stained-glass windows and also in steel decoration of the 1920s and 30s, such as the tiered roof of New York's Chrysler Building.

APOLLO
Apollo, Greek god of the sun, is the slayer of darkness. In this mosaic from Corinth his head, surrounded by flames, symbolizes his divine nature and the ultimate power of the sun.

FIRE

Torch blazes day and night as symbol of liberty lighting the world

Tablet bearing the date of the Declaration of Independence

Crown of sun beams, with 7 rays to represent the 7 seas and the 7 continents

Associated with the sun, fire is purifying, destructive, revealing. It is spiritual power and sacrifice, and plays a part in many rituals and religions throughout the world. The Statue of Liberty, with her crown of sun's rays, stands at the entrance to New York harbor. She holds aloft a burning torch, which is a symbol of safety and assurance. The flame was literally a ray of hope to the thousands of homeless who sailed into the harbor.

CALENDAR STONE
This Aztec stone calendar, with a sun motif, shows the year divided into 18 short months. The central position of the sun emphasizes its importance in the agricultural cycle.

Central face depicts spirit of the sun

SUN MASK
In this Native American spirit mask from northern British Columbia, the face represents the spirit of the sun. It is one of the sky spirits central to its tribe's beliefs.

SUN EMBLEM
This emblem on Siena's cathedral in Italy combines the crucifix within the flames of the sun. It was designed as a symbol of peace.

EARTH & SKY

THE RELATIONSHIP OF THE EARTH AND THE SKY is vital for the well-being of humankind, for it is the combination of sun, rain, wind, and soil that brings life, warmth, and nourishment. The sky is symbolic of transcendence and the heavenly realms, and gods of the sky are linked to the masculine power and the creative aspect of the sun. The earth symbolism complements that of the sky and represents the Great Mother, receiving fertilizing rain, producing crops, and nourishing animals. Rivers and lakes represent the bountiful properties of the earth and share its feminine, nurturing qualities. Some rivers, such as the Ganges in India, are viewed as sacred.

SATELLITE PHOTOGRAPH

EARTH FROM SPACE
Far from demystifying our view of the heavens, space exploration has heightened our sense of awe at the vastness and magnificence of our world.

VOLCANO
Volcanoes, with their terrifying powers of destruction, have always been sacred and highly symbolic to the people who live in their shadow. An eruption may be interpreted as a sign of the fury of the gods. In parts of Southeast Asia a human sacrifice to a volcano used to be made in an attempt to avert such wrath.

RIVER
A river is both a symbol of fertility, since it irrigates land, and an image of the neverending flow of time. Its delta represents the merging of the soul with the Absolute. Meandering slowly to the sea, the river can also symbolize a journey into death. Journeys to the Underworld often involve the crossing of a river, and the four rivers of Paradise are a source of power and spiritual nourishment.

RAIN FOREST
The forest is a magical, heroic realm of danger and enchantment, and it can represent the unconscious mind. The forest is either the fearful haunt of spirits, wolves, and goblins, as in European folklore, or a place of seclusion where ascetics pursue spiritual contemplation, as in Indian culture. In the latter part of the 20th century the rain forest has come to represent the vulnerability of our planet, which is rapidly being destroyed by human encroachment.

THE ERUPTION OF VESUVIUS, JACQUES VOLAIRE, LATE 18TH CENTURY

DOME OF ST. PETER'S, ROME

SKY
Probably because the sun, stars, and moon are above us in the sky, the sky has always been associated with creator gods and the forces of creation. The domed roofs of cathedrals and mosques are often painted blue to resemble the sky, symbolically reminding the faithful of heaven above.

WATCHING A WATERFALL, ZHANG DAQIAN, 1935

WATERFALL
In Chinese symbolism a waterfall represents the feminine while a mountain or cliff is the masculine. Its downward motion is the harmonious counterpart to the upward-striving mountain. Here the tiny figures are deliberately insignificant against the mighty landscape.

SNOWFLAKE
Snow represents coldness and hardness in human nature, but the fragile beauty of a snowflake symbolizes truth and wisdom. The snowflake is also a symbol of individuality, since no two are alike.

THUNDER AND LIGHTNING
This Japanese god of thunder takes the form of a strong man beating his drum. The circle of balls around his head represent the reverberations of the thunder.

WEATHER
Every culture has had an explanation for the whims of the weather. In folktales personifications such as the North Wind and Jack Frost are blamed for miserable weather, while storms are traditionally attributed to the storm god in China and Japan.

Balls of thunder

JAPANESE THUNDER GOD

Drumstick to beat out the rolling thunder

A LONDON FOG, F.D. BEDFORD, 1902

FOG
Fog, like cloud, is a symbol of the mystical and mysterious. It stands for the confusion from which the soul must emerge to attain enlightenment.

WIND CHERUB
This cherub blows the wind, probably to guide a boat on its course across the ocean. Such cherubs were a popular way of representing the winds in Western art.

CHINESE CLOUDS
Clouds symbolize the mystical and the sacred. The Chinese traditionally believe they are formed from the union of female and male, yin and yang.

Dove of peace

NOAH'S ARK, GABRIEL LOIRE, 1975

Rainbow, sign of God's covenant

Noah's ark, symbol of the Christian Church

RAINBOW
In many cultures the rainbow bridges the earth and heaven. It is often seen as a message of hope from the gods. In the Bible God sent a rainbow as a sign of His covenant after the Flood.

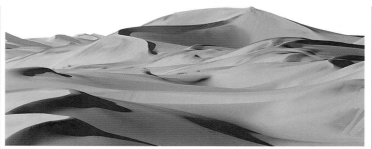

DESERT
A place of abandonment and desolation, the desert also represents peace and contemplation. In the Bible great events occurred in the desert. The children of Israel sojourned there for 40 years and Christ was tempted in the desert.

PRECIOUS MATTER

THE WORLD'S MOUNTAINS, LAKES, AND WATERS are the repositories of hidden treasures – revealing the unexpected presence of pearls inside craggy oysters or substances such as metals and minerals that can be mined and transformed into objects of extraordinary beauty. In the past, the fascination with these materials stemmed from their colors or brilliance, but durability also played a part. Gold could last forever without tarnishing or corroding, and stones, cut and polished, seemed equally impervious to change. In a fragile, uncertain world, such beauty and permanence must have appeared to have magical, almost divine, properties.

Mother-of-pearl

NATURAL PEARL IN OYSTER SHELL

CORAL

In the 16th century it was believed that the only way to cross rivers safely or to calm a raging tempest was to carry a piece of red or white coral. But the alleged powers of coral went far beyond this. Coral was thought to staunch the flow of blood from a wound, cure madness, imbue the wearer with wisdom, and offer protection against enchantments. Sprigs freshly gathered from the sea, such as the one hanging above the Madonna in this picture, are deemed the most powerful. To this day many people give children coral jewelry to protect them from harm.

This Italian child's bracelet with its carved hand clasp was designed to safeguard the wearer

CORAL BRACELET

Coral beads strung overhead afford further protection for the Madonna and child

Sprigs of coral, unworked and fresh from the sea, were thought to safeguard against evil

MADONNA OF VICTORY, ANDREA MANTEGNA, 1496

AN UNBOKEN BRANCH OF CORAL, ITS PROTECTIVE POWERS INTACT

PEARL

Prized in East and West alike, the pearl is a universal symbol of beauty and perfection. It is linked to the realm of the feminine – the moon, chastity, patience, and purity. Chinese dragons are usually portrayed clasping a pearl, symbol of wisdom, immortality, and light. Pearls were once thought to be the tears of the gods.

MOTHER-OF-PEARL

The shell's symbolism is clear from its name – it is the mother of the much-prized pearl and as such represents fertility and birth. Its luster and iridescence make it perfect for honoring the gods. Here, tiny casts have been placed into the shell of this pearl mussel to create images of the Buddha.

AMBER

With its bright golden sheen, amber was thought to be congealed sunlight; in ancient Greece it was sacred to the sun god, Apollo. In Norse and Greek myth amber was thought to be tears – for the Vikings it was Freya's tears for Svipdag, and for the Greeks it was tears shed over the death of Phaeton.

JET

When in direct contact with the skin, jet was believed to become a part of a person's body and soul and to safeguard the wearer. It could protect against poisons, illnesses, and storms. In the 19th century jet became associated with death and mourning, and was worn as a symbol of love for a lost friend.

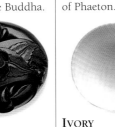

IVORY

Because of its color, ivory is a symbol of purity and so is associated with the Virgin; it was a favored material for crucifixes. Ivory is also associated with moral strength. An ivory tower represents detachment from the world, possibly through arrogance or intellectual pursuits.

GOLD

Regarded as the most precious of metals, gold is a symbol of all that has the highest value or is the hardest to attain. The ultimate prize-winners are gold medalists, perfect times are known as "golden eras," and treasured items as "worth their weight in gold." In most cultures gold is linked to the sun, giver of light, fire, and life. The sun god Apollo, symbol of all that is radiant and beautiful, rode a chariot of gold across the skies.

SILVER
Linked to the moon because of its color, silver is bright, but also tarnishes, symbolizing the corruptible side of human nature, which needs cleansing. In China silver is the lunar, feminine yin; in Christianity it is purity, chastity, and eloquence.

COPPER
The power of copper to conduct has made it symbolic of connection. In alchemy it is in the sphere of Venus, and so is linked to warmth and femininity. Among North American tribes, copper denoted status.

PILGRIM'S BADGE

LEAD
Lead's cheapness made it ideal for pilgrims' badges commemorating a journey to a saint's shrine. As the heaviest metal, lead symbolizes weight, as well as a heavy heart or a person burdened by sin.

IRON
Iron denotes power, durability, and inflexibility; to rule with "an iron fist" is to be harsh and unyielding. In Chinese, Egyptian, and Islamic belief, iron was darkness and evil. In Mexican and Minoan cultures it represented male strength.

OLYMPIC GOLD
Awarded for excellence in a given field, the gold medal is the most highly sought after prize, symbol of exceptional achievement.

SUN KING
Louis XIV of France was known for his extravagant and opulent lifestyle. Nicknamed the Sun King after the sun god Apollo, he adopted the golden emblem of the sun to symbolize his power and his importance in the world.

EMBLEM OF LOUIS XIV, THE SUN KING

The sun's rays symbolize the extent of the King's power

GOLD FEVER
In the 1850s and '60s "gold fever" spread across the American continent as thousands of fortune hunters panned riverbeds for gold. Gold's power to corrupt lends it a negative as well as positive symbolism, representing the sins of idolatry and greed – as in the legend of King Midas.

HUMAN-SIZED JAR
This Chinese ornamental jar, made of beaten gold, is as tall as a woman. The detailed scenes depicted on its surface took a team of goldsmiths more than a year to complete.

GOLDEN OFFERING
In Thailand worshipers honor Buddha by pressing fine leaves of pure gold onto his image. Over the years, the layers of gold render Buddha's form almost unrecognizable.

ROCK
In the Bible a rock represents the strength and protection of God. It is the symbol of St. Peter, the name Peter coming from the Greek *petros*, rock. In Greek myth the wicked king of Corinth, Sisyphus, was punished by having to push a huge stone up a hill and watch it forever roll down again.

LODESTONE
Its magnetic properties imbued lodestone with quasi-sexual powers. In ancient Greece it was believed that a man could ensure his wife's faithfulness by placing a lodestone under her pillow while she slept. In Sanskrit the word for lodestone means "kisser," and in Chinese the word means "loving-stone."

CRYSTAL
Crystal symbolizes purity, clarity, and also the mind. In Christianity a crystal ball represents the world of the light of God. Crystals are widely thought to have magical powers. To Australian aboriginals a crystal is a symbol of the Great Spirit. Crystal balls hold secrets of the future, and wearing a crystal is thought to promote health.

CRYSTAL BALL

PRECIOUS STONES

DIAMOND, SYMBOL OF POWER AND WEALTH

FETISHES, AMULETS, AND TALISMANS have played an important part in every culture and continue to do so to this day. From the early Egyptian and South American civilizations to the oldest cultures in the East, people have imbued stones with supernatural powers. There are stones to control the elements, calm the winds, and still rough seas, and others to work directly on the body, stimulating vital organs or creating a sense of well-being. There are stones for particular days of the week, and stones for the different months. Stones that capture and reflect light, such as moonstones and star sapphires, are deemed to bring good luck. Agates, with central white rings carved into watchful "guardian eyes," can neutralize the power of the evil eye.

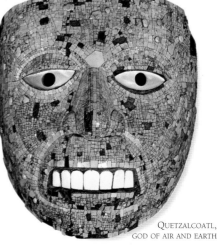

ONYX GOOD-LUCK TOKEN

BUFFALO FETISH
At one time, Native Americans used fetishes to help control the forces of nature and to tackle problems in their everyday lives. The fetish did not contain any innate power; its spirit force was given to it by its owner.

THE MEANING OF GEMSTONES

The symbolism of stones varies depending on their color, their form, and the use to which they are put. For example, cut and faceted gemstones symbolize the soul set free from the base exterior of the human body.

DIAMOND CADUCEUS BROOCH

Wings, symbols of transcendence

Twin snakes of good and evil

Mercury's winged staff, to bring harmony from strife

LAPIS LAZULI
In Mesopotamia this blue stone symbolized the heavens and so was used to decorate the ceilings of temples. In Egypt it was used to adorn statues of the gods, while in Europe it was viewed as a cure for melancholy and fever. In China it symbolized vision, and was used to cure diseases of the eye.

SAPPHIRE
Like lapis lazuli, sapphire symbolizes the blue of the heavens and also the heavenly attributes of truth, chastity, and contemplation. The star sapphire is a powerful good-luck charm. Its three shafts of light are thought to represent faith, hope, and destiny.

AMETHYST
This is the stone of humility, peace of mind, piety, and resignation. It was associated with Bacchus, god of wine, and was thought to cure drunkenness. It became a symbol of sobriety, possibly because water in an amethyst jug looked like wine, but had no intoxicating effect.

RUBY
In India this is the king of stones and is generally associated with royalty, dignity, zeal, and power. In Burma rubies were thought to confer invulnerability, especially if they were embedded in the teeth or flesh so that they became a part of the body. They then allegedly prevented wounding by spears, swords, or guns. Worn as jewelry, rubies may ward off misfortune and illness.

DIAMOND BROOCH
The most prized as well as the hardest stone, the diamond is associated with incorruptibility and invincibility. Its transparency and purity make it also a symbol of constancy and sincerity. Here, diamond snakes entwine a staff of emeralds in a winged caduceus, symbol of medicine as the healing union of opposites.

EMERALD
Legend has it that emeralds are found in the nests of griffins. Revered and powerful stones, emeralds are thought to enhance the memory, sharpen the wits, and, when placed under the tongue, help in predicting the future. The emerald has been used as an antidote for poison and a treatment of eye disease, dysentery, and leprosy. Due to its color, the emerald is a symbol of spring, of fertility, and of rain.

TOPAZ
This stone was also widely believed to cure poor vision. According to St. Hildegard, the patient had to place a topaz in wine for a period of three days. Then, on going to bed, he had to rub his eyes with the moistened stone to effect a cure. In the 15th century topaz was thought to heal plague sores. A Roman physician claimed many successes by touching open sores with a stone that had belonged to two popes.

QUETZALCOATL, GOD OF AIR AND EARTH

AZTEC TURQUOISE MASK
Turquoise was highly valued in Mesoamerica and was often used in representations of gods, or tied to weapons to ensure accuracy. The Aztecs called it the "stone of the gods." In ancient Egypt turquoise was thought to be protective. The stone is symbolic of courage, fulfillment, and success.

BIRTHSTONES

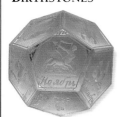

CRYSTAL WITH ZODIAC SIGNS

Wearing one's birthstone is thought to be lucky. These are the most common birthstones:

January – Garnet
February – Amethyst
March – Aquamarine
April – Diamond
May – Emerald
June – Pearl
July – Ruby
August – Peridot
September – Sapphire
October – Opal
November – Topaz
December – Turquoise

OPAL

The opal is the national stone of Australia, as symbolized by this brooch. Shakespeare viewed the opal as a symbol of inconstancy, although its Christian associations are fidelity, prayer, and religious fervor. It is generally held to be unlucky (except for October's children), although this belief almost certainly comes from the fact that opal breaks very easily. Jewelers disliked working with it, and their misgivings turned into popular myth.

AGATE

Agate has been thought to cure insomnia, to ensure pleasant dreams, to protect the wearer from danger, and to endow a person with a bold heart. Its popularity has been widespread. In Sudan, agate amulets – black with a white circle to look like an eye – were carried as guardian spirits to counter the effects of the evil eye. Black agate stands for courage, vigor, and prosperity; red for long life and spiritual love.

MAORI LUCKY CHARM, HEI TIKI AMULET, THAT KEEPS EVIL SPIRITS AWAY

New Year dragons, emblems of good luck   CHINESE DRAGONS

JADE

In China this is the most precious stone, symbolizing purity, perfection, and immortality. Bridegrooms give their fiancées jade butterflies to represent their eternal love. Jade is similarly valued by Mesoamerican Indians, who adorn the masks of their gods with it. The Spanish *conquistadores* believed it healed hip and kidney complaints.

RELIGION, SUPERSTITION, AND MAGIC

The rise of Christianity did little to dispel the belief in the magic properties of stones. Jewelers began to include pectoral crosses and rock crystal reliquaries in their range, and it was not uncommon in Spain and Italy to festoon children with protective jewelry. This Spanish child is armed with an all-powerful red sprig of coral, a protective fist, and a host of Christian symbols of salvation.

Patron saint
The child is safeguarded by her patron saint

Sprig of coral
Amulet with powers against magic spells

Malachite lozenge
Often given to children to help them sleep and keep evil spirits at bay

Clenched fist
The jet hand protects against the evil eye

Crucifix
Large and small crosses ensure God's embrace

Pomander
Contains spices to safeguard against infection

Tooth
Mounted animal tooth, for luck

LA INFANTA MARIA ANA CON SONAJEROS, JUAN PANTOJA DE LA CRUZ, 1602

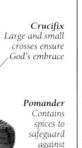

CORNELIAN

Red stones were thought to be stimulating to the circulatory system and the cornelian was deemed particularly valuable to those timid in speech or weak of voice. In the West it is viewed as a stone of self-confidence, courage and health. In the East it is thought to protect the wearer from other people's envy.

MOONSTONE

So named because it captures the sheen of the moon, this stone is sacred in India and is widely believed to bring good fortune. Legend has it that a person who places a moonstone in his mouth when the moon is full will be able to see into the future. It is symbolic of the moon, of tenderness, and of lovers.

BLOODSTONE

This stone was thought to contain the blood of Jesus and to be magical. It could allegedly cause thunder, lightning, and tempests. On a practical level, bloodstone was used to stem nosebleeds and hemorrhaging. When made into jewelry, it is symbolic of peace and understanding.

SEE ALSO

AZTEC TURQUOISE MASK ☞
SUN MASK 35;
SNAKE DEMON MASK 59;
LEOPARD MASK 62;
MASKS 77

DIAMOND BROOCH ☞
ROD OF AESCULAPIUS 59;
ENGAGEMENT RING 87;
CADUCEUS 108

LAPIS LAZULI ☞
BLUE STONE 107

PRECIOUS STONES ☞
CHORTEN 23; CORAL 38;
FLY 56; EYES 72;
MAGIC EYE, POWER TO
PROTECT 79

RELIGION, SUPERSTITION, AND MAGIC ☞ CORAL 38;
FLY 56; LUNAR EYE 72;
MAGIC AND CHARMS 78-79

GARDENS

THE LITERATURE OF EUROPE, the Middle East, and Asia is full of the imagery of the garden: the garden represents Paradise and the abode of the soul. Chinese and Vietnamese emperors had tombs built in exquisite, tranquil gardens, which they visited during their lives and where they were eventually buried. The biblical Garden of Eden symbolized the state of perfection from which Adam and Eve fell, while the walled garden with a narrow opening was a visual representation of the wall of purity that surrounded the Virgin Mary.

Walled enclosure contains garden and provides protection from the unwelcome curiosity of the outside world

Geometric planning symbolizes taming of wilderness

Venus, goddess of beauty, inspects herself in a mirror

15TH-CENTURY FRENCH MANUSCRIPT

GARDEN OF EDEN

THE GARDEN OF EARTHLY DELIGHTS, HIERONYMUS BOSCH, c.1510

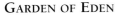

WALLED GARDENS
The medieval walled garden was a symbol of the womb and the feminine, protective principle. It symbolized privacy, secrecy, and virginity. The walled garden had powerful religious symbolism, representing spiritual enlightenment. Chinese and Roman tomb gardens were the earthly counterparts of the gardens of heaven. In medieval literature a "garden of delights" was an allegory for courtly love (as here), with symbols of love, beauty, and other pleasures.

This panel from a triptych, a three-paneled painting, by the Flemish painter Hieronymus Bosch depicts the biblical Garden of Eden. Here, the first humans, Adam and Eve, lived in harmony with nature and the animals in a state of natural innocence – until they were banished from Paradise after the Fall. On the right is a detail showing nature running riot.

DETAIL

FOUNTAINS
In Babylonian tradition, four rivers watered Paradise, and in the Bible, the Fountain of Life is the source of the rivers. This symbolism is echoed in formal European gardens in which four paths lead to a central fountain.

FOUNTAIN GARDEN OF THE ALHAMBRA PALACE

GARDENS OF SPAIN
For Arabs living in the desert, a garden was the earthly symbol of luxuriant Paradise, described in the Koran as a place of "spreading shade," with "fountains of gushing water." The fountain was a symbol of everlasting life. The fourfold, or courtyard, garden with a fountain in the center spread with the Moors to southern Spain. Here, some of the loveliest examples can be seen in the grounds of the Alhambra at Granada.

UNDERGROUND GROTTO

GROTTO
In ancient Greece sacred rites were conducted in grottoes, and so grottoes were created in Greek and Roman gardens as artificial caves to reinforce the magical link between the garden and nature. In Renaissance times, the grotto was reintroduced as an essential element of classical garden design.

ENGLISH ARCHITECTURAL WATER FOLLY

Knot garden at Mosely Old Hall, England

Grand scale of design reflects supreme status of the king

Formal layout of gardens signifies civilization through ordering of nature

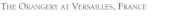

The Orangery at Versailles, France

LOVE KNOTS
Knot gardens are made up of interlaced bands of shrubbery, each with a central motif. They were popular in England in the 16th century, and reflected contemporary needlework designs. Knots, representing links and binding, are symbols of love and matrimony. They also symbolize fate and ward off evil.

SILVER BAY TREE

BAY TREE
The evergreen bay tree is a symbol of immortality and victory. Small bay trees are cultivated in pots as a symbol of honor and longevity.

VERSAILLES
The formal grandeur of Louis XIV's palace and gardens at Versailles have a political significance. Known as the Sun King, Louis wanted to show his supremacy by conquering and reworking the natural landscape so that his surroundings reflected his own status. The grand scale of Versailles was a conscious symbol of the power of absolute monarchy.

Abbot's Garden of Fukuji Temple, Kyoto, Japan

WISHING WELL
A symbol of the feminine, life-giving principle, the well has often been believed to have magical properties. A coin tossed into its depths could make a wish come true.

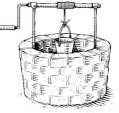

GARDEN GNOME

ORNAMENTS
A garden can be seen as a symbol of the natural world, and so it is considered home to spirits of all kinds. Statuary can represent these spirits, from the gods of Greece and Rome to the humble gnome of Celtic origin.

Maze at Hever Castle, Kent

MAZE
Though the maze is a classical device, it has been used in gardens only since the Renaissance. It provided concealment for amorous pursuits. Mazes were thought to catch and hold evil spirits and also to represent the journey from darkness into light, or secret wisdom discovered after trials.

LOVERS' ROSE BOWER

BOWER
The columns that enclosed a Roman *peristyle,* or courtyard, are echoed in a garden with trellises, overhung with flowering plants to provide shade and fragrance. As an enclosed place of retreat, the bower reflects the safety of the womb; the rose, in this case, eternal love.

PURPLE MAPLE

BONSAI
The Japanese art of growing miniature trees, *bonsai,* symbolizes mastery over nature. As bonsai are often passed from generation to generation, they are also a symbol of immortality.

ZEN GARDEN
Beautiful, bare rock gardens are created in Zen Buddhist monasteries in Japan to represent the universe in microcosm. Some have raked sand; the Dry Landscape garden in Kyoto uses rocks and pebbles to create in miniature the impression of an ocean interrupted by islands. This illusion is intended to represent "ultimate truth," and as such is an aid to meditation.

TREES

THE TREE HAS SYMBOLIC significance in cultures throughout the world. It represents the Great Mother in her nourishing, sheltering form. Rooted in the earth, it draws water from the ground and reaches up to the heavens and eternity, acting as a world axis. It is closely linked to the symbolism of the pillar and the mountain. Individual trees, types of trees, and groups of trees all have particular associations. For example, evergreen trees symbolize immortality, whereas fruit-bearing trees are often seen as trees of life, and forests or groves tend to be magical places where mysterious or momentous events occur.

OLIVE BRANCHES:
SYMBOLS OF PEACE

WILLOW
In the Western world the weeping willow is associated with death and mourning, and it is often depicted in funerary art. In China and Japan however, it is a symbol of spring, of feminine beauty, and grace. In Taoism the willow, pliable in strong winds, represents strength.

PALM
As an important food source the palm was equated with the tree of life in the Near East. In ancient Egypt it was sacred to the sun god, Re, and represented the fertility of the crops. In Judaism it is an emblem of Judea; in Christianity of Christ's entry into Jerusalem.

TREE OF KNOWLEDGE
SPANISH SCHOOL, 12TH CENTURY

Symbol of temptation, the tree of knowledge grows in Paradise and bears the fruit of good and evil. As Adam succumbs to Eve's enticements and takes a bite of the apple, he defies the will of God, signifying both his loss of innocence and his downfall – Adam falls from grace and mankind is doomed. In this Spanish painting, Eve blames the serpent, her tempter and itself a symbol of evil.

SYCAMORE MAPLE
To ancient Egyptians, this was a celestial tree, a form of the sky goddess, Nut. Its leaves provide shade, which symbolized peace and rest in the afterlife. The fruit yields a milky substance, and so was associated with fertility and nourishment.

CHERRY
In China and Japan the cherry is a national emblem and its blossom is a symbol of spring, femininity, and youth. In English lore a cherry tree planted near the house brings luck, and the luckiest lovers are those who meet for the first time under a cherry tree.

LAUREL
Sacred to Apollo and a symbol of immortality and victory, the laurel was said by Greeks and Romans to be physically and spiritually cleansing, and to repel lightning. Worn as a wreath, it symbolized the poet and excellence in the sciences and arts.

BEECH
Associated with death, the beech is sacred to Hades and Cybele, the mother of Zeus, and represents prosperity, divination, and immortality. Because of its leathery leaves and bark the beech symbolizes endurance, and the Freemason's hammer is made of beech wood. The beech tree is the emblem of Denmark.

PINE
As an evergreen the pine symbolizes immortality. In Japan it has come to signify strength of character and vital energy due to its ability to withstand strong winds. In both East and West the pinecone symbolizes life and fertility. It is an attribute of the Greek god Bacchus, and an emblem of Jupiter, Venus, and Diana.

YEW
The yew tree has poisonous seeds and needles and so represents death. It has become symbolic of mourning and is often found in English churchyards; however, as an evergreen it also symbolizes immortality and was grown in Celtic sacred groves. In the Middle Ages it was used as an antidote to enchantment.

THE CHRISTMAS TREE

Widespread throughout Europe and North America, the Christmas tree is a symbol of Christ as redeemer of original sin. The ornaments on its branches represent the apples from the tree in the Garden of Eden. The custom of decorating an evergreen tree goes back to the pre-Christian period of "raw nights" (December 25 to January 6), when people would hang green branches in their houses and light candles to keep evil spirits at bay.

The candles are symbolic of Jesus, the "light of the world"

HOLLY
In Roman times holly was part of the Saturnalia festival celebrated in mid-December. In Christian lore it symbolizes both the crown of thorns, due to its spiked leaves and blood-red berries, and the joy of Christmas.

LIME OR LINDEN
In Europe the lime, or linden, tree represents joy, beauty, and femininity. In Germany and Scandinavia it was believed to repel lightning and to cure disease if touched by someone who was sick.

MULBERRY
This tree's berries ripen in three stages: white represents youth; red the vigorous middle years; and black the ripeness of wisdom, age, and death. This tree symbolizes the sun and is a tree of life in China. In Greek myth it is a tree of misfortune.

CYPRESS
Associated with Pluto, Roman god of death, the evergreen cypress is nevertheless a symbol of immortality. It was thought to have the power to preserve bodies and so was, and still is, often grown in graveyards. In China it represents death, but also the feminine realm.

ACACIA
With its red and white flowers, the acacia was sacred to the ancient Egyptians, symbolizing birth and death. Their gods were said to have been born beneath an acacia tree. The sacred wood of the Hebrew tabernacle was that of the "shittah," or acacia tree. In Europe it symbolizes immortality.

PLUM
In China the plum is an emblem of winter. In Japan the tree represents the fleeting joy and innocence of youth; its beautiful blossom a symbol of spring triumphing over winter, and virtue and courage triumphing over difficulties.

MYRTLE
Sacred to Venus and to the Egyptian goddess Hathor, myrtle brings luck to lovers and was once the English bridal flower. Symbol of immortality, good fortune, happiness, and peace in many cultures, it is also the flower of the gods. In dreams it signifies prosperity and a ripe old age.

SACRED TREES

A reverence for trees, and even tree worship, is widespread thoughout the world. Many traditions speak of a tree of life – a tree that is the central point and pivot of the world. This tree links heaven and earth since it is rooted in the underworld, but its branches reach up to the heavens, symbolizing man's striving for perfection. The Scandinavians have Yggdrasil, Buddhists have the bodhi tree, and Muslims kneel on carpets embroidered with trees of life when praying toward Mecca. Christ is sometimes shown crucified on the tree of knowldge in the Garden of Eden, symbolizing redemption.

The serpent of Midgard encircles the world, representing the eternal cycle

Malevolent serpents attack the roots

YGGDRASIL
Yggdrasil is the evergreen ash tree that, in its mythological form, represents the entire world. Its trunk represents the central axis of the universe, and from beneath its roots bubble the rivers – the waters of wisdom.

Flames of light, or enlightenment, encircle Buddha's body

BUDDHA UNDER A BODHI TREE
The Bodhi tree, a type of fig, is symbolic of the Buddha's Enlightenment, which he attained while meditating beneath its branches. Bodhi trees are often grown in monastery grounds as a reminder of this event.

PRAYER HANGING
In this 19th-century example, a stylized tree of life is intricately woven into the design. Muslim prayer rugs often depict this powerful symbol of ascent and salvation. The faithful kneel and say their prayers on a tree of life.

OAK
Often associated with the thunder gods, the oak is sacred to the earth mother, to Juno, Jupiter, and to the Celtic god Donar. In China it represents fragile strength since it does not bend in the wind and so breaks. To Christians it is a symbol of Christ's steadfastness, while in Judaism it is a symbol of the divine presence. In Europe the oak stands for heroism.

ACORN
As the seed of the "mighty oak," the acorn is a widespread symbol of life. In Scandinavia it is sacred to Thor, and is a symbol of fertility, life, and immortality.

PLANTS

PLANTS ECHO THE CYCLE OF BIRTH, DEATH, AND REBIRTH. They were closely connected with the mother goddesses of many cultures and with fertility. Myths from around the world often feature a human or a god changing into a plant, or a plant sprouting from the dead body of a god. Wheat and herbs, for instance, grew from the body of the Egyptian god Osiris. Often the symbolism of plants is more direct, based on their shape, color, smell, or habitat. The fact that ivy, for example, covers many old university buildings has meant that the term "ivy-league" now symbolizes a respected and long-established place of learning.

ACANTHUS
This thistlelike plant has large, thorny leaves and takes its name from the Greek *ake*, meaning sharp point. The distinctive leaves, carved in stone or marble, are commonly seen on classical buildings, particularly on Corinthian capitals (shown above). Acanthus leaves signify the arts, or a love of the arts, while in Christianity the thorns symbolize pain and punishment for sin.

REEDS
Rushes and reeds symbolize flexibility because they sway in the wind. Pan's pipes were made of reeds.

DEADLY NIGHTSHADE
Also known as devil's berries, the fruits of this plant look edible, yet are highly poisonous. It is a symbol of deception and danger.

BAMBOO
A symbol of pliability, grace, and strength because it bends in the wind but does not break, bamboo is central to the cultures of the Far East. As its shoots are always green, it symbolizes longevity. Bamboo's straight, jointed stem symbolizes the path and the steps toward enlightenment in Chinese philosophy, and it is often depicted in paintings.

Symbolic of fertility and growth

The plant's leaves form the "headdress" of the man

Mandrake's odd-shaped roots give the impression of a man's body

ILLUSTRATION FROM 12TH-CENTURY MEDICAL TREATISE

The mandrake rides on a dog's back – a reference to the method of uprooting it

SHAMROCK
Once an Arabian religious symbol, the shamrock, or clover, was also adopted by Christians. Its three leaves signify the Holy Trinity: Father, Son, and Holy Spirit. The plant is the emblem of Ireland and of its patron saint, St. Patrick. A four-leaved clover is thought to bring the finder luck.

IVY
Like most evergreens, ivy is associated with immortality, but it is also a plant of death, drawing vital moisture from trees. Sacred to Dionysus, the Greek god of wine (shown above trailing ivy), it was thought to cure drunkenness when worn as a garland.

WHEAT
For the ancient Greeks wheat was the symbol of the goddess Demeter, while the Egyptians associated it with the resurrection of the slain god Osiris. Ears of wheat motifs in Christian churches signify Christ's body and also his rebirth.

MANDRAKE
This plant, with its human-shaped roots, has been considered magical since the time of the ancient Egyptians. When uprooted, it was said to utter a shriek that killed anyone in earshot, so a dog was used to carry out the task. Mandrake is a symbol of enchantment, fertility, and prosperity.

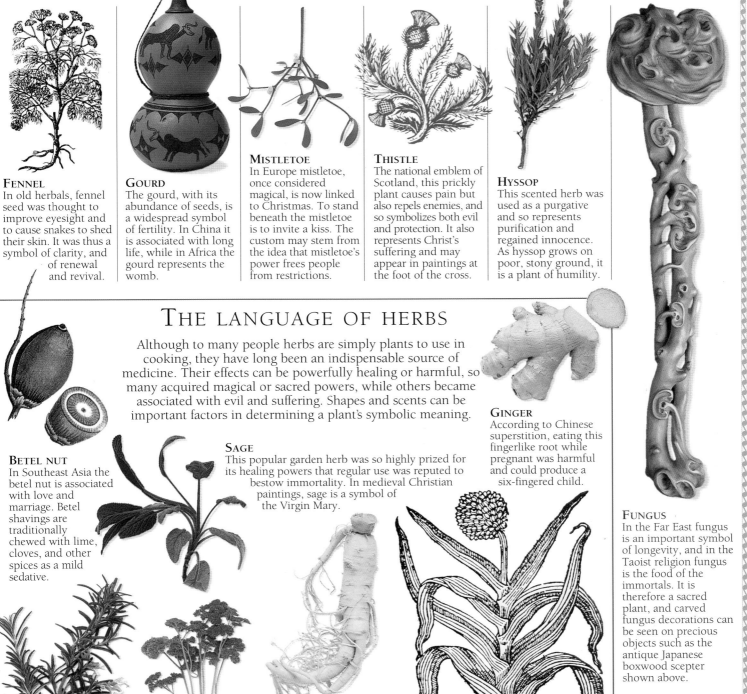

FENNEL
In old herbals, fennel seed was thought to improve eyesight and to cause snakes to shed their skin. It was thus a symbol of clarity, and of renewal and revival.

GOURD
The gourd, with its abundance of seeds, is a widespread symbol of fertility. In China it is associated with long life, while in Africa the gourd represents the womb.

MISTLETOE
In Europe mistletoe, once considered magical, is now linked to Christmas. To stand beneath the mistletoe is to invite a kiss. The custom may stem from the idea that mistletoe's power frees people from restrictions.

THISTLE
The national emblem of Scotland, this prickly plant causes pain but also repels enemies, and so symbolizes both evil and protection. It also represents Christ's suffering and may appear in paintings at the foot of the cross.

HYSSOP
This scented herb was used as a purgative and so represents purification and regained innocence. As hyssop grows on poor, stony ground, it is a plant of humility.

THE LANGUAGE OF HERBS

Although to many people herbs are simply plants to use in cooking, they have long been an indispensable source of medicine. Their effects can be powerfully healing or harmful, so many acquired magical or sacred powers, while others became associated with evil and suffering. Shapes and scents can be important factors in determining a plant's symbolic meaning.

GINGER
According to Chinese superstition, eating this fingerlike root while pregnant was harmful and could produce a six-fingered child.

BETEL NUT
In Southeast Asia the betel nut is associated with love and marriage. Betel shavings are traditionally chewed with lime, cloves, and other spices as a mild sedative.

SAGE
This popular garden herb was so highly prized for its healing powers that regular use was reputed to bestow immortality. In medieval Christian paintings, sage is a symbol of the Virgin Mary.

FUNGUS
In the Far East fungus is an important symbol of longevity, and in the Taoist religion fungus is the food of the immortals. It is therefore a sacred plant, and carved fungus decorations can be seen on precious objects such as the antique Japanese boxwood scepter shown above.

ROSEMARY
Sprigs of this herb, which symbolizes fidelity, were once included in bridal bouquets – tapping your lover with it would ensure constancy. Rosemary signifies remembrance and is often planted on graves.

PARSLEY
This herb is so slow to germinate that people once imagined its roots went down to the devil. Parsley was a symbol of death for the ancient Greeks, who used sprigs in wreaths.

GINSENG
Ginseng's forked root, like the mandrake's, symbolizes the human body. For this reason it is considered a life-giving herb. Ginseng's Chinese name means man-root, and it is a masculine, or yang, herb, reputed to increase virility.

GARLIC
To the ancient Greeks garlic, with its pungent smell, provided protection against evil spirits. Offerings of garlic were left at crossroads for the feared Hecate, goddess of the underworld. In Central European myth the cloves were reputed to ward off vampires. In China garlic is considered a lucky plant that will bless parents-to-be with many children.

SEE ALSO
GINSENG ☞ TWO 102; I CHING 111
HERBS ☞ PASSOVER PLATE 17
IVY ☞ BACCHUS 15; GRAPES 48
OTHER PLANTS ☞ VULVA 74; HENNAED HANDS 83; COLOR OF LIFE 107
PLANTS ☞ FLOWERS 50-53
REEDS ☞ PAN PIPES 81
SHAMROCK ☞ FOUR-LEAF CLOVER 79

NATURE'S FOODS

FOOD GIVES US LIFE and thus unity with all other living things. It grows through the interaction of the earth, the sun, and water. Foods that must be harvested, like corn and rice, are linked to the gods of abundance and fertility. Water is symbolic of life and purity, and milk represents the nourishment of mother earth. Food is part of life's cycle: all that lives must die and return to the earth, fertilizing it for new growth.

PORCELAIN DISH, QING DYNASTY

Peach, symbol of immortality

FIG
The fruit of the fig tree, with its many seeds, represents the feminine realm, fertility, and prosperity. A basket of figs symbolizes woman as goddess or mother. The fruit has erotic symbolism and was sacred to Bacchus, god of wine and vegetation. Adam and Eve covered their nakedness with leaves from the fig tree.

APPLE
The apple, especially if red, symbolizes love and fertility and is an emblem of Venus as love and desire. Its round shape indicates eternity and also the earth. In the Bible the apple represents temptation, although as an attribute of the Virgin Mary, it means redemption.

ORANGE
Sometimes shown in the hand of the infant Christ, the orange represents good fortune and fertility. Like the apple, its shape symbolizes eternity and immortality, and due to its distinctive color it is associated with the sun.

LEMON
A symbol of purity and faithfulness, the lemon was traditionally thought to have protective properties that could counter magic spells and poison. In Judaism the lemon represents the human heart.

PEACH
The peach is a symbol of immortality. In China it brings joy and protects against evil. In the hand of the infant Christ it represents salvation.

CHERRY
In Japan the cherry is associated with self-sacrifice, particularly in relation to samurai warriors – the red flesh of the fruit symbolizing their blood. In Christianity cherries are a fruit of paradise and are sometimes depicted in the hands of the infant Christ.

POMEGRANATE
Because of its color, the pomegranate symbolizes the sun, life, and blood, while its many seeds make it a symbol of fertility. In ancient Rome newly married women wore pomegranate wreaths, and pomegranate juice was used as a remedy for infertility.

GRAPES
Grapes produce wine and are a symbol of revelry and immortality, but also of blood and sacrifice. Grapes brought back from the Promised Land symbolized the promise of a new life to the Israelites. In Islam wine is the drink of the chosen in Paradise, and to Christians it is the blood of Christ.

SWEET ITALIAN GRAPES

Bacchus, god of wine, with his garland of vine leaves

Red wine of revelry

Overripe pomegranates and apples symbolize excess

THE YOUNG BACCHUS, CARAVAGGIO, c.1591-3

PLUM
In the Far East the plum is a symbol of ripening female sexuality, and may be viewed in the same way when it appears in dreams. In Christianity the plum represents fidelity.

DATE
In the desert regions of North Africa, clusters of dates traditionally represent life and fruitfulness. Because of their shape and abundance, dates are seen as a symbol of male fertility.

PINEAPPLE
The pineapple is a life-giving fruit and a symbol of fertility. In parts of America pineapples were a sign of hospitality, and sailors would place a pineapple on the gatepost to tell neighbors that they were home from sea. In the late 1800s, the Scottish Lord Dunmore echoed this custom with a fruit-shaped summer house to announce his return to Scotland from America.

THE PINEAPPLE, DUNMORE, SCOTLAND

EGG
The egg as origin of the universe is found in myths throughout the world. The egg contains the potential for life and so represents the womb, birth, and the universe. It is also a symbol of hope and of immortality, and in Christianity can represent the virgin birth.

SALT
Because of its purity, salt represents immortality. Named after Salus, Roman goddess of health, salt was once used in ceremonies in her honor. A grain dissolving in the ocean symbolizes the union of the human soul with the infinite. In Christianity salt has come to represent suffering.

BREAD
Bread symbolizes spiritual nourishment. It is the food of the body and of the soul. Bread is particularly important in Christian symbolism, where Christ is seen as the "bread of life." Bread at the communion service represents the body of Christ and its consumption represents oneness with Christ. The ceremonial "breaking of bread" may symbolize the death of the sacrificial victim.

The leek, symbol of Wales

The Queen's crown

LEEK
The leek represents victory and was thought to protect against wounds. It appears on the British pound coin as the emblem of Wales, and is also an attribute of St. David, patron saint of Wales.

HONEY
Honey is the food of the gods and represents immortality, rebirth, and fertility. It is associated with the moon and the feminine. To ancient Greeks it represented wisdom, and to Christians it symbolized Christ's gentleness and compassion. Paradise was known as "the land of milk and honey."

FOOD OF THE GODS
The people of Israel are seen below gathering **manna**, food sent by God from heaven to sustain the Jews in the wilderness during their long journey from Egypt. In the Bible it is described as white, like coriander seed, and tasting of wafers made with honey. Manna is also mentioned in the Koran, and is a symbol of God's love.

Nectar was the name used by Homer for the beverage of the Greek gods, which conferred immortality and beauty.

Amritsa is the elixir of immortality that emerged during the churning of the milky ocean and was consumed by the gods in Indian mythology.

Ambrosia was the food of the gods in Greek myth.

GATHERING OF THE MANNA, DIERIC BOUTS, c.1464-8

Aztec corncob vessel

RICE
Rice is an essential food and represents immortality and nourishment, both spiritual and literal. In many parts of Asia it is thought to possess a soul. The spirit of rice is revered and every stage of cultivation is accompanied by ritual to ensure a good crop. In the Western world rice is traditionally thrown over brides at weddings to ensure the happiness and fertility of their union.

CORN
In the Americas corn is a symbol of life, especially when it is intact as corn on the cob, and it is used as a motif in pottery. In ancient Mexico a corn plant depicted with a hummingbird symbolized the Sun Hero and new growth. In Europe and the Mediterranean corn represents peace, plenty, and the fecundity of the mother goddess.

MILK
The first and most nutritious food, milk symbolizes spiritual nourishment and immortality. It is often associated with the moon due to its color, and is seen as the food of the gods. In Hindu legend Vishnu reclines on the cosmic milky ocean from which the wonders of creation were churned at the dawn of time. In the Bible its symbolism is linked to that of honey.

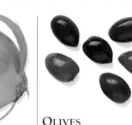

ONION
The many layered onion represents unity. It also symbolizes revelation, as one peels off the layers to reveal the center. Its round shape symbolizes the cosmos and immortality, and, because of its strong smell, it is used to ward off evil. It is said to be particularly effective against the dangerous influences of the moon.

OLIVES
An attribute of Athena and Apollo, the olive is a symbol of immortality and fruitfulness. In ancient Greece, a crown of wild olives, representing Zeus, was worn by the victor at the Olympic games. In the Bible the dove returned to the ark bearing an olive twig. This was a sign that the Flood sent by God was receding, and so the olive represents peace and reconciliation.

OLIVE OIL
The oil from the olive has its own symbolism. In Judaism, it is considered holy and is used as fuel for the sabbath lamp and for the menorah in the festival of Hanukkah.

SEE ALSO
CHERRY ☞ CHERRY 44; SAMURAI SWORD 91

FIG ☞ TREE OF KNOWLEDGE 44; FIG LEAF 84

FOOD OF THE GODS ☞ FUNGUS 47

NATURE'S FOODS ☞ PASSOVER PLATE 17; COMMUNION 19; WEDDING CAKE, CHOCOLATE 83; FOOD OFFERINGS 93

PINEAPPLE ☞ PINEAPPLE QUILT 70

RICE ☞ BLESSINGS 83

FLOWERS

FROM EARLIEST TIMES and in every culture flowers have held a special place in our hearts and lives. In ancient times certain flowers were viewed as earthly forms of the gods. People treasured them, used them in worship, and imbued them with magical powers. A flower in bud is symbolic of new life and potential, but flowers also accompany the dead to the grave. Flower motifs adorn churches and temples, are incorporated into jewelry, and decorate everything from fabric to furniture. Flowers have even wound their way into our language – we view the world through "rose-tinted glasses" or see life as "no bed of roses." Many flowers have taken on particular meanings, but what a certain flower means can differ vastly from one culture to another.

ANEMONE
From the Greek *anemos*, meaning wind, this flower denotes the transitory nature of life. In Greek myth anemones sprang from the blood of Adonis and represent death. In Christianity they are the blood of the saints.

POPPY
An opiate, the poppy symbolizes the ultimate sleep of death. Popular lore has it that the red poppies that sprang up after the Battle of Waterloo grew from the blood of the dead.

IRIS
Named after the Greek goddess of the rainbow, who transported women's souls to the underworld, irises were placed on graves. Louis VII adopted the iris as his emblem during the Crusades, and it evolved from the *fleur-de-Louis* to the *fleur-de-lis*, the three leaves symbolizing faith, wisdom, and valor.

FORGET-ME-NOT
European legend has it that a youth drowned in a river after picking this flower for his beloved. As he went under, he shouted, "Forget me not!", so the flower is a symbol of desperate love.

VIOLET
A Greek nymph was spared Apollo's lust by becoming a violet. In Christianity it is tied to humility.

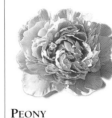

PASSION FLOWER
Often used in stained-glass windows, this flower is a Christian symbol. The Spanish believed it grew around the cross, others saw in its form the wounds of Jesus, and some viewed its flowering as God calling for converts.

PEONY
In ancient times this flower was thought to have magical properties. The Greeks used it to keep evil spirits at bay. The Japanese linked it to masculinity, riches, and good fortune, and adopted it as the Imperial flower. In China it was related to marriage and fertility and much used as a motif on temple walls.

CARNATION
In Renaissance portraits, this is a symbol of betrothal, particularly when held in the sitter's hand. In China the carnation is a common symbol of marriage.

CYCLAMEN
Dedicated to the Virgin Mary, the spot at its center symbolizes her bleeding heart. Once used in love potions, it is now associated with voluptuousness.

PANSY
The word stems from the French *pensées* (thoughts), and the flower is poetically linked to thoughts, thoughtfulness, and remembrance, as well as love. Placed over the eyes of someone asleep, the pansy can impel the dreamer to fall in love with the first person to appear. It is said to be sacred to St. Valentine, and is a Christian emblem of the Trinity.

HYACINTH
The Greek god Apollo created this flower from the blood of his beloved friend Hyacinthus, who was murdered while throwing the discus with him. It is a Christian symbol of prudence.

ORCHID
In China the orchid is a symbol of perfection. In England the purple spots on an orchid's petals are said to represent the blood of Christ.

PRE-RAPHAELITE FLOWER IMAGERY: SHAKESPEARE'S OPHELIA

OPHELIA, JOHN EVERETT MILLAIS, 1852

Driven to madness by her beloved Hamlet's murder of her father, Ophelia drowns herself in a stream. The garlands in her hair and the flowers that surround her are all charged with symbolic meaning. The willow represents forsaken love; the nettle growing in its branches represents pain; and the daisies near Ophelia's hand are symbolic of innocence. The chain of violets around her neck is associated with faithfulness, chastity, and untimely death. The poppy is also a symbol of death; other flowers floating in the water are linked to sorrow; and the forget-me-nots on the bank are an entreaty not to forget Ophelia.

THE LANGUAGE OF THE ROSE

More than any other flower, the rose and its symbolism have entered the human consciousness. In different cultures it has come to represent youth, purity, perfection, earthly love, and rebirth. It is the flower of courtship, of marriage, and even of death. Its essence has been distilled into love potions, perfumes, cosmetics, teas, and medicinal remedies. In the West there was a custom that a rose suspended over the dinner table meant that all confidences were to be held sacred, hence the central ceiling rose of Victorian architecture, and the white rose as a symbol of secrecy. The rose is also intricately linked to Catholicism – the rosary was originally made of rose hips strung together.

RED ROSE

Red roses were sacred to Venus and were – like the goddess – archetypal symbols of love and beauty. Even today these associations continue, roses being considered the messengers of love. In Christian tradition the red rose grew from drops of Christ's blood and the Madonna is sometimes depicted with a red rose in her hand. Also associated with war, the red rose was adopted by the Lancastrians in the English Wars of the Roses.

WHITE ROSE

Considered the flower of the moon or of the light, the white rose symbolizes purity, virginity, charm, and secrecy. It represents water in contrast to the fire of the red rose. It was the emblem of the House of York in the Wars of the Roses.

YELLOW ROSE

Symbol of the state of Texas, the yellow rose is also commonly associated with jealousy and infidelity. In 1759 the Order of the Golden Rose was created by papal decree, an honor reserved mainly for female Catholic sovereigns.

PETALS

In Roman times rose petals were a valuable currency. Ladies used them to make face packs in the hope of banishing wrinkles; guests at banquets dropped petals into their wine to stave off drunkenness, and victorious armies returned to streets strewn with petals.

The design here incorporates roses within roses

The focal point of the window is the classic Madonna and child

THE LITANY OF THE VIRGIN MARY, WEST ROSE WINDOW, REIMS CATHEDRAL, FRANCE

DETAIL OF A TUDOR ROSE

ROSE WINDOW

The rose window, so named because of its petallike shapes of glass, represents both the human aspiration for wholeness and coherence and the realization of those same desires. Rose windows, which first appeared in 13th-century France, are thought to be symbols of eternity. They have been likened to mandalas – Eastern objects of meditation – for their perfection of geometry and of form. The many paths that lead to the center are like the paths that lead to enlightenment.

Rose motifs adorn this lady from her hat to the rings on her fingers

The carnation behind this noblewoman's ear is a sign that she is betrothed

TUDOR ROSE

This 16th-century lady wears a dress embroidered with a feast of Tudor roses. The Tudor rose with its red outer petals and white inner ones symbolized the union of the two royal houses – York (the white rose) and Lancaster (the red rose). Henry Tudor adopted this rose as his standard when he married Elizabeth of York in 1485.

PORTRAIT OF A LADY, BRITISH SCHOOL, 1569

THE LOTUS

One of the most ancient symbols to appear in Asian art, the lotus symbolizes both creation and purity. Its long stem is the umbilical cord that holds Man to his origins, while its perfect flower represents enlightenment and the purity to which the human soul aspires. The thousand-petaled lotus represents the sun emerging from the cosmic ocean, the sun and the waters being vital to growth. The lotus symbolizes divine birth, since the god Brahma emerges from Vishnu's navel seated on a lotus, and then creates the universe. It also symbolizes the sun and the cycle of birth and rebirth, since its petals open at dawn and close at sunset.

FLOWER OF PERFECTION
The lotus emerges unsullied from swamps and lakes. For this reason, and because its petals open and close with the passing of the day, it is highly symbolic in the East.

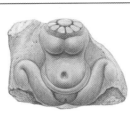

FERTILITY SYMBOL
This 3rd-century Indian figurine represents a mother goddess, shown here squatting in childbirth. She has a lotus – a symbol of fertility – for a head.

CHRYSANTHEMUM
In China and Japan the chrysanthemum is an emblem of fall and long life, of scholarship and contentment. It was thought to hold the key to eternal life. The Japanese have adopted it as a national emblem and as the badge of the Imperial family.

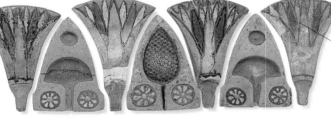

Floral inlays and molds

FIRST FLOWER OF EGYPT
Often appearing in decoration, the lotus embodies royal power. It is associated with the god Nefertem and the sun god, Re, who is sometimes depicted as a child lying on a lotus. Capitals of Egyptian columns are often carved to resemble lotuses, either in bud or full flower.

The gods are standing on beds of lotuses

MARIGOLD
In Chinese belief the marigold is the emblem of long life – "the flower of ten thousand years." Mexicans claim the flower's color is tinted by the blood of the Aztecs, who were massacred by the Spaniards in their quest for gold.

Protective lotus flowers surround the Buddha's halo

In this typically Tibetan example, the Buddha is richly ornamented with jewels

HE-HE GODS
In China the lotus represents purity, perfection, and spiritual grace combined with fertility and the ripeness of summer. Here, both of the He-he, twin gods of prosperity, carry a lotus in a jar. The garment worn by the god on the left is also decorated with a lotus. The He-he themselves symbolize concord and harmony between married couples.

BUDDHIST JEWEL IN THE LOTUS
In Buddhist cosmology the lotus symbolizes both purity and the primordial waters from which all life is created. Because the beautiful flower grows out of mud and water, it is associated with human aspiration and potential. The Buddha is often represented as the jewel in the lotus, seated on a lotus throne, the pinnacle of perfection.

SUNFLOWER
In Greek myth, Clytie is turned into this sun-worshiping flower as a consequence of her blind love for the sun god, Apollo, hence the flower's association with blind infatuation. Some environmentalists have adopted the sunflower as their symbol because it absorbs air pollutants.

The thousand-petaled lotus supports the Buddha (Akshobya), the two together being a potent symbol of enlightenment

A TIBETAN *THANG-KA*, SACRED TEMPLE BANNER

NARCISSUS IN GREEK MYTH

ECHO AND NARCISSUS (DETAIL),
J.W. WATERHOUSE, 1903

In Greek mythology the youth Narcissus spurned the love of the beautiful nymph Echo who could only repeat the last words spoken to her, and she wasted away until only her voice remained. As punishment, the gods condemned the vain Narcissus to fall in love with his own image. When he saw his reflection in a pool of water he was unable to tear himself away and died. He was changed into the narcissus flower which grows at the water's edge.

LILY

A white lily is the most widely accepted symbol of purity and perfection in the West. It is also a symbol of peace, divinity, and innocence. In Greco-Roman mythology the lily was believed to have come from the milk of the goddess Hera/Juno. To the Jews it is the emblem of the tribe of Judah.

LILY OF THE VALLEY

This is the flower of Ostara, Norse goddess of springtime. Throughout Europe it represents spring and new life, and so also symbolizes the advent of Christ. In France, it is the workers' flower, traditionally given to employees on Labor Day, May 1st.

MAGNOLIA

This flower is a Chinese symbol of feminine beauty and gentleness. In ancient China, the plant was the exclusive property of the emperor. A gift of a magnolia plant to a subject was therefore a sign of special favor. Historically it is also associated with a celebrated heroine who shares her Chinese name, *Mu-lan*, with that of the flower. *Mu-lan* disguised herself as a man in order to battle on behalf of her father.

NARCISSUS

The sweet, intoxicating scent of the narcissus was once believed to cause madness. "Narcissism" means vanity, and the flower symbolizes the dangers of vanity. To Christians, the flower is a symbol of divine love. In China its flowering at New Year signals good fortune.

CROCUS

People once believed that wearing garlands of crocuses would ward off drunkenness. The species saffron was highly prized in medieval times when its pigment dyed garments a brilliant yellow, a symbol of light and nobility.

HONEYSUCKLE

Given by the French to their loved ones to symbolize their union, the honeysuckle represents more broadly generous love. It was once used medicinally to charm away boils.

THE ANNUNCIATION, SIMONE MARTINI AND LIPPO MEMMI, 1333

The angel Gabriel holds a lily – a symbol of Mary's chastity

PRIMROSE

The primrose heralds the spring and an end to winter gloom, and is associated with purity and youth. In Germanic folklore, he who wears a primrose will find hidden treasure.

JASMINE

This perfumed flower is prized in India. It is a love symbol, and so is carried in Hindu bridal garlands. In China jasmine is an emblem of beauty; in Christianity a symbol of heavenly happiness.

DAISY

Originally the "day's eye," the daisy represents innocence and is sometimes an attribute of the Virgin. It is an emblem of the Germanic mother goddess Freya.

THE LILY AND CHRISTIANITY

The lily is associated with the Virgin Mary – its whiteness representing her purity, untainted by sin. It is often depicted in paintings of the Annunciation, either held by the angel Gabriel or in a vase. It is the flower of Easter and is sometimes seen with a sword at the Last Judgment, the two together symbolizing innocence and guilt. The lily is associated with chastity and is the emblem of a number of saints, for example Catherine of Siena, Francis of Assisi, Francis Xavier, and Thomas Aquinas. In the New Testament the lilies of the field are referred to by Christ as a symbol of simplicity and of purity.

SEE ALSO

CHRYSANTHEMUM ☞ IMPERIAL FLOWER *115*

IRIS ☞ FLEUR-DE-LIS *105*

LILY ☞ LILY WHITE *106*; LILY *93*

LOTUS ☞ BODHISATTVA *23*

PEONY, ROSE ☞ TRANSITORY NATURE OF LIFE *57*

ROSE WINDOW ☞ YANTRA OR MANDALA *104*; KNOT *105*

SEA CREATURES

ONE OF THE MOST IMPORTANT SYMBOLS in world myth, the fish represents fertility, life, and death, and is generally auspicious. It is associated with the mother goddess, the moon, and the primeval waters from which all life grew. It is one of the earliest symbols in Christianity, signifying both Christ and the faithful, swimming in the sea of life. Jonah was swallowed by a great fish, and similar stories abound in other cultures. In Hinduism the god Vishnu's first incarnation was in the form of a great fish that saved mankind from the flood.

Grapevines, attributes of Dionysus, god of wine

Pirates turned into dolphins

CONTEMPORARY CHINESE CARP

Symbol of courage and good fortune

CARP
This is an important symbol in the Far East. In China it represents perseverance and success owing to its ability to leap formidable rapids. In general, the carp symbolizes patience, determination, and long life. Its armorlike scales are linked to valor; in Japan it is a symbol of the Samurai and of courage.

SEA HORSE
The delicate sea horse is the mount of Poseidon/Neptune, the Greco-Roman god of the sea. It also appears in heraldry, often to signify bravery at sea, and as a civic emblem to show overseas trade.

A phallic-shaped sexual symbol

EEL
The eel plays a part in Polynesian flood myths and also has erotic associations. In Tahiti it is an ancestor figure. In China it is a symbol of carnal love, while in Britain the term "slippery as an eel" signifies a person who wriggles out of trouble.

DOLPHIN
In Greco-Roman myth this noble fish conducts souls to the world beyond, saves the shipwrecked, and symbolizes safety and speed. It is associated with the sun god, Apollo, and is linked to Dionysus, god of wine. The dolphin is a widespread symbol of virtue.

INUIT IVORY CARVING

WHALE
In the Bible, Jonah was swallowed by a great fish, probably a whale, and disgorged alive onto dry land three days later. A similar legend exists among the Inuits. The whale has thus come to signify death and rebirth, and darkness before the light. In Arctic, Slav, and Russian myth the earth rests on the back of a great whale. When the whale moves, there is an earthquake.

SHARK
One of the most potent symbols of terror, the shark is revered as an ancestor figure in the Pacific regions of Polynesia, Melanesia, and the Solomon Islands. In Hawaii, as in parts of West Africa, sharks are also held sacred.

SALMON
Like the carp, the salmon swims determinedly upstream in search of its birthplace and so symbolizes perseverance and courage. It is associated with the moon, and is a symbol of death and rebirth.

SWORDFISH
In the Sepik region of New Guinea the swordfish is a totem figure, and swordfish-shaped masks are worn during sacred dances. The Ainu of Japan worship a sea divinity that takes the form of a swordfish.

The octopus was a familiar sight in Aegean life and art

MYCENAEAN JAR, C.1400 BC

OCTOPUS
Because of its spiraling tentacles, the octopus is related to the symbolism of the spiral – air, water, and rolling thunder and lightning. It is also a symbol of fickleness and changeability since it alters color when under threat.

THE LANGUAGE OF SHELLS

Shells share water's symbolic associations and are linked to the moon and to the feminine, yin principle. Venus, goddess of love, was born in the waters and transported to land on a scallop shell. In China shells symbolize a successful journey and good fortune, and in Christianity they represent the baptismal waters, perhaps because shells were sometimes used to carry water. Those shells that consist of two halves fused together are symbolic of secrecy or sexual passion, and shellfish such as oysters are thought to be aphrodisiacs.

SIENESE SYMBOL

SCALLOP SHELL
The scallop shell is an emblem of Venus, and also represents the female sexual organ. In Christianity it often signifies pilgrimage, particularly to the shrine of St. James in the Spanish city of Santiago de Compostela, where pilgrims wore the scallop on their clothing. The shell was also adopted as an emblem in Siena.

OYSTER
Possibly because the oyster nurtures the pearl, it represents the feminine realm – the womb, the fertility of the waters, and the moon. With its tightly sealed shell, it is also a symbol of secrecy.

EGYPTIAN LUCKY GIRDLE
The Egyptians believed that the cowrie shell had protective powers because it resembled the female sexual organ. For this reason it was deemed particularly effective as a fertility charm, or to safeguard a pregnancy, when worn low down on a woman's body.

SECTION OF EGYPTIAN GIRDLE WITH COWRIE SHELLS

Cowrie shell

Heh, god of "millions of years," symbolizes long life

Beards or sidelocks of youth

Fish amulets, to prevent drowning

To sell

Treasure

CHINESE CALLIGRAPHIC SYMBOLS

COWRIE SHELLS
These small shells were used as a form of currency in a number of ancient cultures. In China the graphic design of the shell became the symbol of money in the writing system. The pictogram was then incorporated with other written symbols to represent concepts related to money.

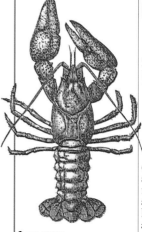

CEREMONIAL BUDDHIST CONCH

CEREMONIAL CONCH
The conch shares the symbolism of the spiral owing to its convoluted shape. In Mayan culture it represents the waters. It is the emblem of Neptune, as well as of the god Vishnu as Lord of the Waters.

CRAB
Because of its protective shell, the crab is associated with the womb and with motherhood. It is the symbol of Cancer, fourth sign of the zodiac, which is ruled by the moon. Due to its habit of walking sideways, the crab also has associations of evasiveness and deceit. In Buddhism it is linked to the periods of cosmic night between the ages of Brahma, or the sleep of death between one incarnation and the next. In Africa the crab is considered a symbol of evil.

LOBSTER
In the East the lobster is viewed as a good omen and is often portrayed without claws. In ancient Greece it was similarly valued and was considered sacred. In Chinese art it is sometimes seen at the feet of the bodhisattva Kuan Yin, and it symbolizes wealth and marital harmony. In Japan it appears on many New Year presents as a token of congratulation and, because of its curved, brittle form, as an emblem of long life.

STARFISH
Seen in Europe as a symbol of the undying power of love, the starfish in Christianity represents Mary guiding the faithful through the storms of love.

SEA URCHIN
In Celtic lore the sea urchin is known as the serpent's egg, and in its petrified form it is viewed as a symbol of the world. It is thought to be able to foretell the approach of a storm when it attaches itself to a rock, using it as an anchor. Blind and largely defenseless, it is also a symbol of all weak creatures in God's care.

INSECTS & OTHERS

INSECTS, SNAILS, AND SPIDERS differ biologically but are commonly referred to as "creepy crawlies" – lowly animals usually shunned and even feared. In ancient times, however, they were the focus of much interest. The Egyptians singled out the beetle as a creature to be revered, incorporating it in the form of a scarab in their art and their jewelry, and even in funerary offerings. For other cultures the spider is particularly important, due in part to its remarkable weaving abilities, and the bee often has powerful associations both because of its poisonous sting and its life-giving honey.

FLY
In many cultures the fly is seen as evil and corrupt, and sometimes represents weakness or insignificance, but in parts of Africa there is a fly god, and among the Navajo of America the Big Fly is a heroic figure. The ancient Egyptians wore fly amulets to keep real flies away.

DRAGONFLY
Probably so-named because of its long, sinuous body, this beautiful insect shares the symbolism of the butterfly, representing immortality and regeneration. It is the national emblem of Japan, which is known as the "Island of the Dragonfly." It also represents unreliability and instability, perhaps due to its hovering and darting movements. In China the dragonfly is symbolic of summer, but also of weakness. To Native Americans the dragonfly symbolizes change and illusion, and also speed, a whirlwind, and activity.

LADYBUG
Named after Our Lady (the Virgin Mary), because of its good works in ridding plants of pests, the ladybug is a symbol of good luck.

WINGED SCARAB

EGYPTIAN SCARAB
The scarab, which takes its form from the humble dung beetle, was the most popular good-luck charm in ancient Egypt. The beetle was deemed sacred because it mimicked the passage of the sun across the heavens in its own heroic struggle to roll balls of dung containing its eggs over long distances. The young hatched from these balls, representing new life emerging from the earth. Scarab amulets were commonly buried with the dead as symbols of regeneration.

DUNG BEETLE

THE SIGNIFICANCE OF BEES

Bees evoke feelings both of fear and admiration. The bee is widely seen as a symbol of immortality and rebirth, as well as of diligence and social organization. It is an emblem of several Greco-Roman and Indian gods, including Cupid and Kama, both gods of love. Kama is sometimes depicted with a line of bees following him, representing the sweet pain of love.

HONEYBEE

BEES IN CHRISTIANITY
In Christian allegory a queen bee sometimes represents the Virgin Mary. As Mary gives birth to Christ, so the queen bee produces honey. The hive is then a symbol of the Church.

"Busy bees" in a "hive of activity"

POPE URBAN VIII'S ARMS
The coat of arms of Pope Urban VIII features the keys to the kingdom of heaven, plus the Barberini bees, symbols of his family. These same bees grace a 17th-century fountain in Rome, *Fontana delle Api*, designed by Bernini to honor the Pope.

The Barberini bees   COAT OF ARMS

BUTTERFLY & CICADA ON CHINESE 19TH-CENTURY PURSE

Butterfly of joy

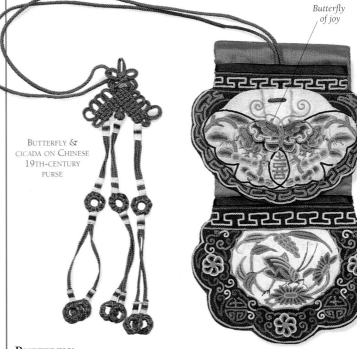

BUTTERFLY
Because of its metamorphosis from a caterpillar, the butterfly is seen as a symbol of rebirth and resurrection. As it emerges from its chrysalis it represents the soul leaving the body. To ancient Greeks the butterfly represents the soul, and to the Chinese and Japanese it is a sign of both immortality and joy. In Chinese art, butterflies combined with plum blossoms symbolize long life, and two butterflies together indicate a happy marriage.

JAPANESE-STYLE "SIGNATURE" OF THE ARTIST WHISTLER

THE TRANSITORY NATURE OF LIFE

VASE OF FLOWERS, JACOB VAN WALSCAPELLE, C.1670

The insects in Dutch flower paintings often enhance the symbolism of the flowers. Here, overblown roses, peonies, tulips, and a variety of other blooms illustrate the transitory nature of worldly joys: youthful beauty soon languishes and fades; love loses its innocence; riches cannot be taken to the grave. The short-lived fly crawling over the white rose in the center is a symbol of transience; the centipede and bugs amid the rose's petals hint at corruption and decay. Butterflies, however – common symbols of everlasting joy – offer signs of hope and renewal.

FLY AND CENTIPEDE

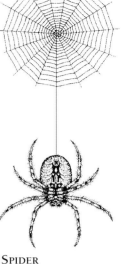

SNAIL

Since it constantly emerges from and withdraws into its shell, the snail is associated with the waxing and waning moon, and symbolizes birth and rebirth. It is generally viewed as lucky, and folklore has it that if a girl places a snail on a piece of slate, it will "write" the name of her husband-to-be.

WORMS

Historically the worm was associated with the devil, and it continues to have rather sinister connotations. In the Bible it denotes degradation and humiliation. More generally this legless creature symbolizes the earth or lowly life emerging from the earth, but also darkness.

SPIDER

Spider myths occur in many cultures. In China a spider sliding down a thread symbolizes good fortune descending from heaven. In general the spider represents the sun, or a Great Mother as weaver of destiny. A spider controls its web from the center just as the sun generates rays from its fiery center. Spider-woman, creator-daughter of the sun, appears in the myths of Native Americans, and in Japan a similar spider-woman can ensnare unwary travelers.

ASHANTI SCORPION TOE GUARD

MOTH

As the moth is irresistibly attracted to the light, so the soul is drawn to the divine truth. The moth is thus a symbol of the soul's quest for truth. Because of its delicate structure and brief lifespan, it also represents fragility and impermanence, frequently dying in its pursuit of light.

ANT

Like the bee, the ant is a symbol of thrift, hard work, and diligence, and also of community life. It is respected in most cultures. To the Chinese the ant represents patriotism, virtue, and orderliness. To Hindus it is more like the moth, symbolizing the transitory nature of life.

WASP

Wasps represent order within a community. However, ancient Egyptians and Persian Zoroastrians linked the wasp with evil, as did the Greeks and Romans. According to Polish legend, bees were created by God, but when the Devil tried to create bees, they turned into wasps.

LOCUST

Because of its voracious eating habits and capacity to strip large areas of vegetation, the locust is widely associated with calamity, destruction, and greed. In the Bible the locust is an instrument of punishment, sent as a plague by God to the Egyptians.

SCORPION

Widely associated with evil, destruction, and death, the scorpion also symbolizes envy and hatred, and represents darkness since it lives below the earth. Ancient Egyptians worshiped the goddess Selket in the form of a scorpion. The Ashanti wore scorpion jewelry to protect against scorpion bites.

SEE ALSO

EGYPTIAN SCARAB ☞ SCARAB 35

SCORPION ☞ SCORPIO 112

SPIDER ☞ WITCH'S FAMILIAR 79

SIGNIFICANCE OF BEES ☞ HONEY 49; VENUS AND CUPID 82

THE TRANSITORY NATURE OF LIFE ☞ ASIAN BADGES OF HONOR 115

REPTILES & AMPHIBIANS

AMPHIBIOUS CREATURES, ANIMALS THAT LIVE both on land and in the water, take on the symbolic associations of water, the source of all life. Reptiles are mostly associated with the earth and therefore assume the fertility symbolism of the earth, although their appearance often inspires fear and disgust. Reptiles that hold a special place in the popular imagination are dinosaurs, ancient inhabitants of the earth. Their symbolism is mixed – they are both giant monsters, terrifying to behold, and among the most fascinating of all the creatures known to us.

TYRANNOSAURUS REX
A formidable 47ft (15m) high, T. rex is certainly the best known and most feared of the dinosaurs. It has been popularized in films, fiction, and children's cartoons, and although a symbol of extinction, is far from extinct in people's minds.

CROCODILE
The crocodile has long been both feared and revered. Living on land and in water it carries the symbolism of each, and is thus very powerful. "Crocodile tears" are false tears, from the belief that crocodiles weep while devouring their victims.

NEWT
The newt is generally thought of as an evil, harmful creature. Such was its reputation that in *Macbeth*, Shakespeare listed "eye of newt" as one of the ingredients in the witches' brew designed to conjure up evil spirits that would reveal the future.

JAPANESE SYMBOL OF LONG LIFE

FROGS AND TOADS

Frogs and toads are both associated with water and the moon, and therefore with fertility and the feminine realm. Both undergo the process of metamorphosis, from tadpole to frog, and so are symbolic of resurrection. The frog was an emblem of Aphrodite, and Heket, Egyptian goddess of birth, took the form of a frog. The toad, however, became associated with witchcraft and with a more sinister symbolism.

Frog motif on Zuni bowl

FROG BOWL
The frogs modeled around this Southwestern bowl indicate the high regard given to frogs in the Americas. They are esteemed as harbingers of rain, and for their cleansing and purifying powers.

QING FROG
In China the frog represents the lunar yin principle and the frog spirit is revered as a healer and bringer of prosperity.

CHAMELEON
The chameleon's changing color symbolizes inconstancy and changing fortunes. Its eyes, which can see in different directions, see into both the past and future. In parts of Africa it is viewed as magical, and brings rain.

TORTOISE OR TURTLE
Linked to the moon and water, the tortoise and turtle symbolize fertility and long life. Various world myths speak of a tortoise supporting the world, and in Hinduism a man-tortoise was the ancestor of mankind. In Aesop's *Fables* the tortoise represents steady determination.

Inlaid turquoise eyes

ANASAZI FROG
The widespread association of the frog with fertility was particularly strong among Native American peoples. The ancient Anasazi people who lived on the border of Arizona and New Mexico used jet and much-prized turquoise in the making of this ornament, reflecting the importance of the frog in their culture.

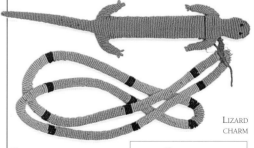

LIZARD CHARM

LIZARD
The lizard's sun-seeking habit symbolizes the soul's search for awareness. The Romans believed that the lizard hibernated, and so it represented death and resurrection. To Native Americans, lizards have magic powers.

SEE ALSO
FROGS AND TOADS ☞ WITCH'S FAMILIAR *79*
ROD OF AESCULAPIUS ☞ DIAMOND BROOCH *40*; CADUCEUS *108*
SNAKES ☞ DOUBLE-HEADED SERPENT, HYDRA *28*
THE FALL ☞ TREE OF KNOWLEDGE *44*; FIG *48*

SNAKES

The snake, or serpent, is probably the most widely revered of all creatures because it embodies so many forces. Its underground lair allies it with the underworld and it is associated with the primal waters from which all life was created. The serpent symbol was widespread in agricultural societies where it was used to represent the fertility of the soil.

PUEBLO
SNAKE STICK

SNAKE STICK
Among the Pueblo peoples of America, the snake is associated with thunder and lightning. Snake sticks such as the one above were used in annual rituals to call down the rain that ensured a good harvest. The snake sticks were themselves symbols of lightning.

Sacred snakes that banish evil spirits

EGYPT
In ancient Egypt the serpent was feared and worshiped. Several deities are depicted in the form of a snake – in this tomb painting a worshiper is seen kneeling before the serpent goddess Meretseger, the guardian of the Valley of the Kings.

19TH-CENTURY
SRI LANKAN MASK

SNAKES & LADDERS
This childhood game represents life's journey. Ladders are positive symbols of success and achievement, whereas snakes represent the slippery slopes of misfortune.

SNAKE DEMON MASK
This Sri Lankan mask of a Naga Rassa, or snake demon, is worn in dances to chase away evil spirits causing sickness. Nagas, or sacred snakes, have the power to be both protective and destructive.

EGYPTIAN
TOMB
PAINTING

THE FALL
The fall from grace of Adam and Eve is inextricably linked with the serpent. It was a serpent, here in female form, that tempted Eve to taste the forbidden fruit of the tree. The serpent is therefore viewed as a symbol of smooth-tongued evil and deceitfulness, and as the embodiment of temptation and sin.

ROD OF AESCULAPIUS
A serpent coiled around a rod was both the emblem and symbol of Aesculapius, the Roman god of medicine. Its association with healing comes from the snake's shedding of its skin, making it a symbol of renewal and regeneration. In alchemy a serpent around a pole represents the harnessing of the metal quicksilver (mercury).

SHIP'S
EMBLEM

MEDUSA
With hair of writhing serpents, Medusa's appearance was so hideous that all who looked at her turned to stone. In addition to being a symbol of terror, she embodied enchantment and cunning.

THE TEMPTATION OF ADAM AND EVE,
TOMMASO MASOLINO, *C.*1427

MAMMALS

BECAUSE OF THEIR COMPLEX AND OFTEN INTIMATE relationships with humans, animals have always played a prominent part in our imagination and in our mythology, literature, and art. Many, especially predatory species, have been worshiped and credited with protective powers. Names of animals were given to the constellations, and people even claimed descent from these powerful creatures. Certain animals have been traditionally paired in conflict – the lion and the unicorn, for instance, which are associated with the sun and the moon. This may represent a balance between the opposing forces in nature.

HARE, MEDIEVAL PSALTER

HARE
A nocturnal animal, the hare is widely associated with the moon, and also with lust and fertility. To Native Americans the Great Hare represents opposing characters: part clown and part god, creator and transformer of our animal nature. In China it is yin, symbol of the feminine principle. The hare's association with fertility probably accounts for the Easter Bunny, representing spring and the growth of new life.

MOUSE
In Western mythology, the mouse is associated with the powers of darkness. The Bible considers it unclean and devilish. Elsewhere, however, the mouse is viewed as orderly and methodical.

EGYPTIAN CAT
In ancient Egypt cats were revered, and the male cat was an emblem of the sun god. Cats were also sacred to the goddess Bastet who had the head of a cat and who represented the power of the sun to ripen crops.
So valued were cats that thousands were mummified after they died and buried in special graveyards in honor of Bastet.

Intricate pattern of bandaging

37348

MUMMIFIED
EGYPTIAN CAT

BLACK CAT
Being largely nocturnal, the cat is associated with the moon. It is also credited with supernatural powers, both good and evil, and is the companion of witches. In Norse legend, if a black cat crossed your path it was a sign that Satan was thinking about you. In America, a black cat crossing your path brings bad luck, but in England and Japan this is a good omen.

THE OLD SHEPHERD'S CHIEF MOURNER, SIR EDWIN LANDSEER, C.1837

DOG, PROTECTOR AND LOYAL FRIEND
In Greek mythology Cerberus was the three-headed dog that guarded the gates of the realm of the dead and acted as a spirit guide. In Judaic and Islamic traditions the dog is considered unclean, while in Zoroastrianism it is regarded highly. Everywhere, however, the dog is a symbol of faithfulness and protectiveness, of blind love and obedience. The dog is the eleventh sign of the Chinese zodiac.

ASS OR DONKEY
A beast of burden, the ass, or donkey, is a symbol of poverty, of stupidity, and also of fertility. Greek writers used the ass to represent foolishness, and we still use the term "silly ass." For the ancient Egyptians, the wild ass of the desert symbolized loneliness and isolation. In Christianity the humble ass is blessed: it bore Mary to Bethlehem and Jesus into Jerusalem.

"The most ill-starred of quadrupeds, pitiful and miserable."
Roman writer

BRAYING ASS

FOX
The fox universally represents cunning and deception. In some traditions it has the power to transform its shape in order to deceive, for instance in the East, the fox can become a beautiful maiden who creates trouble. Also, like the wolf in *Little Red Riding Hood*, a fox sometimes dresses in the clothes of a trustworthy person in order to catch unwary prey. Some Native Americans have fox tribes and clans.

RAM

The ram embodies virility and creative energy. It is associated with many gods and is a common sacrificial animal, its blood symbolically returning fertility to the soil. The Hebrew ritual horn, the *shofar*, blown at the feast of Rosh Hashanah, is made from a ram's horn.

EGYPTIAN CONTAINER

HEDGEHOG

In antiquity the hedgehog was reputed to collect grapes by rolling over them and so catching them on its spikes. Christianity associates it with the Devil and with evil, as this practice was likened to stealing people's souls. The hedgehog sometimes symbolizes witchcraft, as witches were thought to assume the form of hedgehogs to drink milk from cows.

Spiral-shaped horns, historically used by Jews to herald the Jubilee year

Goat's-head wine cup, symbol of Bacchus and drunken revelry

GREEK DRINKING CUP

GOAT

Because of its agility and urge to climb, the goat is a symbol of the far-seeing quest for truth. However, the goat also stands for lawlessness, demonic powers, lust, and fertility. Satyrs were half human, half goat, and the devil is often depicted with the horns and hooves of a goat.

ROMAN CLAY PIG

PIG

The boar is a symbol of courage (its head was eaten as protection against danger), and the sow is associated in many cultures with fertility and a mother goddess. In Judaism and Islam the pig is viewed as the most unclean of all animals, and in Christianity it is linked to Satan and symbolizes gluttony.

HORSES

The horse represents speed, grace, and nobility. It is both a solar and lunar symbol: the heavenly chariots of Apollo and the Indian sun god Surya were drawn by fiery or white horses, as was Neptune's ocean chariot.

BUCKING BRONCO

In parts of the US and Canada men compete at riding untrained horses, the goal being to complete a round without being thrown. This challenge emphasizes the horse's reputation as a wild and noble creature.

20TH-CENTURY WATERCOLOR

Hands kept free to draw bow while riding

MONGOLIAN HORSEMAN

In Mongolia herdsmen had expert cavalry skills: they raced without harness and reins. This custom probably originated when their warlike ancestors rode horses into battle and had to keep their hands free to fight.

MONGOL WARRIOR

OX

The symbolism of the ox has much in common with that of the bull and the buffalo. While clearly symbolizing male power and strength, all three animals, because of their crescent-shaped horns, also have lunar, hence feminine, attributes. The bull is the mount of the Hindu god Shiva, and in Taoism the sage Lao Tzu is shown riding an ox to represent the taming of the ego.

Crescent-shaped horns associated with the moon

Rope, symbol of man's attempt at controlling beast

HUMPED OX, FROM 18TH-CENTURY INDIAN MINIATURE

LION, KING OF BEASTS

The lion is the king of the beasts in most parts of the world. Its golden color, fiery mane, and great strength associate it with the sun, although the lioness may also be linked with the moon and great mother goddess figures. Lions have often been carved into thrones and are also sculpted at entrances, where they act as guardians.

LION FAMILY, 13TH-CENTURY ARAB MANUSCRIPT

ORIENTAL LIONS
In antiquity lions were found not just in Africa, but also in the Middle East and India. They were kept by kings as a symbol of royal power and were used in hunting. The lion is also a symbol of the wisdom of the Buddha.

CHINESE TIGER, 13TH CENTURY

LION GARGOYLE

HERALDIC LION
The lion is the most important animal in heraldic art, probably because nobility wished to be associated with its valor and strength. It is shown "rampant," standing on its hind legs, or "sejant," seated.

Spout for draining water

GUARDIAN LION
A lion's image is often placed on buildings, perhaps to add protection. As a gargoyle it carries water away from the roof, its solar nature combining with water as a symbol of fertility.

CHURCHILL FAMILY EMBLEM

Lion in the "sejant" position, seated with one paw raised

TIGER
Like the lion, the tiger symbolizes royalty, courage, and strength. It is particularly important in the Far East, where it replaces the lion as king of beasts. In China, where it is the emblem of the West, if a tiger devours a man, that man's soul becomes the tiger's slave and preys upon other men.

EGYPTIAN JACKAL-HEADED CANOPIC JAR

JACKAL
The head of the Egyptian god Anubis is that of a jackal. Jackals were thought to haunt graveyards and were reputed to see both by day and night. Clear-sighted Anubis was a pathfinder, guiding spirits to the next world. Canopic jars, which contained embalmed organs, had Anubis-shaped stoppers.

ST. JEROME AND THE LION
There are several stories of a fierce lion helped by a devout man whom it then befriends. Like Androcles in Aesop's *Fables*, St. Jerome is said to have extracted a thorn from a lion's paw. In return the lion renounced its fierce nature and lived peaceably with him. This symbolizes man's mastery of his own animal nature.

St. Jerome removing thorn from lion's paw

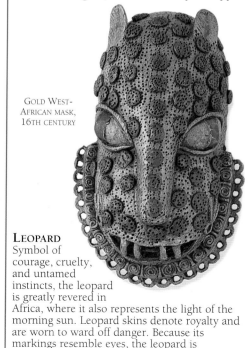

GOLD WEST-AFRICAN MASK, 16TH CENTURY

LEOPARD
Symbol of courage, cruelty, and untamed instincts, the leopard is greatly revered in Africa, where it also represents the light of the morning sun. Leopard skins denote royalty and are worn to ward off danger. Because its markings resemble eyes, the leopard is sometimes known as the Great Watcher.

ST. JEROME AND THE LION, NICCOLO COLANTONIO, 1450

HERALDIC STAG

ISLAMIC PLATE

CHINESE ENAMELED ELEPHANT, 18TH CENTURY

THREE MONKEYS, JAPAN

STAG

Associated with hunting, the stag is a solar animal and an enemy of the serpent. The shape of its antlers recalls the Tree of Life, and because the antlers are renewed each year, the stag is a symbol of regeneration. In European and Asian mythology stag hunts often lead to a supernatural encounter.

GAZELLE

The swift-running gazelle is a symbol of beauty and of the soul, particularly in Arabic literature. It can also be used as a metaphor for the beloved. In Christianity, when the gazelle is shown fleeing from an animal of prey, such as a panther or lion, it represents the soul fleeing from earthly passions.

Ornate enameling, befitting an imperial elephant

MONKEY

The monkey is sacred to some West African tribes, for whom it is an ancestor figure. Generally it represents mischief and inquisitiveness, but the monkey-god Hanuman is highly regarded in Hinduism. From Japan comes a well-known motif of the three Mystic Monkeys, which see no evil, hear no evil, and speak no evil.

AUSTRALIAN BARK PAINTING

KANGAROO

Among some Australian Aboriginals the kangaroo is an ancestor-spirit that protects and guides them and plays a major part in their myths. Each Aboriginal group has a different animal ancestor and feels a kinship with that species. The kangaroo ancestor left many traces of its journey at the time of creation, seen today in features of the landscape.

CANADIAN HEADDRESS

BEAVER

According to Native American myth, the beaver brought mud from the ocean bed to create land. There are many beaver clans and the beaver is seen as an ancestor figure. In Europe it is a symbol of energy and industry.

ELEPHANT

Because of its bulk and strength, the elephant is generally a symbol of power. It also signifies patience, wisdom, and chastity – probably because, according to Aristotle, a bull elephant remained celibate during the two-year long gestation period of his mate. The Hindu god Ganesha has an elephant's head and, with his huge belly, represents prosperity and benevolence. The white elephant is a symbol of royalty and is associated with the Buddha.

NATIVE AMERICAN FEAST DISH

BEAR

In northern countries the bear replaces the lion as king of the beasts. It was an ancestor of the Lapps, who called it grandfather. Because it hibernates, and then wakes in the spring, it symbolizes resurrection. The bear also represents power, and to the Celts, warfare. It is the national emblem of Russia.

CLAY CAMEL, ALGERIA

CHINESE BATS OF HAPPINESS

BATS

The bat is generally seen as unclean and is associated with darkness and death. In Europe it can be a form of the devil, and vampires such as Dracula often took the form of bats. In contrast, to the Chinese the bat symbolizes happiness and good luck.

Water plant denoting water habitat

EGYPTIAN HIPPOPOTAMUS MODEL

HIPPOPOTAMUS

Owing to its natural affinity with water as well as earth, the hippopotamus is associated with fertility. It was known to the Greeks and the Romans as the "beast of the Nile," and it played a particularly important role in ancient Egyptian mythology – the fertility goddess Taueret was depicted with the head of a hippopotamus.

CAMEL

The camel, or "ship of the desert," is highly valued in Middle Eastern cultures. In Arabia it is regarded as ennobled by God – the prophet Mohammed took an oath on one, and where his camel is said to have knelt on the flight to Mecca, the holiest spot in Islam now stands. As a pack animal, the camel represents stamina, obedience, and temperance. It is a classic symbol of Arabia.

BIRDS

THERE IS A WIDESPREAD AND ANCIENT BELIEF that after death, the soul leaves the body in the form of a bird. Consequently the bird is a symbol of the spirit. Birds can be mediators between gods and men, and can act as vehicles for the gods. Many religions have heavenly beings or spirits with wings: angels, cherubs, and seraphim for example. Birds are seen in myths involving a Tree of Life, and are sometimes depicted fighting with or carrying a serpent, symbolizing the uneasy balance between the sun (as bird) and the waters (as serpent). In Christian art this symbolizes the struggle between good and evil.

FALCON PECTORAL

CUCKOO
Because of its habit of laying its eggs in other birds' nests, the cuckoo is sometimes regarded as evil. It is a symbol of unfaithfulness in marriage and, in Japan, of unrequited love. But it also has positive associations, linked to fertility and rain. The song of the first cuckoo heralds the arrival of spring and the sowing of crops. If it is heard too early, it is taken as a sign of frosts and a poor harvest.

SPARROW
In the Old Testament the sparrow is viewed as a symbol of solitude and loneliness, while in the New Testament this small bird represents lowliness and insignificance. However, it is also associated with fertility, and in Greek mythology it is linked to Aphrodite, goddess of love. In Japan the sparrow is traditionally a symbol of loyalty, perhaps because of its sociable nature.

SWALLOW
Returning north from its summer habitat only with the arrival of warmer weather, the swallow symbolizes spring, renewed life, and fertility. Because the swallow is almost always airborne, in parts of Africa it is seen as a symbol of purity – it does not soil its feathers by walking on the ground. In China two swallows flying together represent marital happiness.

PELICAN
The pelican stands for self-sacrifice and parental devotion. According to early Christian legend, either the female pelican or a serpent killed the newborn chicks. The female then mourned them for three days, after which she stabbed her own chest to resuscitate them with her blood. Thus, for Christians, the pelican represents Christ, who shed his blood for mankind and was raised from the dead after three days. The bird is often carved on church lecterns.

FALCON
In general, the falcon is a symbol of the sun and the masculine powers in nature. It is particularly important in Egyptian mythology where it was sacred to Re, Egyptian god of the sun. It was also a popular form of the god Horus. Like the eagle, the falcon, with its strength and high flight, represents freedom of the spirit, which perhaps explains its popularity as a sporting bird in Renaissance Europe. In China the falcon has both the healing power of the sun and the destructive power of war.

ROOSTERS AND HENS
Roosters and hens have long been used in ritual. In some places roosters are sacrificed so that their blood returns fertility to the soil, and seers foretell the future from the entrails of the hen.

ROOSTER
The rooster is associated with courage and battle, with masculinity and the sun. Its crow heralds the dawn and symbolizes the victory of light over darkness. It is equated with fertility, and its sacrifice forms part of many harvest rites. In Christianity the rooster is a symbol of resurrection, and on a weathervane it represents vigilance.

ROMAN MOSAIC, 1ST CENTURY BC

HEN
The hen is widely seen as a symbol of maternal care and protectiveness. In Christianity the hen with its chicks represents Christ and his believers.

NATIVE AMERICAN TOTEM

RAVEN
Although often seen as an evil omen and a sign of war, illness, or death, the raven was viewed in China, Japan, and Persia as a messenger of the gods and as a symbol of the sun. In Norse legend the god Odin is accompanied by two ravens, and according to Native American myth the earth was created by a raven that dropped pebbles to make islands in the sea.

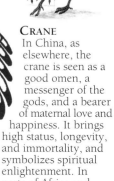

CRANE
In China, as elsewhere, the crane is seen as a good omen, a messenger of the gods, and a bearer of maternal love and happiness. It brings high status, longevity, and immortality, and symbolizes spiritual enlightenment. In parts of Africa and North America the crane was associated with wisdom.

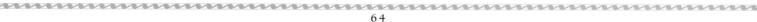

CROW

The black crow is widely regarded as a bird of ill omen and to many Native Americans, a crow's black feather spells death to an enemy. To the Chinese the black crow paired with the white heron represents the yin/yang, male/female principle, and in Japanese Shintoism the crow is a messenger of the gods.

Talon holds the "shenu" symbol of eternity

PARROT

The parrot symbolizes spring and fertility, as well as imitation and mockery due to its gift of mimicry. It is held sacred by the Hopi peoples of North America. In Hinduism the bird is associated with Kama, god of love, and also with prophecy and rain-making.

KINGFISHER

In the East the kingfisher denotes married bliss and its feathers are prized for their color and are thought to be magical. According to medieval legend, after the Flood the kingfisher flew too close to the sun and scorched its breast red while its back took on the color of the sky.

KIWI

According to legend, the kiwi, which is flightless and without a tail, was created from a gourd by Tane, a Polynesian ancestor god. It is the emblem of New Zealand.

MAGPIE

The magpie is a bird of ill omen in the Western world, where its chattering foretells trouble between husband and wife. But in the East, particularly China, it is a bringer of joy, and its call heralds the arrival of welcome guests. Two magpies together symbolize marital bliss.

PEACOCK

This royal bird with its fan-shaped tail is a symbol of the sun; its circular tail represents the vault of heaven and the "eyes" the stars. In Buddhism the many eyes symbolize watchfulness, although the feathers are often thought to be unlucky, a form of the evil eye. In Hinduism the peacock is the mount of Karttikeya, the god of war. The male peacock courts its mate with such pride that it has become synonymous with vanity.

DOVES OF LOVE AND PEACE

The dove is a symbol of the soul, and of peace, innocence, gentleness, and purity. Two doves together are considered a sign of marital love and fidelity. Doves are held sacred in many countries. In Greek legend the dove was linked to Aphrodite, the infant Zeus, the Fates, and the Furies.

SEVEN GIFTS OF THE SPIRIT

In Christianity the white dove is a symbol of the Holy Spirit and sometimes of martyrdom. Seven doves encircling a cross represent the seven gifts of the Holy Spirit: wisdom, understanding, counsel, fortitude, knowledge, piety, and fear of the Lord.

GREENPEACE DOVE

Greenpeace, the international movement for protecting the environment, has adopted a dove bearing an olive branch as its emblem. It is symbolic of peace and also of hope.

CONDOR

To the Incas condors were revered and were thought to be the embodiment of the gods of the air. Condor feathers were prized and used in religious ornaments.

GOOSE

The goose is a bird of the sun. It was associated with many Greek and Roman gods and was kept to guard temples. It thus came to symbolize watchfulness and love. In Hinduism the goose is the mount of the god Brahma and in China and Japan it is associated with the fall moon and is a bearer of good news.

SWAN

In Greek myth Zeus took on the form of a swan to seduce the beautiful Leda. The swan is also associated with Venus/Aphrodite: her chariot is sometimes borne through the air by swans. In Native American lore the swan is a symbol of trust and submission. The song of the dying swan is said to be one of joy at the prospect of entering the afterlife.

DUCK

In Native American myth the duck acts as mediator between the sky and the water, and it was one of the creatures that helped renew the earth after the Flood. According to Hebrew tradition the duck symbolizes immortality, while in China and Japan it represents contentment, marital bliss, and fidelity.

STORK

In ancient Egypt and Greece young storks were believed to treat their elders kindly, and so they symbolized filial duty. In Europe the stork is associated with the spring and with birth: babies are said to have been "brought by the stork."

EAGLES

State symbols of power and strength

ASHANTI THRONE DECORATION

Universally viewed as the king of birds, the eagle is a symbol of the sun, royalty, and the gods, especially sky gods. It represents authority, strength, victory, and pride, and in China the male yang principle, keen vision, and fearlessness. The eagle is often identified as the mythical Indian garuda, seen in deadly combat with the serpent. Like the hawk, the eagle is reputed to gaze straight at the sun as it flies upward and so, in medieval Europe, it came to be associated with prayer ascending to God, and with the ascension of Christ. In Australian lore the sea eagle carries the souls of the dead back to Dreamtime.

JAY
Although viewed as a chatterer and a sign of bad luck, to Native Americans the jay is a creator bird that helped recreate the world after the Flood. It is a guardian spirit of some tribes and warns of the approach of an enemy.

BIRD OF PARADISE
The feathers of this magnificent bird, found in New Guinea, are so beautiful that it was thought in Europe that the bird came from paradise. The bird achieved mythical status – people believed that it lived on dew drops and would moan in pain if captured. Its feathers were prized and were once worn as a fashion item.

NAPOLEONIC EAGLE
Perhaps inspired by the Roman practice, every French regiment in Napoleon's army carried a bronze standard in the form of an eagle. The example shown here was the emblem of the 105th regiment, and was captured by the British at Waterloo. In its right talon the eagle holds Jupiter's emblem of a thunderbolt.

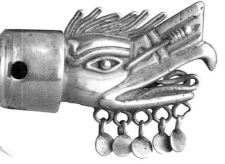

NAPOLEONIC EAGLE

US BALD EAGLE

In 1782 the United States adopted the bald eagle as a national emblem. It appears both on US coins and paper money and is symbolic of power and strength. The eagle's outstretched wings demonstrate its strength, and it rests above an olive branch of peace.

Jupiter's thunderbolt

GOLDFINCH

Essentially a Christian symbol, the goldfinch represents both the soul and the passion of Christ. Goldfinches like to eat thistles and thorns, and so the bird has become associated with Christ's suffering on the cross. The red spot on its throat is said to represent the drop of blood that fell as the goldfinch drew a thorn from Christ's brow.

HUMMINGBIRD

The hummingbird is seen as a symbol of joy, giving pleasure through its loveliness. In Native American myth it is a truthful bird that represents beauty, harmony, and enjoyment. The Aztec war god, Huitzilopochtli, and Quetzalcoatl, the Mayan god, both wore its feathers, which were widely thought to have magical properties.

Eagle feathers representing success in hunting and war

LIP ORNAMENT
To the Aztecs the eagle symbolized the rising sun and celestial power. It was associated with the warrior clans, and this eagle head was worn as protective jewelry.

EAGLE FEATHERS
To the Sioux the spotted eagle represents the essence of all life. The eagle's feathers are regarded as rays of the sun, and the eagle-feathered headdress is a symbol of Thunderbird, the Universal Spirit. By putting the headdress on before battle the warrior identified himself with the power and strength of the eagle god.

IBIS
In ancient Egypt the ibis was a symbol of the soul. It was sacred to the lunar deities Isis and Thoth, and represented the moon (with the hawk as the sun). However the ibis also had a solar significance when seen in battle with serpents, emblems of the water. In Christian art the ibis symbolizes devotion and perseverance.

BLACKBIRD
The much-loved blackbird was sacred to the Greeks for its sweet song, but because this song is so alluring the bird is also a symbol of the temptations of the flesh. In some Christian writings the black plumage makes the blackbird a symbol of evil.

NIGHTINGALE
The song of the nightingale, both sweet and plaintive, was particularly meaningful in Persia, where it was seen as a symbol of love, longing, and pain. Because its song heralds the dawn, it is said by Christians to represent the soul's yearning for Christ.

DODO
The dodo, which was hunted to extinction in the 17th century, has become a symbol of final death, hence the phrase "dead as a dodo."

OWLS
In ancient Greece the owl was sacred to Athena, goddess of wisdom and night, and came to symbolize the city named after her, as well as wisdom. The owl was then incorporated into the design of Greek coins, and was so popular that countries such as Italy, Egypt, and Turkey issued similar coins.

BIRD OF THE NIGHT
Because of its association with the night, the owl is widely seen as a bird of ill omen with a cry that heralds death and misfortune. To the Celts the owl was a "night hag" linked to corpses. In parts of Africa it was associated with magic, and its head was used in preparing spells.

ROBIN
The robin is a symbol of compassion. Its red breast is said to be the result of scorching when it carried water to the parched souls in hell. Alternatively, the robin was pricked when trying to remove nails from Christ's cross.

WREN
Although killing a wren is considered unlucky, it was not always so. In England and France it was once a part of Christmas rites to hunt and kill wrens, burying them in the churchyard as a symbol of the ending of the old year.

HAWK
This predatory bird is one of the great solar birds, with similar associations to the eagle and the falcon. To Greeks and Romans it was the messenger of Apollo. The god Horus was also depicted with the head of a hawk. In Native American myth the hawk helped fire the sun and recreate the world after the Flood. The eagle hawk is a deity and totem for Australian Aboriginals.

ALBATROSS
Because of its ability to fly great distances over water, the albatross is a symbol of the sea and long ocean journeys. When it circles a ship it is thought to herald the advent of a storm and is symbolic of rough weather. In the West there is an ancient belief that the albatross embodied the soul of a dead sailor, and so it was considered extremely unlucky to kill one, as reflected in Coleridge's *Rime of the Ancient Mariner*.

WOODPECKER
The woodpecker was widely believed to have magical powers and to bring good luck. It was sacred to Mars, Roman god of war, and was seen as a symbol of lightning and fire by Germanic peoples. The Ainu of Japan viewed it as evil, but also believed that the woodpecker was sent by God to show them how to hollow out tree trunks to make boats.

OSTRICH
In medieval times the ostrich was reputed to leave its eggs to hatch in the heat of the sun. In some cultures this was seen as a sign of cruelty to its young; in others as a symbol of belief in the power of the heavens. The ostrich also represents those who hide from the truth, owing to its reputation for burying its head in the sand. An ostrich egg is a symbol of rebirth.

HOOPOE
The hoopoe has conflicting symbolism. In Egypt it is known as the "doctor bird," and in Arab literature it is described as a messenger of love. However, it also has negative associations. It is said to betray secrets, and in Europe it is a symbol of the devil and of witchcraft.

QUAIL
In Russian lore the quail symbolizes the sun, with the hare as the moon. The quail was also a symbol of the tzars. To the Chinese, as to the Romans, it was a symbol of courage and victory in battle, although when caged it symbolized the soul imprisoned in the body. Elsewhere it is associated with good luck and the spring, and because it is thought to have an extremely amorous nature, it has sexual associations.

HERON
The heron, like the stork and the crane, represents both the sun and water and is thought to predict changes in the weather. In ancient Egypt the heron was associated with renewal and the annual return of floodwaters to the Nile, but in Greece it was a symbol of treachery, because its wading in shallow waters revealed a fordable path to enemies.

VULTURE
Closely associated with several Egyptian deities, the vulture is seen as feminine and represents maternal instinct, as vultures were supposed to feed their young with their own blood if necessary. Zoroastrians view them as "compassionate purifiers" since, according to their rites, the dead are left for vultures to devour. However, vultures are also feared because of their carnivorous appetite.

SEE ALSO
DOVES ☞ HOLY SPIRIT 18; MOURNING JEWELRY 87
EAGLES ☞ GARUDA, GRIFFIN 31; EAGLE, CRESTED EAGLE 114
PELICAN ☞ CHRISTIANITY 18
RAVEN ☞ RAVEN 92
ROOSTER ☞ ROOSTER 113
VULTURE ☞ HARPY 31

PEOPLE

*A*ncient societies believed that our very bodies were microcosms of the universe, and that our actions, particularly in ritual, reflected our relationship with nature. Still today, much of our behavior can be seen as symbolic, from donning ceremonial gowns and dressing baby girls in pink to participating in the complex rituals surrounding birth and marriage.

SEX & FERTILITY

FOR MANY PEOPLE NOWADAYS, especially city dwellers, the fertility of soil is a rather remote concept. But for thousands of years the fertility of the earth, along with human fertility and thus the continuation of the species, was the greatest preoccupation of humankind. All societies have had fertility gods and goddesses. And there are countless images imbued with sexual symbolism, which thus essentially have to do with fertility. Many are straightforward sex symbols and relate to the union of man and woman; others have to do with the earth's bounty.

BRAZILIAN WAIST ORNAMENT

Pomegranate of fruitfulness

Fish of fertility

Key to womanhood

SILVER CHARMS
This richly decorated waist ornament includes many items connected with fertility and may have been a gift to a young bride. Hanging from its garland of flowers are silver keys, a fish, pomegranates, grapes, and a festive tambourine.

Three stripes of Shiva worship

Shiva's face protected by two cobras

LINGA AND YONI
The *linga* is the most commonly worshiped form of Shiva, its phallus-shaped pillar representing the god as the male creative principle. Here it is set into the *yoni*, the vulva-shaped feminine element. Together they represent fertility and creation.

FERTILITY DOLLS
Dolls such as these were worn by women and young girls in Angola to enhance their fertility. They are made variously of corn cobs or forked sticks and beeswax – the corn cob being itself a symbol of fertility.

PINEAPPLE QUILT
This American bridal quilt is ornamented with pineapples, symbols of life and fertility, and also with meadow lilies and tulips, which symbolize love. Quilts are traditionally made as part of a bride's trousseau when she marries, and are often designed to promote "fruitfulness."

SEX SYMBOLS

The symbolism of sex varies greatly from culture to culture according to lifestyle, social etiquette, and taboos. In the Western world classic sex symbols tend to be young and glamorous, and are often film stars or musicians. Objects that symbolize male sexuality tend to be associated with a phallic shape and with power, whereas female sexuality is related to rounded shapes, receptivity, and abundance.

USA 32

ELVIS
Known as "Elvis the pelvis," the king of rock 'n' roll was revered as much for his gyrating hips and simmering good looks as his voice.

MARILYN
Idolized by millions, Marilyn Monroe was the classic Hollywood sex symbol, doomed to die young.

STILETTO SHOE
The high-heeled shoe operates on two levels: it elongates the leg, thereby accentuating a Western symbol of femininity; and its spiky heel suggests domination.

ROCKET
The rocket is a classic phallic shape and an object of great power and thrust. In addition, it is symbolic of what is essentially a male urge to conquer: man-the-hunter sets out to penetrate the ultimate new frontier – space.

Sprouting leaves of plenty

CARVING, NORWICH CATHEDRAL, ENGLAND

GREEN MAN
The foliate head has continued to be a symbol of life and fertility from pre-Christian times well into this century. In church architecture it stands for the regenerative force of Christ. More recently it has been adopted as an ecological symbol for preserving and protecting nature.

BIRTH
Giving birth is the ultimate symbol of creation, and as such is mythologized throughout the world. In the West babies often appear as if by miracle, snatched by storks from the cosmic waters. In other parts of the world the process is more direct – resulting from the blessed union of man and woman.

BIRTH PLATE
In this commemorative plate a stork delivers a baby to its crib. In folklore storks became associated with birth because of their renowned devotion to their young.

PERUVIAN CHILDBIRTH
A single act of creation mirroring the whole of creation, childbirth is seen as a moment of spiritual vulnerability and is often accompanied by rituals. The umbilical cord is treated with respect as a link between worlds and sometimes, as in Peru, may be preserved by the family.

Woman giving birth, helped by two women

PINECONE
This vast bronze pinecone is part of an ancient Roman fountain. As the fruit of the pine tree it is a powerful symbol of life and fertility. The Romans associated it with Venus, goddess of love, and it is one of her emblems.

WHEAT SHEAF
A sheaf of wheat or corn is a well-known symbol of the fertility of the earth and of growth and abundance. It represents the fruitful union of the sun and the soil.

CORNUCOPIA
The cornucopia is the horn of plenty, spilling over with fruit. It is a symbol of fertility and an attribute of the gods of vegetation. Its shape, – a hollow horn – is both female and male.

GODDESS OF FERTILITY
This gold figure represents Astarte, the Canaanite goddess of fertility, and dates from the 16th century BC. Although highly stylized, with a pubic triangle set within a larger one, the sexual organs are clearly defined.

The breasts are a prominent feature

Stylized pubic triangle

LOVERS
This Japanese print is an illustration from an 18th-century "pillow poem." It is one of thousands of erotic paintings depicting the union of male and female. The union can be seen as a purely sexual act or as the male and female principle combined in a symbolic act of creation. Illustrated stories about men taking their pleasure with courtesans were highly popular at the time.

THE POEM OF THE PILLOW, UTAMARO, 1788

SEE ALSO
BIRTH ☞ STORK 65; BREASTS 74
FERTILITY SYMBOLS ☞ EMERALD 40; ACORN 45; APPLE, DATE, FIG, ORANGE, PINEAPPLE, POMEGRANATE 48; EEL 54; VULVA 74; ELECTRIC GUITAR 80; BASKET 96
PHALLIC SYMBOLS ☞ SCEPTER 89; PLOW 90; GUN, SPEAR 91; SKYSCRAPER 94

HUMAN BODY

THE HUMAN BODY is seen by many people as a microcosm of the universe. In some parts of the world buildings are laid out with this symbolism in mind. A Southeast Asian house, for example, has sections that correspond to the human head, body, and feet, the head area being the most sacred. In other parts of the world the body is referred to as the "temple of the soul." Composed metaphorically of the four elements, it can be seen as representing life, and linking gods and humans. Gods, in fact, frequently appear in human form, and the Bible tells us that "God made man in his own image."

HAMLET AT THE GRAVE

EYES

The eye symbolizes the sun, the all-seeing eye of God, and eternal watchfulness, as well as the power of evil. It is the window of the soul and the light of the body. The eyes on Buddhist shrines symbolize wisdom and omniscience, whereas the widespread belief in an "evil eye" – and the consequent need for a "lucky eye" – reflect the fear that curses can be transmitted with a single glance.

Watchful eyes of Buddha

LUNAR EYE
In ancient Egypt the right eye of Horus, the sky god, was his solar eye, and the left eye his "wadjet eye," or eye of the moon. This wadjet eye symbolizes the power of light and was one of the most sacred and powerful protective amulets in Egyptian magic.

ALL-SEEING SHRINE
Four pairs of eyes mark this Buddhist stupa in Nepal. These represent the eyes of the all-seeing Buddha, gazing out in all directions. The question-mark-like nose is a symbol of unity, and slightly above each pair of eyes is a third eye, which represents the Buddha's clairvoyant powers.

EYE OF WISDOM
This 15th-century eye is an Islamic illustration based on an almond-shaped mandala. It represents the spiritual gateway that leads to the soul and to ultimate truth and wisdom. Within the soul's outer circle is a smaller, inner one, which stands for a person's true spiritual center.

Eye of sea monster wards off evil

PROW OF BOAT
The prow of this Portuguese fishing boat is painted with *oculi*, or great eyes, which see the dangers that lie ahead and ward off evil. The eyes cause the boat to look like a great sea monster, thus deceiving the dangerous spirits of the ocean into keeping away.

EYE IDOL
This alabaster figure with oversized eyes (3500–3000 BC) is one of thousands of similar such idols found at the Eye Temple at Tell Brak, in present-day Syria. The temple derived its name from its cache of visionary figures.

SKULL
In this famous scene from Shakespeare's play, the prince holds the skull of Yorick, a former servant. The scene stresses the impermanence of life and the pointless vanity of worldly matters, both symbolized by the skull.

SKULL-AND-CROSSBONES
In the 1600s, variations of the skull-and-crossbones emblem were adopted by pirates as a sinister warning of their evil intentions. The emblem filled sailors with dread, and signaled death to all who saw it.

TONGUE
The tongue is likened to a flame because of its color and quick movements. It can be a fertility symbol and also represents the voice of the deity. In some churches, devotees speak "in tongues." Here the Indian goddess Kali's protuding tongue is a symbol of her creative and destructive energy.

Golden head of god-king

TROPHY HEAD, ASHANTI

EARS
In the East, large earrings were once worn by kings and princes. The Buddha is usually shown with long ears, perhaps stretched by such earrings during his youth as a prince. Long ear lobes thus signify both royalty and spiritual authority.

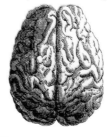

BRAIN
The brain is equated with the intellect and its location in the skull gives the head its Western connotation as being the seat of the intelligence.

NOSE
The nose may signify arrogance if it is raised or wrinkled. In literature it is often linked to the phallus – its size used as a veiled reference to male prowess. In the story *Pinocchio*, a big nose symbolizes dishonesty since the puppet's nose grew with every lie that he told.

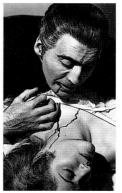

TEETH
In many parts of the world teeth are ritually filed at puberty as a sign of beauty. In the animal world baring the teeth is a sign of defense or threat, but in the well-known story of *Dracula* the fangs of the vampire draw blood from innocent victims.

GROTTO ENTRANCE

HEAD
The head is widely seen as the seat of the life force within us and so as the most sacred part of the body. Head hunters sought to capture this life force, which was equated with fertility and power. People in authority are known as the head of an organization, and in Japan heads are bowed in greeting as a sign of respect. This golden head is that of an West African Ashanti king killed in battle.

MOUTH
The mouth gives judgment and so symbolizes the word. It can represent the all-devouring earth or a door into the realm of the unconscious. The demon above, from a Baroque Italian garden, invites passers-by into his cavernous mouth.

HAIR
Hair is often seen as holding the strength and energy of the body as it grows from the head, seat of spiritual power. In popular stories, hair worn loose denotes a free spirit, even wantonness, although in Christianity it represents penitence or the virgin saints. Often when hair is covered it is a sign of respect for God. Christian nuns cut their hair short to symbolize their renunciation of worldly vanity.

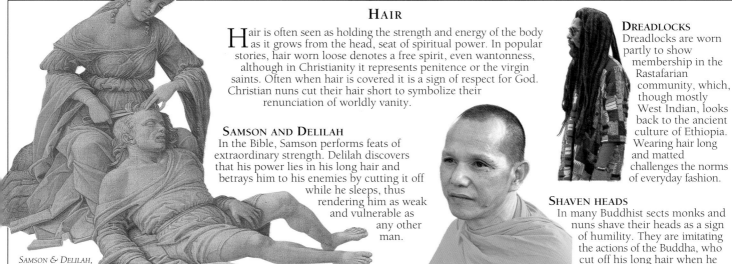

SAMSON AND DELILAH
In the Bible, Samson performs feats of extraordinary strength. Delilah discovers that his power lies in his long hair and betrays him to his enemies by cutting it off while he sleeps, thus rendering him as weak and vulnerable as any other man.

SAMSON & DELILAH, ANDREA MANTEGNA

DREADLOCKS
Dreadlocks are worn partly to show membership in the Rastafarian community, which, though mostly West Indian, looks back to the ancient culture of Ethiopia. Wearing hair long and matted challenges the norms of everyday fashion.

SHAVEN HEADS
In many Buddhist sects monks and nuns shave their heads as a sign of humility. They are imitating the actions of the Buddha, who cut off his long hair when he embraced a life of asceticism.

THE HEART

To Christians the heart is the source of love, joy, sorrow, and compassion. Many Christian saints hold a heart as an attribute, sometimes pierced by arrows or crowned with thorns. In ancient Greece, the heart was the center of thought, feeling, and will, while in Islam, it is the spiritual center.

SACRED HEART
This French greeting card depicts the sacred heart of Jesus within a stylized crucifix. It combines a flaming heart surrounded by a crown of thorns with other Christian imagery.

LOVE
This is the classic symbol of love: Cupid's arrow pierces a heart and his victim is struck by the unexpected pleasure and pain of desire.

PLAYING CARDS
Hearts are one of the four suits in a standard pack of playing cards. They represent warmth and the heart of the world. The queen of hearts stands for love. The king is more powerful than her, but the ace is generally even more so, and to be "ace" is thus to be best.

HUMAN SACRIFICE
In Mesoamerica, human sacrifice was ritually practiced as a form of communion with the gods; the deities were periodically fed to maintain cosmic order. For the Aztecs the heart was the center of the life force, and it was this that had to be offered to the gods to ensure the fertility and the renewal of crops.

SPLEEN
In European and Arab countries the spleen is the seat of the humors: laughter, anger, ill-humor, and melancholy. To be "splenetic" is to be melancholy.

LIVER
In China the liver is linked to courage and filial duty. Elsewhere, to be "lily-livered" is to be cowardly.

INTESTINES
The twisting nature of the intestines gives them their symbolic relationship with the labyrinth of life. In some places the intestines are associated with compassion.

SKELETON
The personification of Death, the skeleton is often shown carrying a scythe or an hourglass as a reminder of the speedy passing of time.

RIBS
In the Bible, after God created Adam, he decided that Adam needed a companion. He therefore caused him to fall into a deep sleep, and, according to Genesis, took out one of Adam's ribs and fashioned it into a woman – Eve. The rib is thus a symbol of wife, born from the body of man.

EARLY CHALK MAN, ENGLAND

PHALLUS
As symbol of fertility the male sexual organ represents the generative forces of nature and the Creator. An erect phallus is depicted in the art of many countries as a powerful symbol of regeneration and renewal. This English chalk figure from Cerne Abbas is 180ft (55m) high.

COCO-DE-MER, SOUTH INDIA

VULVA
This strange palm nut, known as a double coconut or coco-de-mer, is seen as a symbol of the female genitalia and so of fertility and creation. In India it was worshiped as a manifestation of the vulva of the earth goddess, and thus of all creative energy.

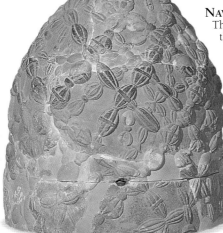

NAVEL
The ancient Greeks placed this huge stone carving in the sacred city of Delphi to mark the center of the world. They believed that two birds flying from opposite ends of the earth would meet here, and so erected the *omphalos*, or navel, to physically represent the center of the world, from which all creation originated. Its rounded top was a symbol of the point of connection between the realms of the gods, of humans, and of the dead.

BREASTS
Nowadays breasts are often seen as simply erotic. However, in the past, and still in many cultures, they have primarily symbolized motherhood and abundance. Fertility goddesses thousands of years old are depicted as large-breasted women, sometimes in the act of giving birth, making the link with creation clear.

STONE-AGE VENUS, AUSTRIA

HANDS

Hands, by their gestures, can signify blessing, protection, justice, and authority. Healers often work through the "laying on of hands," and we speak of giving a "helping hand" when we assist someone. Two people holding hands is a sign of love and affection.

HAND OF THE FUTURE
This Roman hand was used in divination. It bears symbols such as a rooster's head and a pinecone, which were linked to the cult of Bacchus and the visions of the future that arose out of drunken revelry.

HANDPRINTS OF THE STARS
In Hollywood film stars leave their handprints in wet cement as a lasting testament to their fame. Thousands of fans try out the impressions to see how they match up to their idols.

JOINED HANDS
In 1973 a special fifty-pence piece was minted to commemorate Britain joining the European Economic Community. It features a series of hands clasped in a continuous circle of friendship.

HAND OF GOD
This Jewish symbol of strength and power is worn as a good-luck charm.

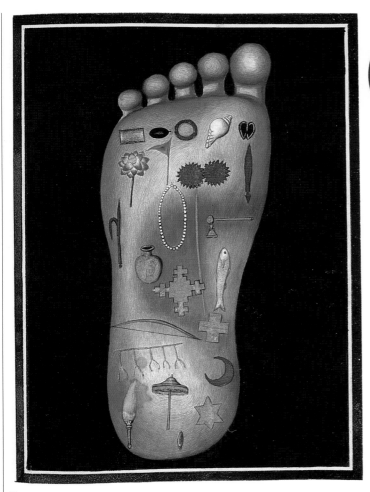

LEGS
The three-legged symbol has various meanings. It represents the swift-footed sun as it rises, sets, and ebbs each day. It is a symbol of good luck, like the swastika, symbolizing fertility and regeneration with its continuous cycle of footsteps, and it is also the chosen emblem of Sicily and the Isle of Man. The motto of the Isle of Man is *Quocunque Jeceris Stabit* – whichever way it is thrown, it will stand.

ARMS
If raised, the arms may signify supplication or prayer. They may be raised in battle (bearing weapons) or in surrender (open-palmed). Generally, the arm symbolizes action. The arm of justice is a common metaphor, as is the "strong arm of the law." In Eastern religious iconography arms represent power. Thus a many-armed deity represents the many-powered nature of the god.

SPINE
This Egyptian *djed*-pillar represents the backbone of Osiris and symbolizes stability – both the stability of the Pharaoh's rule and that of the heavens, which the pillar supported. The spinal column as the central support of the body is a symbol of the world axis.

FEET
In the West, bare feet are a sign of humility and poverty, thus pilgrims often went barefoot. The foot is the most lowly part of the body and in parts of Asia it is rude to sit with one's feet pointing at another person. In the footprint of Vishnu, above, the symbols on the sole relate to his nature or incarnation. Buddha's footprints bear auspicious symbols of the universe to demonstrate how far above worldly considerations he has risen.

VIETNAMESE NOBLE, *c.*1880

FINGERNAILS
In the 19th century, long nails were evidence of wealth in eastern Asia, since they implied an absence of manual work, which was left to others. Some African cultures share this belief, although often restricting the practice to the little finger.

SEE ALSO

EYES ☞ MAGIC EYE *79;*
WINDOW *94;*
LUCKY EYE *100;* TRACING
BOARD, SIGN LANGUAGE *109*

FEET ☞ FOOTPRINT *22*

HANDS ☞ HAND OF GOD
24; CORAL *38;* LOVE RING,
MOURNING JEWELRY *87*

LEGS ☞ TRISKELE *105*

TEETH ☞ TOOTH FAIRY *79*

DANCE & THEATER

DANCING IS MOVEMENT, ENERGY, EXCITEMENT. It is a part of everyday life as a symbol of pleasure and as a ritual of courtship. In different cultures it is associated with initiation ceremonies, fertility rites, rain, war, and death. It is used in harvest festivals to improve the crop and in war rituals to induce a state of frenzy. Many of today's dances have developed from earlier rituals; the maypole dance, for example, has its roots in Greek and Roman rites of spring. Drama, with its more controlled actions and gestures, provides us with a symbolic representation of the world we live in.

WAR DANCE
Native American tribes of the plains, such as the Hidatsa, were formed into military "Dog Societies." The Dog dancer, Pehriska-Ruhpa (Two Ravens), enacts a war dance to enlist the aid of spirits and to prepare the warrriors for battle.

WHIRLING DERVISHES
In their ecstatic dances the whirling dervishes (holy men) of Turkey pace out the turning of the earth on its axis as it orbits the sun. Through the dance, a dervish symbolically brings the spiraling of the universe into being.

LORD OF THE DANCE
Encircled by a ring of fire and on the back of the dwarf of ignorance, the Hindu god Shiva dances out the end of one age and the start of another. He enacts death and rebirth in one frenzied dance. With his drum, Shiva beats out the pulse of the universe and the pounding of the heart.

The Ganges River borne in the hair of Shiva

Shiva's hand drum

PUPPETS

Puppets are scaled-down versions of men and women, or the gods they believe in, and their performances often concern human behavior. The design of the puppets, their clothing, and their actions are all symbolic.

JAVANESE SHADOW PUPPET

MARIONETTES
In Burma string puppets are used to act out epic stories involving princes and deeds of valor. These moral fables leave their audiences with food for thought.

SHADOW PUPPET
The famous shadow puppets of Java and Bali enact the great epics of Hinduism. The flickering shadows, projected onto a white screen, create a world of mystery in which the stories of the gods and heroes are filled with symbolic meaning.

SWORD DANCE
Dances involving swords occur all over the world. They were probably originally used to ward off evil spirits and to strengthen the power of the sword in battle. Some sword dances end with a motion symbolizing the cutting off of a head, suggesting a link with ancient rites of sacrifice.

The ribbons form a pattern around the pole

MAYPOLE DANCE
The dance around the maypole has been performed since Greek and Roman times to celebrate spring. It is often associated with May Day celebrations. The maypole represents the earth's axis and also acts as a phallic symbol, representing male fertility.

GREEK TRAGEDY

In ancient Greece drama presented a powerfully symbolic portrayal of human behavior and emotions. By resolving huge issues such as jealousy, love, and incest, such performances enabled the audience to identify with the characters and overcome anxieties in the process. Thus drama often had a healing effect.

MIME

Mime is a symbolic form of drama that is enacted without words. It uses only expressions and gestures to convey meaning, and so can be "read" universally.

MASKS

Because they present other faces and other realities, masks are used everywhere in dance and drama. In many sacred rituals they are worn to represent the gods or ancestors. In Japanese Noh theater the actors are masked and they "dance" the moments of greatest intensity. The masks are very stylized and denote gods, character types, or moods such as rage or vengefulness.

GREEK COMEDY MASK

GREEK TRAGEDY MASK

Flames in ring of fire symbolize purification and destruction of illusion

THAI DANCERS

The costumes of Thai dancers make them look like heavenly creatures. Their stylized dance movements reinforce this impression.

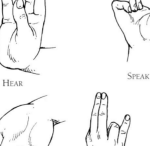

CHANGING FACES

Native American Kwakiutl dancers can take on more than one identity with a "transformation mask." When the dancer pulls levers and strings, the outer mask opens up to reveal another.

Strings pull back to form beaked eagle head

KWAKIUTL TRANSFORMATION MASK

CLASSICAL INDIAN DANCE GESTURES

Hand gestures used in classical Indian dance are also used in modified form in Southeast Asia. They represent moods, actions, and objects or creatures. Every movement of the dancer is symbolic and has meaning.

HEAR

SPEAK

BEAUTIFUL

SORROWFUL

BIRDS

FLOWER

Dwarf of ignorance under Shiva's feet

NOH MASK

Japanese Noh theater is distinctive for its use of painted wooden masks. The masks represent five general groups – male, female, the aged, deities, and monsters – as well as certain emotions.

HUSK MASK

Native American Iroquois dancers wear masks of braided corn husks for their midwinter ceremonies, when they call on spirits for a good harvest.

"THE DYING SWAN"

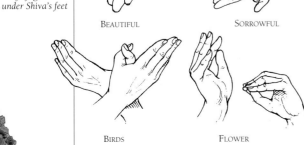

BALLET

Like other dance forms, ballet uses costume and gestures to convey meaning. A ballerina fluttering in white tulle, for example, can convincingly suggest the death throes of a swan.

MAGIC & CHARMS

THROUGH FAIRY TALES WE BECOME AWARE OF the world of magic and ritual at an early age. As adults, many things in life remain mysterious to us – what we cannot explain by rational means we may try to explain by magic. Similarly, when we find ourselves powerless to control the forces that affect us, we may look to magic. Many people still use spells to cure illness, to harm enemies, or to ensnare a lover. Even the skeptical among us may wear lucky charms, avoid walking under ladders, and consult fortune tellers. Magic and ritual, though disparaged by some as superstition, are still practiced by many people throughout the world.

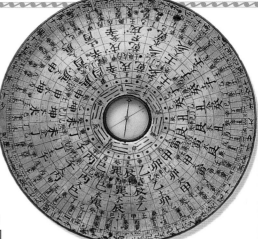

FENG SHUI COMPASS
Feng Shui is an ancient Chinese art based on living in harmony with one's surroundings. Using this compass, Feng Shui diviners locate the right combinations of elements, such as time, wind, and water, which determine the best sites for homes, temples, or burial grounds.

WITCH
According to folklore, witches could fly on broomsticks, brew magic potions, and cast spells. Once they were thought to be in league with the devil and thus were symbols of evil. Women healers were often branded as witches. By 1700 more than 200,000 had been put to death.

LOVE POTION

THE LOVE POTION, EVELYN DE MORGAN, 1903

EGYPTIAN MAGIC KNIFE
Serpent armed with knife

EGYPTIAN KNIFE
This curved knife of animal bone was used in ancient Egypt to strengthen the weak parts of a house. It would have been drawn against the relevant area to create a magical protective barrier. The various animals and patterns depicted on it endow the knife with their collective power.

FIVE-POINTED STAR
An upside-down five-pointed star was a symbol of evil. Right-side up, as here, it symbolized light and spirituality, and was painted on houses to ward off witches.

CHINESE COIN SWORD

Coins strung together to cover sword shape

MONEY CURES
Money is a symbol of power, and so by extension it has come to be imbued with spiritual, as well as practical, properties. In China a sword made of coins was hung over the bed of a sick person to dispel the demons or evil spirits that might be causing the illness.

MIRROR OF TRUTH

MIRROR
The mirror symbolizes divine truth and the wisdom of the universe. This "vision" is shattered if a mirror is broken, and it is a popular superstition that seven years' bad luck will follow.

When all else fails, unsuccessful lovers often resort to magic to beguile the object of their desires in literature. This could take the form of love potions, usually made from phallic-shaped ingredients such as the mandrake root, ginseng, or ginger, plus an appropriate spell. Many foods are reputed to be aphrodisiacs or love enhancers, and are used in much the same way as the age-old love potion.

LOVE-STRUCK PAIR

NATIVE AMERICAN LOVE CHARMS

LOVE DOLLS
These male (right) and female (left) dolls are traditional Native American medicine charms. In the Menominee tribe, the dolls were given the names of a couple and tied facing each other to make sure they remained faithful to one other. In the Potawatomi tribe they were used as love charms to draw two people together.

FOUR-LEAF CLOVER
Finding a clover with four rather than three leaves is so rare that a four-leaved clover has become a widespread symbol of good luck. The four leaves represent fame, wealth, a faithful lover, and good health – all important components of happiness.

HORSESHOE
The horseshoe is made of iron, which has power over the Evil Eye. It brings luck if it is hung on a door with the open end uppermost, because it will then catch good luck and hold it safely. If it is hung upside down, it is considered unlucky – the luck will run out.

DICE
Dice represent chance – the random pairing of numbers symbolizing life's unpredictability. Thus the phrase "the die is cast" means that one's fate has been decided. Dice are also a Christian symbol: after the Crucifixion, soldiers threw dice for Christ's cloak.

MAGIC EYE
A belief in the Evil Eye is widespread in the Mediterranean and the Near East. Charms that look like eyes are thought to turn away the Evil Eye or deflect the look of anyone with evil intentions. Such charms are often made of glass to make them seem lifelike.

MAGIC CARPET
Riding on a magic carpet is the stuff of many dreams. Flying symbolizes release of the spirit and the overcoming of all physical limitations. King Solomon had a flying carpet that carried him, his throne, and both his armies wherever he wished. In *The 1,001 Nights*, Aladdin also flew on a carpet.

ALADDIN'S MAGIC CARPET

POWER TO PROTECT
Many people wear charms to protect themselves from illness and danger. Certain objects and images are also used in healing the sick and are thought to be able to absorb illness, thus ridding a sick person of disease. Other objects are thought to give off energy, repel evil, or instill powers.

ROMAN VOTIVE LEG

LIGHT CURE
A crystal will refract light in many directions. It is thought that when a crystal is placed on the body, its energy will be absorbed and have a healing effect.

HEALING CRYSTAL

TOOTH FAIRY

VOTIVE LEG
Gifts are often promised to gods in return for a favor, such as curing an illness. This bronze votive leg, dedicated by a Roman named Caledus, was probably a symbol of his gratitude for having been cured of a leg injury or infection.

Nutshells

TOOTH FAIRY
Fairies people children's stories as well as their imaginations. They have magical powers and are generally symbols of good – fairy godmothers can right the wrongs of the world. Here a tooth fairy guards a lost tooth, and collects money for it.

WEST-AFRICAN CHARM

FOR GOOD HEALTH
The Nte'va people of the Upper Congo in West Africa use little figures, such as this one made up of rags, bone, leather, nuts, and wood, to "watch over one's body," providing protection from illness.

THE SPIRIT OF SMALLPOX

PROTECTIVE GARMENT
This Burmese undershirt is covered with charms, spells, and horoscope details. It was made to protect its wearer, probably in battle. In the past, many Burmese men had tattoos with similar markings.

WITCH'S FAMILIAR
Because toads eat spiders, they are thought to be able to repel evil and poisonous things. Parts of a toad were often included in magic potions.

AFRICAN CURE
This Nigerian figure, covered in spots representing the smallpox rash, symbolizes the disease itself. When treated with spells and incantations by witch doctors, the figure can cure the illness – or cause it.

MUSICAL INSTRUMENTS

MUSIC REPRESENTS THE ORDERED PATTERN of the universe, and musical instruments symbolize harmony and oneness with nature. They bring pleasure but may spell danger, pipes in particular having the power to lure listeners to their doom. Stringed instruments represent the sounds of the heavens, while percussion instruments are associated with divine truth, revelation, and ecstasy.

BURMESE GONG CIRCLE

DRUMS

The drum symbolizes the first sounds, divine truth, and speech. It is associated with the symbolism of thunder and lightning and to Native Americans it represents the heart of the universe. Drums were traditionally used to accompany dance throughout the world and were a vital component of ecstatic dance.

The motto "Celer et audax" means "speed and courage"

MILITARY DRUM
Once used to accompany soldiers into battle, the rousing, regular beat of the drum became associated with warfare. Nowadays this military rhythm is an integral part of the brass or marching band.

AFRICAN DRUM
In Africa the drum is highly symbolic and forms an essential part of ritual dance. It represents the beat of the human heart and is played to summon up magic powers.

INDIAN TABLAS
The *tabla*, or drum, is an attribute of the Indian god Shiva, who beats out the pulse of the universe on it as he dances his great dance of birth, death, and purification.

Dragons symbolize celestial power

GONG
The gong is traditionally used in Buddhist temples to mark the stages of the service and to ward off evil spirits. It is a valued religious object in the East and is often highly ornate, as in this example found in Borneo. In secular use, sounding the gong signals a call to dinner, particularly in a formal setting.

CYMBALS
These ancient percussion instruments date back to 3000 BC and are still widely used today. In worship they symbolize contact with the heavens, and in Tibetan temples they are sounded in the worship of Buddhist deities.

MU-YU
Mu-yu means wooden fish in Chinese. These instruments are played in temples and are symbolic of ceaseless prayer because, like fish, they never seem to rest.

BELL
The bell symbolizes contact between heaven and earth. It rings out the voice of the divine and the harmony of the cosmos. In the Western world the church bell is a call to prayer, but can also be sounded as a warning. The sanctus bell at the altar announces the coming of Christ. In Buddhist countries it is rung or struck after devotions, while small bells sounding in the wind represent the gentle sounds of heaven.

Headdress of Buddhist monk

TIBETAN BELL

ELECTRIC GUITAR
Since the 1950s the electric guitar has come to symbolize youth and rebellion, with groups vying with each other to create the loudest sounds. The guitar itself has male associations, with certain musicians using it in performance as an exaggerated phallic symbol.

CHINESE ZITHER
A Chinese scholar should be accomplished in the four arts – literature, painting, chess, and music – and the zither, or *qin*, was the symbol of music. According to Chinese lore, a zither played by a sage had the power to reveal to him the essential truth. The mother-of-pearl disks mark finger positions.

ORPHEUS'S LYRE
Orpheus, musician to the gods, enchanted all animals through his playing of the lyre and even succeeded in calming a storm-tossed ocean. In his hands the music of the lyre calmed all beings, causing them to be aware only of him. The lyre's seven strings corresponded to the seven known planets, and its sides to the relationship between heaven and earth.

LUTE
Popular in Europe from the mid-15th century, the lute is an attribute of music. It is also a symbol of purity and faithfulness. In Western art, when shown with a broken string it signifies discord.

TRUMPETS
The trumpet or bugle was blown as a call to arms in Roman times and has been associated with battle or fame ever since. Traditionally, a trumpet fanfare heralds the arrival of royalty or important persons. Fame personified is often shown holding a trumpet.

Royal Horse Guards flag

BUGLE
The bugle is a valveless trumpet. In military camps it is sounded to play the reveille that heralds the morning and taps to mark the end of the day.

THE LAST JUDGMENT
Both the Bible and the Koran state that the trumpet will be sounded on the Last Day, when the dead shall be raised.

THE LAST JUDGMENT (detail), Michelangelo, 1536-41

CEREMONIAL TRUMPET
The trumpet, with its masculine and authoritative associations, is used at ceremonies and grand occasions in many countries.

Moroccan ceremonial trumpet

Gold Irish shamrocks on national green

IRISH HARP

HARP
An attribute of King David in the Bible, the harp symbolizes sacred music in both Judaism and Christianity, and angels are frequently depicted playing harps. St. Augustine explains the ten commandments in terms of the ten strings in David's harp. In Celtic lore the harp is an attribute of the fire god Dagda, and the harp is a symbol both of Ireland and of Wales.

SHENG
The Chinese mouth organ originated 3,000 years ago and is made up of 17 individual bamboo pipes bound together and held within a mouthpiece. It is a very ancient symbol of the phoenix, which it is said to resemble. The sheng is played at weddings and funerals.

KRISHNA'S FLUTE

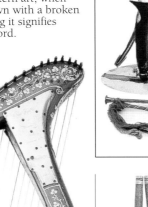

FLUTE
The shape of the flute gives it a phallic masculine dimension, while its tone is gentle and feminine. In Hinduism Krishna's flute is said to be the voice of eternity calling all living beings to himself. More generally, the flute is sometimes associated with anguish and extremes of emotion. In Christianity it symbolizes the soul's longing for God.

PAN PIPES
Played nowadays in the Andean region of South America, pan pipes represent the harmony of nature. In Greek legend they were carried by the god Pan and by satyrs, and had the power to entrance all who heard them.

ORGAN
A church instrument, the organ has come to symbolize the praise of God. St Cecilia, patron saint of music, is said to have invented it and dedicated it to the service of the Lord.

SEE ALSO
BELL ☞ PIECE OF CAKE 83
BUGLE ☞ SHOFAR 16
DRUMS ☞ LORD OF THE DANCE 76
GONG ☞ BUDDHISM 22-23
KRISHNA ☞ KRISHNA 20; KRISHNA'S LOVE 82; BLUE-SKINNED GOD 107

LOVE & MARRIAGE

A POPULAR VIEW IS THAT LOVE MAKES THE WORLD GO ROUND. Love is central to life – its force has inspired poets, writers, and artists from time immemorial the world over. Love binds man to woman, mother to child. It can be sexual, the powerful attraction of opposing and complementary forces found in nature, or platonic, the deep, binding emotion that forms the fabric of our society. In a more spiritual context, love reflects the longing of the soul for God or ultimate truth. The sexual act is then an expression of the soul's urge to merge with the cosmos.

THE TWO SIDES OF LOVE

VENUS AND CUPID, LUCAS CRANACH THE ELDER, 1545

This painting shows Cupid at his mother's side, in tears because he has been stung by bees. Venus, in response, reproves Cupid for inflicting more painful wounds on others than bee stings. Both Venus and Cupid are gods of love and here represent the two sides of love – the pleasure and the pain. Cupid covered in bees is symbolic of love's sting in the tail.

HONEYCOMB OF PURITY AND SWEETNESS

LIPS
Lips pursed into a kiss are a classic symbol of love or sexual attraction – the red lipstick kiss ends many a passionate love letter. Lipstick on the collar, though, signals infidelity.

Lovers transformed into doves

The willow, which shed its leaves as the lovers made their escape

CHINESE WILLOW-PATTERN PLATE

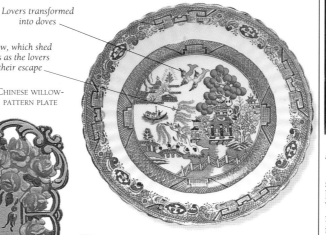

WILLOW PATTERN
This plate shows the Chinese story of Koong-see and her lover, Chang. The girl's father forbids their marriage, so the lovers flee just as the leaves fall from the willow. Soldiers pursue them and kill Chang, so Koong-see, heartbroken, sets fire to herself. The lovers are then transformed into doves, emblems of their constancy.

Winged Cupid

Twin hearts aflame

Red roses, symbols of passionate love

Valentine's card speeding to its destination

White turtle dove of love and fidelity

Forget-me-nots, symbols of yearning

VICTORIAN VALENTINE CARD

VALENTINE CARD
The valentine card first appeared in the 16th century, with its imagery reaching the height of sentimentality in Victorian times. Exchanged on Valentine's Day, February 14, these cards often depict love symbols such as hearts, doves, and cupids. Valentine's Day was originally known as the "birds' wedding day" due to an old belief that birds selected their mates on that day. People then followed suit, and made it a day for declarations of love.

KRISHNA AND RADHA, KANGRA MINIATURE, c.1785

KRISHNA'S LOVE
In this scene Krishna sits in a forest glade with Radha, his favorite *gopi*, or milkmaid. All the *gopis* love Krishna, the embodiment of heavenly love, but Radha is the one who captures his heart. The love of the *gopis* for Krishna represents the longing of the soul to merge with God.

MARRIAGE

The ritual of marriage is conducted in some form in every society and is traditionally a contract uniting two families. In some cases a man may marry more than one wife, while occasionally, as in Nepal and Tibet, a woman marries several brothers. Whatever form the marriage takes, it is a celebration that symbolizes the union of god and goddess, heaven and earth, man and woman, and the uniting of opposites to form a complete whole.

Bright clothes symbolize luck and fertility

CHINESE WEDDING
Chinese legend recounts how the man in the moon ties invisible threads around the legs of newborn boys and girls to link their destinies. When they grow up, they are irresistibly drawn to each other, and marriage is inevitable.

WEDDING BANDS
The custom of giving engagement rings goes back to Roman times although the traditional diamond ring – symbol of faithfulness – dates only from the 15th century. The plain gold band of the wedding ring symbolizes eternity and the cycle of life.

ENGAGEMENT AND WEDDING RINGS

CONFETTI

RICE

BLESSINGS
The practice of showering newly married couples with confetti or rice comes from the East, where rice is a symbol of fertility. It is thrown so that the couple might be blessed with many children. In Saxon times red and white rose petals were thrown to represent the union of passion and purity.

PIECE OF CAKE
The wedding cake has been part of wedding celebrations since Roman times. Bride and groom must cut the first slice together to symbolize lifelong harmony, and their eating of the cake is associated with sexuality. Sharing the cake among the guests represents the union of the two families.

Bride and groom, united on the cake, united in life

Silver bells to ward of evil spirits

A chimney sweep wishing a bride happiness is a good omen

Red roses of love and passion

Horseshoe of good luck

Symbol of good luck, particularly when tied to back of newlyweds' car

INDIAN WEDDING
An Indian bride's red sari stands for fertility. Here the bridal couple is literally bedecked with good wishes. The fragrant garlands of roses and tuberoses represent beauty and happiness, while the bank notes are symbolic of prosperity.

Decorative lace-like tracery is considered auspicious

HENNAED HANDS
In the Middle East and India brides' hands are intricately painted in red for good luck. The red coloring comes from the dye of the henna plant. A bride's appearance would be incomplete without it.

LOCKET

SILVER LOCKET
The heart is the classic symbol of love, although it also represents sincerity and compassion. Heart-shaped lockets, with a photo of a loved one, or perhaps a lock of their hair, are common gifts of friendship.

WINGED HEART INSIGNIA

WINGED HEART
This symbol combines the emblem of the heart, representing love, with the characteristic wings of Cupid or Eros, god of love. A doubly powerful image, it represents the power of love to fly into the heart of anyone.

BUMPER STICKER

HEART AS WORD
In the "I love New York" logo the heart is universally recognized as a symbol of love, making the use of the word itself unnecessary. This is one of the most familiar latter-day pictograms in use today.

CHOCOLATE

CHOCOLATE HEART
With aphrodisiac as well as romantic connotations, chocolate has long been the food of love, given at times of celebration or as a token of affection. This heart-shaped chocolate is probably a Valentine's Day gift.

BROKEN HEART

HEARTBROKEN
The phrase "to be brokenhearted" has wound its way into our language and imagery. The heart splits in two, representing the ultimate pain of grief or loss. Spurned lovers have broken hearts, as do those separated from the ones they love.

SEE ALSO

CLOTHING

CLOTHING IS AN EMOTIVE ISSUE, reflecting the ways in which society regards individuals in terms of sex and status, and also how individuals regard themselves. What you wear says a great deal about who you are, or who you wish to be. More powerful members of society tend to wear more elaborate clothing in public, for instance, and it is often of finer, more expensive, cloth. Clothes can be sensible or seductive, businesslike or frivolous. Youth characteristically dons clothing to denote rebellion, although youth fashions often develop into mainstream fashions.

MATERIALS

The materials we choose to wear are highly significant. Slinky synthetics, for example, show a pride in one's body and flirtatiousness. Cotton, by contrast, is functional and economic; Gandhi spun his own as a symbol of India's independence and would wear nothing else.

SILK
Spun by silkworms fed on mulberry leaves, silk has always represented luxury.

LACE
Lace was a symbol of privilege. It was made by working women for the upper classes.

COTTON
Traditionally worn by working people, homespun cotton is a symbol of simplicity.

TARTAN
The checkered patterns of tartans are like heraldic devices, each denoting a Scottish clan.

FUR
Functional in some cultures, fur is a luxury item, or a symbol of cruel death, in others.

LEATHER
Leather is functional and readily available. Today it is often associated with youth culture.

FIG LEAF
The fig leaf, as the very first item of clothing, symbolizes a loss of innocence and a fall from grace. Adam and Eve donned fig leaves when they first noticed their nakedness.

RUSSIAN NAVY SAILOR'S SHIRT

SAILOR'S TOP
The traditional sailor-suit, or matelot shirt, is woven with horizontal blue and white stripes. The blue of the stripes is called navy blue, or just navy, and is thought to represent the color of the sea.

17TH-CENTURY BUCKLE

ORNATE SILVER BUCKLE

BELT BUCKLES
For men, buckles are one of few outlets for showing individuality. The lower one belonged to a South-American gaucho.

BLUE JEANS
Jeans are essential items for young people throughout the world. Designs seen as fashionable can be surprisingly expensive.

KENYAN TRIBESMAN
This East-African warrior wears simple clothing and distinctive jewelry. This suits his active hunting lifestyle – and he would feel undressed without his staff or spear. In this and many similar societies, individuality is expressed more through jewelry than through clothing.

FASHIONS IN FOOTWEAR

Shoe styles reflect social and cultural attitudes and tell us something about a person. To remove shoes on entering a temple or home is symbolic of leaving earthly matters outside the door as a mark of respect.

JAPANESE CLOG
These Japanese shoes are for outdoor use. Their deep wooden soles – some 4in (10cm) high – add stature to the wearer and induce a delicate gait.

DOC MARTEN
Doc Marten first made protective working boots in 1967, and they were the runaway success story of the '80s and '90s, symbolizing a reaction against glamour by both men and women.

GLASS SLIPPER
In the tale of Cinderella, the glass slipper represents truth and transformation. When Cinderella's foot fits into the shoe she left at the ball, the prince recognizes her, and she is transformed from pauper to princess.

CHINESE SHOE
Until early this century it was common in China to bind women's feet. Symbolically, tiny feet reinforced the image of women as delicate and helpless, and it also prevented them from straying.

PLATFORM SHOE
Platform shoes have been in and out of fashion for centuries. These date from the 1970s. They are the literal embodiment of the human desire to "walk tall."

14TH-CENTURY SHOE
These shoes, worn by noblemen, reached an amazing 18in (46cm). A status symbol to some, the clergy viewed them as the work of the devil.

SNEAKER
Sports shoes have become the status symbols of our time, with accompanyingly high prices. They are worn not for their original purpose, but as everyday wear for both men and women.

HEADGEAR

In most cultures the covering or uncovering of the head is redolent with meaning. Depending on the religion, places of worship require covered heads or uncovered ones. Hats are a sign of respect as well as an immediate indication of status and occupation.

LINE COOK

SOUS CHEF

MASTER CHEF

TOP HAT
Immortalized by the dancer Fred Astaire, the top hat came into fashion in the 1820s and remains the ultimate symbol of male elegance. Worn less often nowadays, it complements the tailcoat at weddings and other formal occasions.

CHEF'S ORDER
The relationship between height and status is evident in the range of chef's hats, from lowly dishwasher to respected master chef.

BERET
The circular beret is associated both with peace and war. In navy blue it is the classic symbol of the French working man; in other colors, notably red and green, it is a symbol of military courage and excellence.

18TH-CENTURY WIG
Wigs were worn by both sexes in the 18th century. They were a sign of affluence and high status.

FEZ
This was part of Turkish national dress until the country became a republic in 1923, and the hat was outlawed.

CHADAR WITH VEIL
In orthodox Muslim countries women are veiled outside the home so as not to draw male attention.

MORTARBOARD
Derived from a cap worn by the Roman Catholic clergy, the mortarboard is now a symbol of erudition.

EXTRAVAGANZA
At Ladies Day at the Ascot race course in England, women traditionally wear outrageous hats.

TURBAN
Made of bright material, this West-African turban is worn on important occasions and confers status.

CLASSIC
S-SHAPED CORSET

CORSET
Corsets of the early 1900s were reinforced with whalebone and were designed to exaggerate the natural curves of a woman's body. A tiny waist was the ideal, and corsets have come to symbolize the way in which women willingly subject themselves to pain in the pursuit of fashion.

KID GLOVES

GLOVES
Originally gloves were a symbol of power and were presented at investiture ceremonies. Until recently, a lady or a gentleman was always expected to wear gloves in public. To handle with kid gloves is to treat someone or something with the utmost care.

HEDGEHOG
PRESERVATION

"ART"
TIE

TIES
Given the fairly rigid code of dress that men are expected to conform to, ties are one of the few areas of self-expression open to them. A man may choose to wear a club tie or military tie to signify his affiliation to that organization, or he can strike out in any number of more individual ways.

EDWARDIAN DRESS
This fashionable figure shows how Edwardian dresses distorted the body. The bust was pushed forward and the hips back in what was known as the S-shape. It was not unusual for women to faint from the pressure on their lungs.

The high lace neck suggests modesty

Diminutive waist – fashion fights nature

Gloves as symbols of feminine elegance

SEE ALSO

BELT BUCKLES ☞ VICTORIAN BUCKLE BRACELET 87

FASHIONS IN FOOTWEAR ☞ STILETTO SHOE 70

FIG LEAF ☞ FIG 48; THE FALL 59

FUR ☞ ERMINE 88

HEADGEAR ☞ LAUREL 44; CROWN 89; EAGLE FEATHERS 66

JEWELRY

TRADITIONALLY JEWELRY IS BOUGHT AS A GIFT, usually celebrating the important stages or events in a person's life – from christening presents to 21st birthdays, weddings, and anniversaries – or a particular relationship of love or friendship. Its symbolism lies not so much in its form as in what the item represents; whether it is the plain gold ring that binds a man and woman together or a locket with a loved one's photograph. Much of our jewelry has ancient origins – a child's charm bracelet is essentially a modern version of amuletic jewelry: the charms protect the wearer from harm.

SERPENT NECKLACE, c.1870

THAI EARRINGS
A love of intricacy and delicacy is visible in these 18th-century earrings. Made from gold-painted animal skin, they represent mythical creatures.

ROPES OF BEADS WORN AS NECKLACES AND WAISTBANDS

White beads indicate love

Pink beads usually indicate "bride price"

BEAR CLAWS
This necklace, made from the claws of several bears, was the prize possession of a Native American chief. Like other pieces made from nails, teeth, or tusks, it denoted status, partly because of the prowess involved in killing the bear to obtain the claws.

EGYPTIAN COINS
Although jewelry often symbolizes wealth, in many cultures the relationship is more direct – jewelry actually is wealth. On marrying, girls are given coin necklaces, headbands, and even belts as part of their dowry. The wealthier the family, the greater the value of the coins.

AFRICAN BEADS
In Africa, beads are a form of communication as well as decoration. They have particular meanings according to their color and the order in which they are strung. Young girls will make "love letter" necklets for their boyfriends to wear. After marriage, girls are allowed to adorn themselves with more and more strings to show their heightened status.

FRUITFULNESS

Symbols of fertility abound in the jewelry of different cultures, from Egyptian cowrie-shell amulets to the Spanish *higa*, or clenched fist. The concern with fertility may be less marked now, but the symbolism still abounds, as in the decorative examples of fruit shown here.

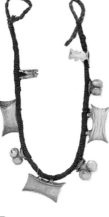

LEG ORNAMENT
In parts of Africa, jewelry denoted the wealth of a woman, just as the number of goats or sheep signified that of a man. Leg ornaments were prized both for their craftsmanship and their bulk, some weighing as much as 33lb (15kg). This leg ornament shows Islamic influences, as Muslims prefer silver, signifying purity, to gold.

PACIFIC CHARM
This 17th-century necklet from the Cook Islands conferred power and protection on its wearer. Although jewelry made from wild beasts was quite common in many cultures, this piece is unusual. The bones and teeth are carved into talismanic shapes, rather than worn in their natural state.

VICTORIAN VINE BROOCH

AMETHYST GRAPES
This cluster of grapes may well have been a wedding present from groom to bride – the grapes are an ancient symbol of fertility. Grapes were associated with all the pleasures, and excesses, of wine.

ANCIENT GREEK PENDANT

POMEGRANATE
This pendant was made by a Mycenean craftsman c.1300 BC and would almost certainly have been worn by a young bride. The many-seeded pomegranate has widespread associations with fertility.

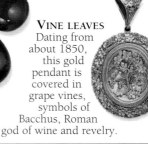

VINE LEAVES
Dating from about 1850, this gold pendant is covered in grape vines, symbols of Bacchus, Roman god of wine and revelry.

SIGNET RING

Examples of swiveling signet rings date back to the 15th century BC. They were both functional and a mark of status since only a person of considerable wealth could have his image carved onto a stone. By pressing the ring onto damp clay the owner was able to seal and identify his goods.

MOURNING JEWELRY

The death of a loved one is marked by a series of ritual and symbolic acts. People adopt different colors of dress and shed their everyday jewelry in favor of more somber forms of adornment, demonstrating that they are in mourning. In the Western world, black is the traditional color of mourning, and jet the classic stone.

RING
In the 17th century, finger rings such as the one above would have been handed out to relatives at a funeral.

LOCK OF HAIR
The brooch below swivels so that it can be viewed from both sides. The back holds a lock of hair, symbol of an absent friend.

This dove bears the heart of a loved one

GLOVED HAND
This jet brooch is of a gloved hand holding a funeral wreath.

UNDYING LOVE
Jet became popular during Queen Victoria's reign when mourning jewelry was at its most fashionable.

CHARM BRACELET

Silver charm bracelets are thought to protect the wearer – often a child – from harm. This one has a lucky horseshoe, a wishing well, and a wise monkey, plus a fish and a frog for fertility. The fashion of wearing charm bracelets is relatively recent, a specifically Western, 20th-century form of amuletic jewelry.

CHINESE PADLOCK
This lock is traditionally given by a father to his young child in order to lock in the child's spirit and stop evil forces from stealing it. One hundred families contribute toward the purchase of the lock. In so doing they become the child's honorary guardians, bound to protect the child throughout his or her life.

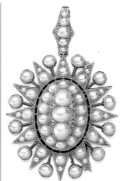

30TH ANNIVERSARY
A symbol of beauty and perfection, the pearl has long been the jewel of love. If the diamond is the "king of jewels," the pearl is the queen. Pearls are the birthstones of those born in June and also the gems that mark a 30th wedding anniversary.

ENGAGEMENT RING
The custom of giving engagement rings goes back to Roman times. The rings were often plain iron circles, the shape symbolizing the cycle of life and eternity. In the 15th century diamonds – emblems of fidelity – were added to these simple bands. In addition to fidelity, diamonds were thought to protect against all the forces of evil.

FORGET-ME-NOT
Flower jewelry takes on the symbolism of the particular flower involved. In giving this brooch, an admirer was probably hoping that he would not be forgotten.

VICTORIAN BUCKLE BRACELET

Jewelry with buckles was popular in the 1800s, both as rings and as bracelets. What they all represented, however subtly, was an era of male dominance. The man gave the piece to a loved one and, in doing up the buckle, she willingly – or unwittingly – acknowledged him as her owner.

LUCKY AT THE HUNT

During the heyday of hunting, jewel-studded foxes, hounds, and riders were very much in vogue. The items were worn for luck and were also symbols of the landed gentry.

SYMBOL OF LOVE
This 18th-century choker with clasped hands is a classic emblem of love. Hands are often represented in jewelry and take on different meanings depending on the position of the fingers. A single hand with thumb and forefinger touching, for example, is a talisman against evil; a fist, instead, is a symbol of fertility.

FAMILY MEMENTO

Before the era of the camera, those who could afford it commissioned miniature enameled portraits of their loved ones. Fashionable ladies could then keep their children close to their heart at all times.

LOVE RING

Love rings became fashionable in the 18th century. Made of interconnecting hoops, they had hands that clasped together to enclose a central heart. Part of their romantic symbolism lies in the fact that the rings can be pulled apart, but can never be separated.

ROYALTY

THE INSTITUTION OF ROYALTY is highly symbolic. Many Asian courts were laid out as microcosms of the universe, with the throne, at the center of the palace, representing the sacred mountain at the axis of the world. A king had four chief queens and four chief ministers, symbolizing North, South, East, and West. The health of the nation and the land depended on his health. In parts of Africa and southern India the king was ritually sacrificed while still strong and virile, so that the shedding of his blood might renew the fertility of the soil and thus ensure the well-being of his people. Kings have been widely believed to rule by divine right, and in some cultures to be semi-divine.

Crown
The crown is a symbol of sovereignty and honor

Scepter
Originally a magical symbol, the scepter signifies the king's responsibility for his people's prosperity

Ermine
The winter coat of the weasel, ermine is a royal fur. It symbolizes purity and incorruptibility

Mantle
The mantle denotes protection, as well as mystery and transformation

Orb
The king symbolically holds the whole world in his hand

Throne
The throne is the seat of authority. It marks the spiritual center of the kingdom and the metaphorical center of the world. Its ornate appearance denotes the rank of the ruler. The Virgin Mary, who was crowned in heaven, is often depicted enthroned.

QUEEN
As the feminine counterpart of the king, the queen is associated with a mother goddess or Queen of Heaven. Together the king and queen represent the perfect union of opposites, two halves of the whole, the sun and moon, and day and night.

KING
The king is the ultimate symbol of power. Traditionally the monarch was surrounded by courtiers, who had the same function as the heavenly beings surrounding God. He was thus seen by his subjects as an earthly counterpart of God and a symbolic link between heavenly and earthly power. The king is also a symbol of consciousness, the ruler over our unconscious urges.

PHARAOH
The famous mask found on the mummy of the boy king Tutankhamun reflects the glory of the pharaoh. For the ancient Egyptians the pharaoh was more than a monarch, he was a god. He was the center of all existence, son of Re, the sun god, and an intermediary between heaven and earth.

CHESS
The ancient game of chess is a symbolic playing out of the conflict between opposing forces in life. The black and white squares represent negative and positive, male and female principles. The pieces, representing the king, his court, and his army, carry the symbolism of their roles, although in the game of chess the queen is more powerful than the king. Each game is an epoch, and each piece makes a possible choice in life.

POWER GAMES

Many games are based on the balance of power and involve kings, queens, courtiers, and armies. The object of the game can be to defeat the other players by conquering their court and army, or to build up a royal power base with which to trump one's opponents.

CHINESE CHESS PIECES

KNIGHT   BISHOP   QUEEN   KING   CASTLE   PAWN

CARDS
Playing cards are divided into four suits, each of which is headed by its own king, queen, and jack (or prince). Packs of cards also include two jokers or jesters, more powerful than their lowly title suggests. In many games the goal is to build up cards to complete the suits, symbolically placing the king in his personal court.

EMPEROR
In China and Japan the emperor is the Son of Heaven, symbol of the moral order and responsible for maintaining harmony between heaven and earth. The Moghul emperors of India took on a similar role. Here the first Moghul emperor, Babur, receives envoys.

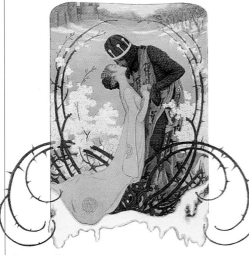

PRINCE & PRINCESS
The prince is usually seen in legends as a hero, an embodiment of courage and moral action. The princess is a symbol of the highest good and beauty. The prince endures hardship to bring about change or rescue a captive princess. In the same way truth can be obtained only after a spiritual struggle.

KNIGHT
When seated on a horse, which represents speed, the knight denotes a superior human. He maintains order in the kingdom and symbolizes moral courage, devotion to duty, and nobility. Clad in shining armor, he represents invincibility.

FOOL OR JESTER
As a simpleton the fool was exempt from court etiquette. But often he was the wisest member of the court and the only one able to speak his mind to the king. The fool represents innocence in a world of human experience.

UMBRELLA
The umbrella, or more properly the parasol, represents the canopy of heaven and, with its raylike spokes, the sun itself. It is a symbol of royalty in parts of Asia.

SEAL
All documents of state or letters written by a king would be sealed with the monarch's own seal, representing authority and power. The seal can be a symbol of belonging to God.

FLY WHISK
Possibly originating from the flail, an instrument of submission, the fly whisk is a symbol of royalty in Eastern and African cultures.

CROWN JEWELS
The crown jewels, the essential accoutrements of royal office, have assumed almost mystical significance for a ruling monarch. Without them, he or she would lose all authority. The crown jewels, orb, and scepter are essential in the coronation ceremony, when they are worn or carried by the newly crowned monarch.

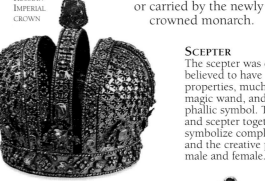

18TH-CENTURY RUSSIAN IMPERIAL CROWN

CROWN
Made of precious metal and jewels, a crown symbolizes sovereignty. It adorns the noblest part of a person, the head, or intellect. Jesus was crowned with an ironic crown of thorns. A crown also denotes supreme accomplishment, as in "crowning glory."

ORB
The orb is composed of a globe, representing the world, with a cross on top, which symbolizes the king's spiritual authority over his subjects, mirroring that of God over mankind.

SCEPTER
The scepter was once believed to have magical properties, much like a magic wand, and is a phallic symbol. The orb and scepter together symbolize completeness and the creative power of male and female.

PRUSSIAN SCEPTER

GERMAN ORB

CORONATION CEREMONY
Queen Elizabeth II of England was crowned in Westminster Abbey in 1953 in a solemn and highly symbolic ceremony. She was invested with the state regalia, which symbolized her role as head of state and the Anglican church.

AMPULLA & SPOON
The new monarch is anointed with holy oil, poured into the anointing spoon from the ampulla, here in the shape of an eagle.

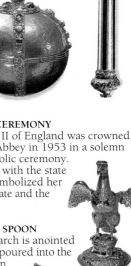

PALACE
As the residence of royalty, a palace can symbolize heaven or the heart of the realm. A palace figures in many legends and fairy tales. Of its many chambers, some are secret, holding treasures, and represent the unconscious with its hidden spiritual truths.

SEE ALSO
CROWN ☞ TORAH 17; CROWN OF THORNS 18; FOOTPRINT 22; FIRE 35; LEEK 49; SACRED HEART 74; STATUS SYMBOLS 114
KING ☞ PERSONIFICATION OF SUN 34; SUN KING 39; HUMAN SACRIFICE 74
KNIGHT ☞ KNIGHTING 91
QUEEN ☞ PERSONIFICATION OF MOON 34

TOOLS & WEAPONS

ALTHOUGH THEY ARE PRACTICAL OBJECTS, tools and weapons make powerful symbols of the inner or spiritual world. In myth, their obvious functions take on symbolic meaning. Gods are often associated with the implements they use, and while these may appear purely functional, they always symbolize concepts such as fertility, death, and war. Sometimes the implement itself denotes the god. Weapons generally represent power, protection, and destruction. In the hands of the gods, they symbolize the defeat of ignorance and thus liberation. Weapons also stand for the state of conflict that the god or hero overcomes.

STATUE OF JUSTICE
Sword of retribution
Balanced scales signify impartiality

SCALES OF JUSTICE
A pair of balanced scales represents justice and judgment, both in court and in the afterlife. In the Egyptian Hall of Judgment, the heart of the deceased was weighed against the Feather of Truth before the god Osiris, who passed judgment. In Roman art, Justice holds a sword and a pair of scales. The archangel Michael weighs the souls of the dead before Christ.

THOR'S HAMMER

CRETAN AX

LADDER
The ladder represents our urge to climb from ignorance into the light. In ancient Egypt an image of a ladder was placed inside the tomb with the dead. In the Bible Jacob dreamed of angels ascending and descending a ladder to heaven. Buddhists believe the Buddha climbed a ladder to preach to his mother in heaven.

ANVIL
The anvil is often seen as the feminine, receptive counterpart of the hammer, with its masculine associations. Together they represent the opposing but complementary forces of the active and the passive.

SCYTHE
Because it is a harvesting tool, the scythe symbolizes death, the moment when life is cut short. It also stands for the liberation of the soul. The figures of Father Time and Death, the Grim Reaper, are both depicted carrying a scythe.

HAMMER
Widely seen as a symbol of thunder, the hammer is an attribute of the Norse god Thor, whose hammer always hit its target and came back to him. The Greek god Hephaestos, the blacksmith, also wielded a hammer. In Japan the hammer is an attribute of Daikoku, god of riches. Along with the nail, the hammer is a symbol of the Passion of Christ.

HAMMER & SICKLE
The sickle lends its name to the new moon because of its shape. It therefore symbolizes time and death, but also the annual cycle of renewal. The Greek goddess of agriculture, Demeter, carries a sickle. The hammer and sickle were brought together in the symbol of the former Soviet Union. That symbol now represents the communist movement.

AX
The ax is an emblem of sky gods such as Zeus. It is a symbol of power, associated with many deities, for example, Shiva and Agni in India, and the Yoruba storm god of West Africa. In China it represents justice, authority, and punishment. The ax is also symbolic of death ordered by a wrathful deity. For Hindus and Buddhists, the ax removes ignorance and thus severs the cycle of birth, death, and rebirth.

SIMON AND ANDREW, GABRIEL LOIRE, 1975

NET
The net symbolizes the power of the gods to bind and hold humans helpless in the mesh of life. In Christian art, a net with fish represents the church. St. Peter (originally the fisherman Simon) was a "fisher of men," and St. Andrew (also a fisherman) carries a net.

ROPE
Rope represents bondage and captivity. It also connects heaven and earth, acting like a cosmic umbilical cord. In the form of a noose, it is a symbol of death and despair. In Christianity it is a symbol of the betrayal of Christ who was bound by his captors.

PLOW
The plow is usually an attribute of Greek pastoral gods such as Demeter and Dionysus. As a phallic symbol it represents impregnation of the earth by the gods, the furrow being feminine and receptive. It also represents the act of creation, when primal matter broke up into different life forms.

SPINNING WHEEL
The spindle is an attribute of goddesses concerned with destiny. They are often shown as three spinners who govern birth, life, and death. The turning wheel is a symbol of the universe. The loom is the loom of life, with masculine, active threads and feminine, passive threads united in harmony. According to Buddhism, the loom weaves the fabric of illusion.

GUN

The gun is a symbol of masculine power and aggression. Because of its projectile capabilities, the gun is associated with virility, along with other firearms and missiles. In Freudian thought the gun is an obvious phallic symbol, an association echoed in gangster movies, where it has become linked to male prowess.

MUSLIM KRIS

DAGGER

The dagger is generally a phallic symbol and stands for masculinity. It is an attribute of military gods such as Mars and Mithras. To Muslims the sacred dagger kris represents the word of Allah and absolute truth. The kris, with its characteristic undulating form, is usually beautifully decorated, often with words from the Koran.

SWORDS

In all cultures the sword stands for power and strength. A sword taken from an enemy is a symbol of victory, and to receive a sword – when knighted, for example – is to be given authority. The sword divides good from evil and cuts through ignorance. Many gods, heroes, and saints, including St. George, hold a sword.

ASHANTI SWORD

This late 19th-century sword of the Ashanti kingdom of Ghana has an unsharpened iron blade because it was used for ceremonial purposes only. The gilded beads on the handle are symbols of wealth and fertility.

SAMURAI SWORD

In Japan the sword is a symbol of courage and strength. For the aristocratic warriors of Japan, the Samurai, the sword was the chosen symbol of honor. It represented the noble cause and the fight for truth and justice.

Double-edged sword for truth and justice

CROSSED SWORDS

The arms of Saddam Hussein hold the crossed swords of the Martyrs' Monument in Baghdad, Iraq. The arch faces east (for birth) and west (for martyrdom).

KNIGHTING

The custom of knighting is very ancient. By touching both shoulders with the blade, the monarch confers authority. As a symbol of purification, the sword also cleanses the soul.

Curved sword for God's power

Quoit – round throwing weapon

SIKH EMBLEM

The Nishan Sahib, the emblem of the Sikhs, contains a two-edged sword, symbolizing truth and justice, and two crossed swords for God's spiritual power. In the center is a *chakram*, a circular throwing weapon, or quoit.

EMPEROR SIGISMUND DUBS HEINRICH OF ULM, 1473

BOW & ARROW

With its crescent shape and powerful function, the bow is both feminine and masculine and represents the moon and the arc of heaven. With the arrow, a penetrative, masculine symbol, it is an attribute of Diana and Apollo. To Chinese Taoists it is "the Way," the Tao.

SHIELD

The shield protects and has come to symbolize feminine power and chastity. In some cultures, however, it personifies the power of a male god or ancestor and can also represent a hero. It is an attribute of the Greek goddess Athena.

Indian shield covered in hide and decorated with mythological figures

SPEAR

With its elongated, phallic shape, the spear represents war, power, and fertility. In Christian art an animal impaled on a spear or lance represents a vice overcome. For this reason, figures personifying virtue often carry a lance. Because of the spear thrust into Christ's side when he was on the cross, it is also a symbol of the Passion. The spear can be a symbol of the earth's axis as well.

DEATH & MOURNING

THE CERTAINTY OF DEATH unites us all, rich, poor, and of every culture or faith. The many different rites and rituals surrounding death and mourning illustrate how each society deals with its fear of the unknown. Ancient beliefs speak of the body being reunited with Mother Earth, or the soul rejoining the cosmic ocean or entering heaven. In other words, life returning to a state of oneness with nature. In other beliefs death can be the door into another future that will be favorable if the deceased was devout in this life. A source of great fear and an occasion for both sorrow and joy, death is laden with symbolism. Many death rituals are symbolic enactments to aid the soul's journey into the afterlife and to console the bereaved.

DAY OF THE DEAD
On November 1, Mexicans celebrate the Day of the Dead. Images of Death in the form of skeletons are made, and to welcome the dead back to earth candles are lit in the graveyards and offerings of food set out. This is a symbolic way of maintaining a link with the past.

RAVEN
Although viewed in many cultures as an auspicious symbol of wisdom, fertility, and creation, the prophetic raven is seen in the Christian tradition as a bird of ill omen. It heralds evil, warfare, and death. This is probably due to its black color, associated with the night. The raven is thought to haunt graveyards and foretell death and destruction.

CHINESE PAPER FOR RITUAL BURNING AT A FUNERAL

DANCE OF DEATH, AFTER HOLBEIN, 1786

DEATHLY DANCE
The *Danse Macabre* was used to illustrate the concept that death is the great leveler. A procession of figures representing the various classes – from Pope to peasant – each alternating with a skeleton, is led towards a grave, showing all are ultimately linked by death. Another popular medieval belief, the Dance of Death, held that the dead rose at midnight and danced about in the graveyard. The two themes were often intermingled.

HEARSE
This magnificent hearse is typical of a bygone era. The hearse and the horses were always black, symbolic of mourning, as was the livery. Though modern funerals are more streamlined, such old-fashioned formalities are still preferred by some for the solace the ritual and sense of occasion provide.

LUCK FOR THE DEAD
At Chinese funerals it is the custom for mourners to burn auspicious squares of colored paper on the funeral pyre to bring good luck to the soul of the deceased on its journey to the afterlife.

TAROT CARD
In the Tarot, Death is not the last card but marks a transition from one state to another. This might signify the end – or death – of one phase of life and the beginning of a new one. Either phase would be accompanied by profound inner changes. Death is shown carrying the scythe, with which he mows down the living.

Black livery of horses extends to dyed ostrich plumes

Black stove-pipe hat with crêpe band

Black gloves and black formal attire

Black trappings on hearse

Black pall to cover horses' hindquarters

HORSE-DRAWN HEARSE

GRAVESTONE
The site of a Christian burial is marked by a memorial stone, often accompanied by symbolic reminders such as a wreath, a Bible, or an angel. An angel is an intermediary between heaven and earth and so symbolizes the passage of the soul to the heavenly realm.

HEADSTONE, 1913, NAPIER, NEW ZEALAND

ROMAN CREMATION URN

FUNERARY URN
After a cremation the ashes of the deceased are often placed inside a funerary urn. As a large, round-bodied vessel of containment, the urn is a symbol of the feminine. The urn with a lid is a good-luck emblem, symbol in Chinese Buddhism of supreme intelligence that triumphs over birth and death.

GRAVE GOODS

In many cultures precious goods are buried with the dead as a sign of their prestige in life and also to accompany them on their journey to the afterlife. Once upon a time even slaves were buried along with their dead owner.

VIKING GOLD
The Vikings buried items of gold, the most precious metal, in the graves of important men. These objects may have belonged to the deceased or they may have been made specially for burial.

VIKING GOLD TREASURE

FOOD OFEERINGS
Bowls containing food were a common offering in many cultures. They symbolize the spiritual nourishment of the soul after death. These Japanese funerary bowls date from the 3rd century.

Steering oar

Rigging up for the afterlife

Helmsman

SHIP OF DEATH
There is a widespread association of death with a journey across water. Model ships buried in a grave were believed to carry the deceased to the afterlife.

EGYPTIAN SHIP OF DEATH

RITUAL MOURNING
Mourners at a Taoist funeral in Gansu province in China are completely covered out of respect for the dead. The chief mourners wear white robes, and the principal mourner carries a green sash. Hessian veils are used, as it would be disrespectful to use fine cloth. Mourners will not eat fine food for the first two or three years after the death.

ETERNAL FLAME
At the tomb of the unknown soldier a flame burns continually as a constant reminder of all those who have died nameless in battle. The unknown soldier is a particularly poignant reminder of the indiscriminate slaughter of war.

ETERNAL FLAME, MOSCOW

FLAG AT HALF MAST
The custom of flying a flag halfway up the pole as a sign of mourning began as a naval custom in the 17th century. The top of the mast was left empty for an invisible flag of death. The custom continues as a public sign of mourning.

Flag hoist at half mast in mourning

WHITE LILY

LILY
The white lily, the flower of the Madonna, is traditionally associated with purity in the West, and this may explain why it has become customary to place lilies on the grave at a funeral. Death is seen as a return to a pure state – white as opposed to the black of death.

POPPY WREATH

WREATH OF RED
Red poppies have become a symbol of lives lost during the two World Wars. The flowers stem from a poem by Canadian John McCrae: "In Flanders fields where poppies blow/ Between the crosses row on row …" The poppy is also a symbol of sleep and dreams.

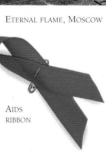

AIDS RIBBON

RIBBON
The red ribbon, devised in New York in 1991 by a group called Visual AIDS, has become a world-wide symbol of the fight against AIDS. Wearing the red ribbon symbolizes support for the fight against the disease and the need for continuing research toward a cure.

TAJ MAHAL, AGRA, INDIA

MAUSOLEUM
The Taj Mahal is the tomb of the wife of the Indian emperor Shah Jahan. Built in the 17th century, it was planned as the most magnificent memorial on earth, a symbol of the emperor's great love for his wife. His own tomb, across the river, was never finished, so he is buried beside her.

SEE ALSO

DEATH ☞ CYPRESS 45; RAVEN 64; SKELETON 74; SCYTHE 90

MOURNING ☞ MOURNING JEWELRY 85; BLACK, WHITE 106

RAVEN ☞ RAVEN 64

RED WREATH ☞ POPPY 50

TAROT CARD ☞ THE LANGUAGE OF THE TAROT 111

ARCHITECTURE

THE SYMBOLIC MEANING OF A BUILDING and its components can be very complex, especially in religious buildings. Stepped terraces may represent heavenly levels and a spire points symbolically to heaven, while a dome represents the vaults of heaven itself. Differently shaped buildings represent differing symbolic ideals: skyscrapers, for instance, represent status and achievement in the material world, while modern, environmentally sensitive buildings symbolize union with nature. Separate elements have their own symbolism: doors and windows, often mark boundaries between worlds.

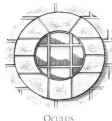

OCULUS

WINDOW

Just as the eye is known as the "window of the soul," the window is the "eye of the soul," symbolic of consciousness and of an individual's perception of the world. A round window is appropriately called an oculus or ox-eye window. Since it lets in light, the window also symbolizes the light of truth entering the soul.

INDIAN BALCONY

BALCONY

The balcony represents mystery and ambivalence due to its partly concealing, partly revealing nature, and also its position, both inside and outside a building. Enclosed balconies add to the mystery. In colder countries bay and oriel windows act as enclosed balconies.

Angel at top protects church and those who enter

Mythical beasts symbolically keep evil at bay

ENGLISH CHURCH DOORWAY, 12TH CENTURY

KNOCKER

Door knockers in animal shapes protect a house and keep evil spirits at bay. The ominous knock at the door has long been a symbol in literature – and music – of inexorable fate or death.

DOORWAY

The doorway marks the passage between the sacred and profane, between safety and danger. It also symbolizes the transition from one stage of life to another or the passage from life to death. Temple doorways in particular are often carved with guardian spirits and fabulous beasts to dispel evil and offer protection.

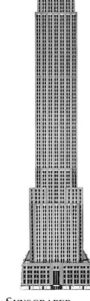

102nd floor observatory

REACH FOR THE SKY

Humankind has always been fascinated by tall buildings that reach upward to the sky, building them both for religious reasons and for reasons of power. Whether ancient pyramids or modern skyscrapers, such buildings represent man's need to reach up to the heavens and also to gain supremacy over his surroundings.

PYRAMIDS

For the ancient Egyptians the pyramid stood symbolically as a world axis at the center of the universe. Its apex represents the highest level of spiritual attainment. A stepped pyramid signifies the stages of consciousness through which the soul must pass on its ascent.

THE TOWER OF BABEL, PIETER BRUEGHEL THE ELDER, 1560

SKYSCRAPER

The Empire State Building in New York was for decades the tallest building in the world. It stands as an obviously phallic symbol of man's achievement, instantly recognizable to people all over the world.

TOWER OF BABEL

The fabled tower of Babel was a ziggurat, or stepped pyramid, in ancient Babylonia. It is a symbol of man's arrogance. In the Bible the Babylonians were determined to build such a tower to reach the heavens. God divided the speech of the builders into many languages so that they could not understand each other, and the tower was never completed.

THE BERLIN WALL

WALL

A wall encloses and protects the sheltering interior of a building or a garden, suggesting strength, privacy, and containment. In the case of the Berlin Wall, above, it may be divisive, signifying the separation of East and West.

BRIDGE OF SIGHS, OXFORD

BRIDGE
The bridge is a symbolic link between heaven and earth. It is the passage from life to death, and from death to immortality. The original Bridge of Sighs in Venice led from the courtrooms to the dungeons.

STAIRS
A staircase represents the steps in spiritual development. Its symbolism is related to that of the ladder and the stepped pyramid. One can either ascend toward Enlightenment or descend into darkness and ignorance. A spiral staircase, with its winding steps leading towards an unknown and unseen end, represents the mysterious.

LIGHTHOUSE
A lighthouse provides a beacon of light to guide ships to safety. It is a symbol of the teachings of Christ, which guide the soul to the safety of faith and understanding.

THE PARTHENON, ATHENS

CLASSICAL TEMPLE
Temples in Greek and Roman times were believed to be the houses of gods. They could be square, polygonal, or round. Round has been considered the perfect form, because the circle itself is a symbol of the cosmic mind and nature's perfection. Classical temples were erected in commanding positions, for example, the Acropolis in Athens, site of the Parthenon.

ARCH
The arch symbolizes passage from one state to another. Victorious Roman armies marched through triumphal arches. In initiation rites, to pass under an arch is to be reborn.

ARCH OF CONSTANTINE, ROME

THE NATURE SANCTUARY BUILDING, FINDHORN, SCOTLAND

EARTH DWELLING
In many countries people live in houses made entirely of natural materials found around them, from adobe huts in Africa to igloos in the Arctic. This keeps them, literally, in touch with nature and more in tune with their surroundings. A modern earth-integrated house, roofed with turf, represents a return to this more natural way of life with its related symbolism of union with nature.

NATURE HOUSE, SWEDEN

GLASS HOUSE
Mainly built of glass, this house provides full access to the natural elements and all their associated symbolism – a window to the world. The glass lets in the maximum amount of light and stores heat. The garden is visible and fresh air from it is scented with flowers and plants.

CATHEDRAL, FLORENCE

DOME
The dome is used as a symbol of the heavens. Religious buildings often incorporate a dome that may be decorated on the inside with paintings of the sun, moon, and stars, as well as angels.

NOBLES' HOUSE, INDONESIA

ROOF
The roof symbolizes the feminine, sheltering principle. Some societies hang treasures and powerful hunting trophies in the roof space to increase its protective power.

CHARLES D'ORLEANS IN THE TOWER OF LONDON, FLEMISH, c.1650

Holding place at top of tower to prevent rescue or escape

Castellated tower

TOWER AND CASTLE
The tower is a symbol of inaccessibility and protection. With its castellated towers, moats, and drawbridge, the castle is a symbol of territorial power and security, and is often a heraldic symbol. A castle is also seen in fairy tales as an enchanted place that houses a giant or demon. In order to release the captive princess or treasure inside (symbols of spiritual knowledge), the giant (the burden of ignorance) has to be defeated.

SEE ALSO
ARCH ☞
SQUARE WITHIN SQUARE 104
CLASSICAL TEMPLE ☞
TEMPLE 21;
SIGN LANGUAGE 109
TOWER AND CASTLE ☞
PRINCE & PRINCESS 89
STAIRS ☞ LADDER 90

EVERYDAY OBJECTS

THERE ARE MANY ORDINARY OBJECTS that do not fit easily into obvious categories but which are so much part of our everyday world that they have become imbued with symbolic meaning. These range from different types of container, associated with the feminine, secrecy, or protection, to objects connected with human frailty and the passage of time. Items linked to fire or light are also rich in meaning, signifying enlightenment, as are keys, which unlock secrets or mark a coming of age.

KEY
The key has the power to open and close. It gives access to another realm, symbolizing wisdom, maturity, or success. Many keys dangling from a key chain symbolize power and status, since they denote the ownership of valued property. Keys are the attribute of St. Peter as the guardian of the gates of heaven.

BASKET
The basket is an attribute of the four seasons and, when full, it symbolizes fertility, fruition, and abundance, therefore also life. In Buddhism the "three baskets" are the scriptures of the Buddhist canon.

FAN
The fan is a common symbol of high rank or royalty. It is also thought to ward off evil spirits, and to Taoists it represents the flight of a bird and release into the world of the Immortals. In contrast, the fan also has long-standing associations with femininity and flirtation.

PANDORA OPENS THE BOX

EGYPTIAN DRINKING CUP

CUP
Because they are containers, cups, like bowls, are symbols of the receptive, feminine realm. In this Egyptian example, the lotus pattern shows the flower's relationship to water, and thus adds to its links with the feminine.

BOX
The box is a feminine symbol. When closed, it symbolizes the unconscious, and when opened, it may unleash a storm of devastation, disease, and death upon the world, as did Pandora's box.

THE SWING, JEAN-HONORE FRAGONARD, 1767

Gold and silver coins, symbols of wealth and greed

MONEY PURSE
The purse represents worldly vanity and the transience of wealth. In Christian art a purse is an attribute of Judas Iscariot and of St. Matthew, the tax collector. Coins spilling out of a purse are a symbol of worldly attachment and greed.

SWING
The swing is associated with fertility because its movements represent the rhythms of the seasons and the rising and setting of the sun and moon, as well as the rhythms of love-making. In this charming 18th-century French painting, the swing, with its backward and forward motion, is a playful symbol of amorous flirtation. A stone Cupid presides over the secluded corner of the garden, while the lush vegetation provides a fertile backdrop for the lovers' games.

LAMP
The flame of the oil lamp represents life and the light of the spirit, wisdom, and immortality. Through the stories of the *Arabian Nights* the lamp has become associated with the genie who lives within it and grants wishes to the person who sets him free. Aladdin's lamp is thus a symbol of magic as well as of good fortune.

LIGHTBULB
Invented *c*.1880, the lightbulb has become the archetypal symbol of a bright idea. Cartoon characters often have one "flashing" over their head to signify a moment of inspiration.

MEASURING TIME
People have always been fascinated by the concept of time, and have linked the many objects related to it to their own mortality. Thus the aging process may be seen as "time marching on," and heart problems as a failure of the "old ticker."

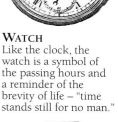

HOURGLASS
This simple instrument for measuring time operates on the principle of sand filtering down over a period of an hour under the force of gravity. The process has given rise to the notion of life being like "sand ebbing away."

EARLY HOURGLASS

WATCH
Like the clock, the watch is a symbol of the passing hours and a reminder of the brevity of life – "time stands still for no man."

SUNDIAL
The sundial shows the time via the shadow cast by the sun as it moves through the heavens. This ancient method thus relied on the activity of a sun god.

18TH-CENTURY SUNDIAL

ANCHOR
The anchor is a symbol of safety, stability, and hope. Christ is often referred to as an anchor in the sea of life. An anchor depicted with a dolphin is a symbol of Christ on the cross, and to be anchored means to be rooted.

MIRROR
Since thought is reflection, the mirror indicates truth, clarity, and self-knowledge, as well as vanity; thus to break a mirror brings bad luck because it is a form of harming oneself. To Taoists a mirror is the calm of the sage and the reflection of the universe.

CANDLE
A candle is a symbol of the individual soul and the flame that lights the darkness of ignorance. It is the sun and spiritual illumination, and an extinguished candle can signify death. Candles play a part in many religious rites and in Christianity the lighted candle represents Christ as the resurrected light of the world.

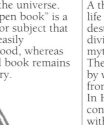

OPEN BOOK
Books are symbols of knowledge and the wisdom of the universe. An "open book" is a person or subject that can be easily understood, whereas a closed book remains a mystery.

THREAD
A thread is a symbol of life and of human destiny spun by a divine power. In Greek myth, Ariadne gives Theseus a ball of yarn by which to escape from the labyrinth. In Hinduism a thread connects this world with the next, and high-caste Hindus wear a sacred thread.

LIPSTICK
Bright red lipstick is a symbol of sexuality. It accentuates the erogenous zone of the lips, and, with its winding, upright mechanism, combines male and female imagery.

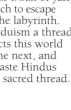

COMPASS
The compass points out the four primary directions, North, South, East, and West, and the four secondary directions, echoing symbolically the directions of the cosmos. Egyptian pyramids are built on an east/west axis, with the entrance facing the Pole Star.

French fleur-de-lis

PEN AND INK
Like the brush used in Chinese calligraphy, the pen is a symbol of learning and the intellect, and it marks out destiny on the blank sheet of life. It is also a masculine symbol, dipping into the bowl-shaped inkwell to derive its power.

SILVER SPOON
In Europe, a silver spoon is often given to a baby at the time of its christening and symbolizes nurture and life. The expression that someone is "born with a silver spoon in their mouth" indicates that they were born into a life of privilege.

SYMBOL SYSTEMS

*C*ertain signs and symbols have evolved
over thousands of years. These include
scripts, gestures, and stylized images,
often used as instant means of communication.
As technology shrinks the modern world,
these signs and symbols increasingly transcend
other languages.

PICTURE WRITING

IN CULTURES THROUGHOUT THE WORLD, picture writing represents the earliest attempt at setting down words in a non-verbal, non-gestural form of communication. Picture writing differs from drawing in that it uses a standardized set of picture signs, or "pictograms." These picture signs came to represent particular objects that were then easily recognized by the reader. As the need for more complex forms grew, signs that represent actual word sounds were introduced, and in addition, simple signs were combined to create a more complex script.

IDEOGRAMS

These Hittite ideograms are a more abstract development of pictograms. A picture of a foot, for example, may mean the verb "to walk."

CITY KING
STOOL GOD OX GREAT

CLAY TOKENS

These Sumerian tablets date from c.3000 BC. Large numbers of representational clay tablets have been unearthed in modern Iraq and Iran. Some 1,500 different symbols have been decoded, most of them relating to agricultural and commercial matters.

COW
DOG
HEART, WOMB
WOOL
STONE VESSEL

SEAT
OIL
GRANARY
ONE

PICTOGRAMS

These particular pictograms are quite modern, dating from the early 1900s. King Njoya of Bamum, in a remote area of Cameroon, set about creating a written language for his people. Bamum has only single-syllable words, and so each picture sign is also just one syllable. The meanings of the symbols are fairly easy to decipher.

NO
HOUSE
PLATE
TO GO

TO GIVE
THREAD
CHILD

EGYPTIAN HIEROGLYPHS

Hieroglyphs, literally "sacred writings," originated long before 3000 BC, but were not deciphered until the 19th century, when the Rosetta Stone was discovered in Egypt. This had inscriptions in three scripts, one of them Greek, which could be translated and compared with the hieroglyphs. Hieroglyphs are a combination of pictograms – mostly stylized drawings of animals, plants, and flowers – and "phonograms," or signs representing sounds. This script was therefore a true form of writing in the modern sense.

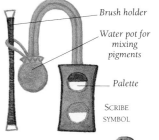

Brush holder
Water pot for mixing pigments
Palette
SCRIBE SYMBOL

LUCKY EYE

The "wadjet eye," or Eye of Horus (sky god), was thought to have magical powers. Scribes often included this symbol in their writing for good luck.

K L E O P A T R A

CARTOUCHE

The names of Egyptian kings and queens were always enclosed in oval borders, known as cartouches. The cartouche was a symbol of the ruler's power, signifying that he or she reigned over "all that the sun encircles." It was a French Egyptologist, Jean-François Champollion, who in 1822 cracked the code of these particular royal hieroglyphs.

This stela, or carved stone, contains symbols that act as clues to the meaning of the writing

FUNERARY STELA, C.2250 BC

The owl indicates the flow of the text

Four lines of inscription detailing the King's funeral offering for the priest Merra

OWL
WATER SNAIL
REEDS LION

READING THE STELA

A hieroglyphic text can be read from left to right, right to left, or top to bottom. The symbols of animals or people tell you which way to read. Here the faces point to the right, so the text is to be read from right to left.

CHINESE

The Chinese script, the oldest script still in use today, is more than 4,000 years old. The earliest examples were inscribed onto tortoise shells or carved into ox bones. Some pictographic elements remain, but the Chinese characters also include phonetic components and an added element to characterize the word.

日 + 月 = 明

SUN + MOON = BRIGHT

Some Chinese words are compounds, being the sum of two other words.

一 ONE

上 GO UP

小 LITTLE

天 SKY

日 SUN

月 MOON

心 HEART

去 TO GO

汁 JUICE

冰 ICE

魚 FISH

信 LETTER

屋 HOUSE

金 GOLD

收 TO RECEIVE

來 COME

細 TINY

親 DEAR

駡 SCOLD

龍 DRAGON

CHEROKEE

Cherokee script was invented in 1821 and shows the influence of the Latin alphabet. It is a phonological system, that is, there is a clear relationship between the written symbol and the sound, shown here in phonetic symbols.

G wa
4 se
Ʉ ga
β ye

B yʌ
ω ya
Ꮁ gwa
W la
Ꮹ gwa
Ᏽ nah
f ga

MAYAN

Mayan script is made up of compounds of signs and is a mixture of pictograms and phonetic elements. It is written in double columns from left to right and top to bottom. The hieroglyphs below are phonetic-syllabic – they each contain several elements and sounds, and yet are still representational.

BURDEN

OPEN

SOUTH

WEST

TURKEY

VULTURE

The inscription records the names and dates of Mayan rulers

MAYAN STORY

This panel comes from the temple of Yaxchilan, close to the present border between Mexico and Guatemala. It depicts the sacrificial offering of blood to bring forth ancestral spirits. Lady Xoc, the wife of Lord Shield Jaguar, is gazing up at Yat-Balam, a spirit who has emerged from the jaws of a huge, double-headed serpent.

CUNEIFORM

This form of writing was used for more than 3,000 years throughout the Near East by Sumerians, Assyrians, Babylonians, and Hittites. It developed from a system of pictograms and changed gradually to a more complex phonological system. The script is made up of wedge-shaped signs created with a stylus. At first, symbols were written vertically, as shown in the table to the right, but later many symbols were reversed and became abstract.

MEANING	3000 BC	2400 BC	650 BC
BIRD			
HAND			
HEAD			
REED			
WALK OR STAND			
WATER			

NUMBERS

IN MOST CULTURES numbers are imbued with symbolic meaning. The practice of numerology is the study of their influence. Numbers have long been seen as expressions of cosmic order, possibly deriving from ancient Babylonian observations of regular cosmic events, such as night and day, the phases of the moon, and cycles of the year. Viewed symbolically, numbers represent more than quantities; they also have qualities. To the Greek mathematician Pythagoras, even numbers were feminine, divisible into two equal parts, and were considered passive; odd numbers were masculine, and active.

0 Zero was invented in ancient India. Represented by a continuous circle, it signifies non-being and eternity. To Pythagoras it was the perfect form, containing all and from which all is created. In Islam it is limitless light and the Divine Essence.

1 To be number one is to be the best. Spiritually, one stands for the state before the creation of the myriad forms of life. It also symbolizes the oneness to which all living things must return. It is God, but also the individual.

2 Many cultures view the world as made up of opposing dualities: life and death, light and dark, male and female, heaven and hell. Others see these pairs as complementary, such as the Chinese yin and yang (left). Two is the number of discord and conflict, but also of balance and marriage.

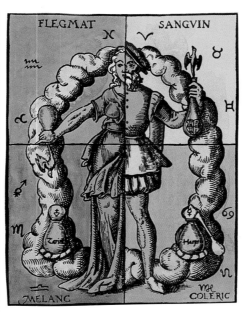

4 Four is the number of the square; the four elements – earth, fire, water, and air; and the cardinal points of the compass. It is associated with the Earth and with completeness. In medieval Europe human nature was characterized by the four humors (seen above): phlegmatic, sanguine, choleric, and melancholic.

NUMBER SYSTEMS

DEVANAGARI
Most Western languages use Arabic numerals. These derive from those written in Devanagari, the script used for Sanskrit, the classical language of India.

| ONE | TWO | THREE | FOUR | FIVE |
| SIX | SEVEN | EIGHT | NINE | ZERO |

ROMAN
The Roman system uses seven alphabetical signs: I, V, X, L, C, D, and M. Numbers are formed by adding (6 = V+I = VI) or subtracting (4 = I less than V = IV). Larger numbers come from Latin words, for example C=*centum*=100; M= *mille*=1,000.

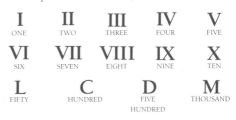

I ONE	II TWO	III THREE	IV FOUR	V FIVE
VI SIX	VII SEVEN	VIII EIGHT	IX NINE	X TEN
L FIFTY	C HUNDRED	D FIVE HUNDRED	M THOUSAND

HEBREW
Numerals in Hebrew (read from right to left) correspond to the alphabet. One is the first letter, aleph; two, the second; and so on. After the tenth letter, the value of each letter goes up in tens.

| FIVE (HE) | FOUR (DALETH) | THREE (GIMEL) | TWO (VETH) | ONE (ALEPH) |
| TEN (YOD) | NINE (TETH) | EIGHT (HETH) | SEVEN (ZAYIN) | SIX (VAV) |

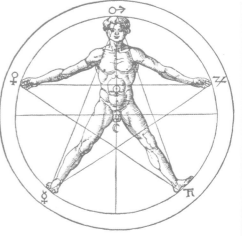

THREE

3 Sacred to most religions, the number three combines the numbers one and two and so includes all life and experience. It is birth, life, and death; mind, body, and soul; past, present, and future; man, woman, and child.

HINDU TRINITY
In India Brahma, Vishnu, and Shiva form a powerful trinity of gods. Between them they create, sustain, and destroy life in an endless cycle of birth and rebirth.

TREFOIL OF THE TRINITY
Three geometric shapes coming together can express the Christian Trinity, one God in three persons: the Father, the Son, and the Holy Spirit. Thus the architectural device of the trefoil is often found in churches.

NEPTUNE'S TRIDENT
The trident is a symbol of the Roman sea god, Neptune, possibly representing the past, the present, and the future. The trident of the Hindu god Shiva stands for his function as creator, preserver, and destroyer. Satan also holds a trident.

5 As the sum of two, a feminine number, and three, a masculine number, five is important in many cultures. It is a symbol for man. There are five human senses. On a human figure, a line joining the head to outstretched arms and legs forms a pentagram. Muslims pray five times a day, and there are five pillars of piety in Islam.

THE CREATION, FRENCH BIBLE, 14TH CENTURY

6 According to the Bible, God created the world in six days and rested on the seventh. Six represents balance, love, health, and also luck, because it is the winning throw of a die.

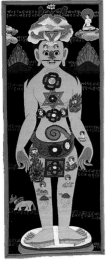

BUDDHIST WHEEL OF LIFE

8 As the first cubic number (2 x 2 x 2), eight is considered the perfect number. Chinese life is ruled by eight: at eight months a child has milk teeth; at eight years he loses them; at twice eight he reaches maturity; and at 8 x 8 he loses the power of procreation. The Buddhist wheel of life has eight spokes, for the eight-fold path to Enlightenment.

SYMBOL FOR NINE

9 Nine is the sacred number: three multiplied by itself to give eternity, completion, and fulfillment. The Norse god Odin hung for nine days and nine nights on the tree Yggdrasil to win the secret of the runes for mankind. In China it is the number of celestial power: the nine-storied pagoda is a symbol of heaven.

COMMANDMENT TABLETS

10 As the number of the fingers, ten is the foundation of most counting systems. Ten also figures strongly in the Bible: there are ten commandments, ten Egyptian plagues, ten virgins, and ten lepers. According to some theories, in the decimal system ten is symbolic of the return to unity.

THE LAST SUPPER, LEONARDO DA VINCI, 1495-98

13 In Christian countries 13 is an unlucky number because there were 13 at the fateful Last Supper. In Leonardo's fresco above, Jesus has just announced that one of the disciples will betray him. In ancient South America there were 13 Mayan heavens and the Aztec calendar was divided into 13-day periods.

21 Originally the age at which a citizen was entitled to vote (though now lowered in many countries), 21 is still considered a major landmark in life. A symbolic key signifies entry into adulthood. In many countries this is the age at which a person is allowed to buy and drink alcohol.

40 Representing wholeness, the number 40 is especially important in the Bible. Moses' sojourn on Sinai lasted 40 days, as did that of Christ in the wilderness, and Noah's ark floated in the Flood for 40 days and 40 nights. Forty was also significant in terms of years – the Jews spent 40 years in the wilderness, and the reigns of David and Solomon were both 40 years.

50 This is the number of joy and celebration. It marks the completion of seven 7-year cycles and signifies new beginnings.

60 This marks the division of the minute and hour, and is associated with time. In ancient Egypt it represented a long life.

SEVEN

7 Seven is a sacred number, representing the union of divinity (number three) and earth (number four). Each of the four phases of the moon lasts seven days and there are seven days in the week.

MENORAH
The branches of the Jewish candlestick indicate the seven days of the week as well as the sun, moon, and five principal planets. The three U-shaped arms represent wisdom, strength, and beauty.

WHEELS WITHIN
In Hindu philosophy there are seven chakras, or wheels, in the body. These stand for needs or levels of consciousness, ranging from the lowest for physical survival to the highest for spiritual enlightenment.

SEVEN DEADLY SINS
The seven deadly sins (clockwise from top) – gluttony, sloth, lust, vanity, anger, envy, avarice – are the counterparts of the three theological and the four cardinal virtues.

12 As the multiple of the masculine three and the feminine four, 12 represents both spiritual and earthly order. There are 12 signs of the Zodiac, 12 months of the year, 12 hours of day and night. There are also 12 knights of the Round Table, 12 days of Christmas, 12 disciples, and 12 tribes of Israel.

SHAPES & PATTERNS

MANY SHAPES AND PATTERNS are universal. For example, similar patterns may decorate objects separated by thousands of miles and thousands of years. Symmetrical shapes appeal to our need for order, intricate shapes, such as puzzles and knots appeal to an urge to unravel mysteries, and labyrinths can express our need to find our true path, despite obstacles. Shapes may be mystical symbols. They are also often used symbolically in architecture – a square temple surmounted by a circular dome, for instance, represents the solidity of the earth topped by the dome of the sky.

YANTRA OR MANDALA

A sacred Hindu diagram, the yantra is used as a focus for meditation. Concentrating on the geometric shapes draws the mind into the diagram and beyond, into ultimate reality. Yantras often form the basis for the ground plans of temples. The mandala is a circular yantra, usually enclosing a square.

DOORS OF PERCEPTION

The four projections from the middle of each side of the inner square are the "doors" of the yantra, through which the mind may enter or leave the center during contemplation.

SQUARE WITHIN SQUARE

The square represents the earth, solidity, order, and safety. It also represents the four compass directions and the balance of opposites. The immense Grande Arche in Paris seems to embody these qualities by its location, size, and function. Where one square sits inside another, the outer square symbolizes awareness of the physical world, the inner square the unconscious.

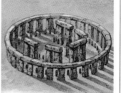

STONE CIRCLE

Certain stone-age peoples have left behind huge standing stones as monuments. The original function of the stone circle at Stonehenge in England is still a mystery. It was probably a form of temple, maybe representing the eye of a great goddess.

STAR

The star symbolizes light in darkness and wisdom shining through ignorance. To many people stars are the spirits of the dead, set in the sky. To "reach for the stars" is to set the highest goal. In the US the star is a badge of honor.

SHRI YANTRA, NEPAL, c.1700

CIRCLE

The enclosing circles serve to unify the opposing triangles. They are made up of lotus petals to signify the unfolding of reality as perceived by meditating on the yantra.

TRIANGLE

The upward-pointing triangles represent the male principle and the downward-pointing triangles the female principle. They interlock to show the creative activity of the cosmos.

WHEEL

This wheel, which is one of twelve from the base of the Sun Temple at Konarak, India, symbolizes *samsara*, the endless round of existence. The wheel in Buddhism is a symbol of the Buddhist law, or doctrine, set in motion in the Buddha's first sermon.

LONGEVITY

This is *shou*, one of the three ways of representing the Chinese symbol for longevity or immortality. It is often seen with other symbols of longevity, such as the pine or the tortoise. When paired with a peach, it is a wish for a long and happy marriage.

SWASTIKA

The swastika is a very ancient and auspicious sign with complicated symbolism associated with the sun. Found in most parts of the world, it is especially popular in India. However, in the West it is now a symbol of evil because of its association with Adolf Hitler.

FLEUR-DE-LIS

Emblem of French monarchy, the *fleur-de-lis* may be a sylized iris. Legend also claims an angel gave a lily to Clovis, King of the Franks, in AD 496 when he accepted Christianity.

ALMOND

Also known as the mandorla, the almond-shaped halo is formed from two intersecting circles. It is used to symbolize Christ's ascension to heaven.

Four corner knots stand for the four directions

KNOT

This engraving by Leonardo da Vinci is, like a yantra, a contemplative diagram. It is a knot made from a single thread that, if followed, will lead to one's inner self. The knot binds, but also holds the promise of release. A knot can be tied for protection, and to "tie the knot" means to get married.

THRESHOLD STONE, NEW GRANGE, EIRE, 3RD/4TH MILLENNIUM BC

SPIRALS

Energy was once believed to flow in spiral form. The spiral symbolizes masculine and feminine energy and the energy of both sun and moon. It is the great swirling force of the whirlwind and the movement of the heavens. It is a manifestation of the energy in nature, and is related to the powerful imagery of the serpent. The spiral also symbolizes the circlings of the soul, which eventually return to the center, or truth.

MAZE

The maze, or labyrinth, has appeared in the art of the Egyptians, Indians, Celts, and Mediterranean peoples. Some mazes have a clear path leading to the center, where truth lies; others are puzzles, with the path constantly dividing. Such mazes often occur in dreams, representing indecision. The labyrinth is difficult to enter, but also difficult to leave, and only those with wisdom can find their way through it.

Pillar of the god Osiris

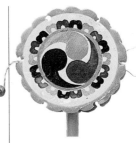

TRISKELE

This Chinese drum bears the triskele symbol, which, like the swastika, was originally a symbol of good fortune. It may represent the movement of the sun across the heavens.

ANKH

The ankh is an ancient Egyptian symbol. By combining the Tau cross of the god Osiris and the oval of the goddess Isis, it signified life. It was later adopted by the Coptic Christian church in Egypt.

SEE ALSO

MAZE ☞
MINOTAUR 28; MAZE 43

STAR ☞
STAR OF DAVID 16;
SEAL OF SOLOMON 108

SWASTIKA ☞
SWASTIKA 21; FOOTPRINT 22

TRIANGLE ☞
ALCHEMICAL SYMBOLS 108

YANTRA ☞ ROSE WINDOW
51; EYE OF WISDOM 72

COLOR

WE ARE SURROUNDED BY COLOR, and its immediate visual effect on our senses has powerful emotional and symbolic overtones. Red is equated with blood, for instance, and green with grass. The two colors traditionally associated with death are black and white. Though it differs from culture to culture – and even from person to person – color symbolism is among the most universal. Certain colors, such as red, advance, and are considered lively and stimulating; others, such as blue, retreat, and tend to be soothing. Rainbows, which contain the full spectrum, are viewed as lucky.

ORANGE

Like red, orange symbolizes flames, but also luxury and splendor. In China and Japan it is equated with love and happiness.

RED

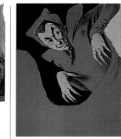

Red is the color of life – of blood, fire, passion, and war. It is worn by brides in India and China as a symbol of good luck and fertility. Christian calendars marked holy days in red, hence red-letter days. But red is also the color of danger, and warning signs are often marked in red.

SAFFRON ROBES
These young initiates wear the saffron-colored robes of Buddhist monks to indicate that they have taken vows of humility and renunciation.

WHITE

White symbolizes purity and perfection, also the Absolute. It is the color most associated with sacredness: sacrificial animals are often white. In the Western world brides usually wear white, but it is the color of mourning in much of Asia. Ghosts are thought to be white because it is a color that conceals nothing. A white flag signals truce, and therefore peace.

BLACK

In the West, black is the color of death, mourning, and the underworld. It also has associations with evil magic. In Hinduism, Kali, the terrible goddess of destruction, is black. In China it represents the north and winter.

JET EARRINGS

JET BLACK
Jewelry made of jet, a black, semiprecious stone, was commonly used by those in mourning in Victorian times. Queen Victoria of England, in perpetual mourning after her husband's death, thought that displaying bright jewelry showed a lack of respect for the deceased, and this led to a fad for jet jewelry.

RED FLAG
Symbol of revolution and the communist party, the red flag was first raised during the French Revolution. It was adopted during the Paris Commune in 1871, and then by the Russian communists.

RED DEVIL
Since medieval times Satan, or the Devil, has been depicted with red clothes or skin. Red is the color of hellfire and damnation and also of unbridled passion and lust.

BROWN

Brown symbolizes the earth and fall. It is also, as the color of the earth, humility and degradation.

HOLY RED
To celebrate a mass commemorating martyrs, a Christian priest wears a red chasuble, the color symbolizing shed blood. Red is also the color of Christ's Passion.

MONK IN BROWN HABIT

STATUS-SYMBOL RED
The association of red with virility, danger, and sexual excitement makes it one of the most popular colors for flashy sports cars – the ultimate symbol of masculine success in wealthy countries.

MONK
In the Middle Ages brown was the color of mourning. Several Christian orders adopted it to signify retreat from the world.

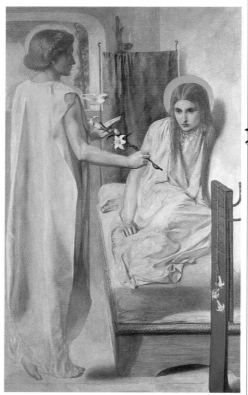

ECCE ANCILLA DOMINI (ANNUNCIATION), ROSSETTI, 1849-50

LILY WHITE
Sometimes called the Madonna Lily, the white lily is a symbol of purity and the Virgin Mary. The angel Gabriel is traditionally depicted with a white lily when he announces to Mary that she is to bear the son of God. In the Christian church white is associated with the priesthood, baptism, and first communion.

YELLOW

Yellow is gold, light, and the sun. In Islam golden yellow represents wisdom and good advice, while pale yellow is deceit and betrayal. In Egypt yellow is the color of envy and disgrace, and in Europe it is associated with cowardice. In China yellow was the color of royalty. Yellow is the most visible color and is used internationally for warning.

TREACHEROUS YELLOW

Since the Middle Ages yellow has come to signify, in Europe, betrayal and treachery. Here, Judas envelops Jesus in his yellow cloak as he identifies him with a kiss, a sign to the chief priests that they should arrest him. The color symbolism would have been evident to Renaissance viewers.

BETRAYAL OF CHRIST, GIOTTO, 1305-6

IMPERIAL YELLOW

In China yellow is symbolic of the masculine principle, yang, and the power of the sun. During the Ch'ing dynasty (1644-1911) only the emperor could wear yellow. This 18th-century imperial throne cushion is decorated with dragons, also the emblem of the emperor.

FESTIVE YELLOW

During the Somavati Amavasya festival in India, pilgrims scatter vast amounts of turmeric powder over the god Khandoba. The yellow powder represents the power of the sun. The festival marks the conjunction of the sun and moon – the new moon – when it falls on a Monday.

GREEN

Green is the color of life, spring, and youth. It represents hope and joy. It is associated with ecology, the concern with preserving the earth's resources. However, green also represents decay and jealousy. In Christianity it is the color of the Trinity.

FLAG OF PAKISTAN

ISLAMIC GREEN

Pakistan's flag declares the nation's faith. Green, Islam's sacred color, is combined with white for purity. The crescent became a symbol of Islam in the 14th century and the star was later added as a symbol of sovereignty.

GREEN FOR GO

Green is used universally as a sign giving the go-ahead. Along with red and yellow, it was originally used for railroad signaling before it was adopted on the road.

VEGETARIAN SOCIETY LOGO

COLOR OF LIFE

Chlorophyl gives plants their green color. A stylized seedling forms the V of the Vegetarian Society. Its logo is increasingly used in the Western world to draw attention to manufactured foods suitable for vegetarian consumption.

BLUE

As the color of the sky and water, blue symbolizes calm, reflection, and the intellect. It is also the infinite, and the void from which all life develops.

BLUE STONE

Ground lapis lazuli produced a pigment highly prized in Mesopotamia for decorating temple ceilings. The color signified divine favor.

BLUE-SKINNED GOD

Rama, an incarnation of the Hindu god Vishnu, is usually depicted with blue skin, as is Krishna, another much-loved incarnation. Blue is an appropriate color for Vishnu, since it represents the vastness of the heavens.

BLUE DOME

The blue dome of this Russian church, with its gold stars, represents the heavens, with the cross above indicating that Christ's dominion encompasses all life.

Gold stars in blue heaven

PURPLE

In the West purple signifies royalty and imperial power as it did in ancient South America. It represents pride and grandeur, and also justice.

DYED PURPLE

In ancient Greece purple dye, extracted from mollusks, was a luxury that only the rich could afford. Thus the color now symbolizes wealth.

PURPLE HEART

In 1782 George Washington created the first US military medal, a heart-shaped badge of purple cloth. It was revived in 1932 as the Purple Heart, awarded to those wounded or killed in battle.

PINK

In Western traditions, pink is the color of flesh, and hence sensuality. A softer tone of red, it is primarily associated with the feminine.

BABY PINK

More muted than red, pink suggests sensuality in a less aggressive way. Pink is the traditional color for young girls. Baby girls are still often dressed in pale pink, in contrast to the traditional pale blue for boys.

GRAY

Gray is associated with gloom and depression. But as a balance between black and white it is the color of mediation. Things that are not certain are considered gray areas. In Christianity gray represents the immortality of the soul and is worn by religious groups.

SEE ALSO

BLACK ☞
JET 38;
MOURNING JEWELRY 87;
RAVEN, HEARSE 92

BLUE ☞ LAPIS LAZULI 40

LILY WHITE ☞ THE LILY
AND CHRISTIANITY 53; 93;
LILY, RITUAL MOURNING 93

RED ☞ GOLDFINCH 66;
ROBIN 67;
INDIAN WEDDING 83

SAFFRON ROBES ☞
BUDDHIST MONKS 23

ALCHEMY

ALCHEMY, THE MEDIEVAL FORERUNNER OF CHEMISTRY, was a richly symbolic science that united practical discovery with a mystical view of nature. The goal of alchemists was to discover the Philosopher's Stone, or the Elixir of Life, which would create gold from base metals. This change was known as transmutation, but could also be understood as a quest for spiritual perfection. One way of achieving it was to unite opposing elements, such as water and fire, earth and air, the four primary elements. The fifth element or essence, "quintessence," symbolized the spirit.

ALCHEMISTS IN A LABORATORY

UROBOROS

THE TAIL OF THE DRAGON

In alchemy a dragon, or more often a serpent, eating its own tail is known as the uroboros. The dragon was a symbol of the god Mercury and the circle a powerful symbol of the eternal cycle of nature. Because the uroboros recreates itself by feeding on its own body, it is a symbol of transforming matter, i.e. alchemy itself.

CADUCEUS
According to alchemical lore, Mercury, messenger of the gods, cast his magic wand between two warring serpents. They coiled themselves around it, forming what is called the caduceus, a symbol of opposing forces held in balance.

EARLY ALCHEMISTS
Alchemists were philosopher-chemists. Their goal was to distill an elixir that would transform common metals, such as lead, into gold. Through their ceaseless laboratory experiments, they forged a path for modern chemistry.

ALCHEMICAL SYMBOLS
Alchemists believed all matter was made up of earth, fire, water, and air. The symbol for water flows down like water, the symbol for fire rises up like flames. Sulfur and mercury are often paired together as masculine and feminine symbols repectively. The sun was the symbol of gold; the moon of silver.

WATER

FIRE

MERCURY

SULPHUR

MOON

SUN

OPUS MEDICO-CHYMICUM, AFTER J. D MYLIUS, 1618

SEAL OF SOLOMON
This six-pointed star, one of the most powerful magical symbols of all time, combines the alchemical signs for fire and water. As the water descends and the fire ascends, air and earth are created. The seal, therefore, represents the union of the four elements in the quest for the Philosopher's Stone.

SEAL OF SOLOMON

IMMORTALITY
Because of fear of persecution, alchemists developed a complex vocabulary of symbols to convey their knowledge. This diagram shows what an alchemist must do to arrive at the Philosopher's Stone, the key to immortality. The alchemist brings together all the vital elements around him – water and fire, earth and air.

PHOENIX
This mythical bird is the alchemical symbol of rebirth through fire. In medieval legend, the phoenix lives in Arabia but flies to Egypt, the home of alchemy, to undergo its ritual death and regeneration. Here it cradles the all-powerful elements of fire and water under its wings.

SEE ALSO
CADUCEUS ☞ DIAMOND BROOCH 40; ROD OF AESCULAPIUS 59
EARLY ALCHEMISTS ☞ GOLD, LEAD 39
PHOENIX ☞ PHOENIX 31
SEAL OF SOLOMON ☞ STAR OF DAVID 16; ISRAEL 115

FREEMASONRY

FREE AND ACCEPTED MASONS form the world's oldest association of men. Its members belong to a lodge presided over by a master and wardens. Its principles, or craft, as freemasonry is called, is to "build" good men. Initiation rites, or degrees, concern the biblical Temple of Solomon and use the stonemason's tools as symbols of personal or spiritual growth.

MASONIC EMBLEM
As essential tools of a stonemason, the square and compass have become the main symbol of freemasonry. Together they help create better citizens.

LEVEL
The level is used to lay bricks horizontally. It is the symbol of a Senior Warden and signifies equality.

SQUARE
This is the emblem of a Master of a Lodge. It is an instrument that gathers scattered elements into order, and so represents a moral code.

PLUMB RULE
Builders use the plumb rule to obtain true verticals. For Masons it is a symbol of rectitude, indicating their upright behavior. It is the emblem of a Junior Warden of a Lodge.

APRON OF GRAND MASTER

APRON
Masonic aprons are richly decorated emblems of office. They hark back to the lambskin aprons worn by stonemasons in ancient times. That of the Grand Master bears the sun – as the sun rises in the East announcing the day, so too the Grand Master opens a lodge, sitting in the East.

TRACING BOARD
The principles of freemasonry are explained to new members using tracing boards covered with symbols. This tracing board, with its three pillars of wisdom, strength, and beauty, represents the first degree of initiation into the fraternity.

Jacob's ladder
This connects the pathway between heaven and earth, with the three principal rungs of Faith, Hope, and Charity

Compass points
The cardinal points of the compass are shown on the border

Pillar
The three pillars stand for the "Rule of Three": the wisdom, beauty, and strength displayed in the building of the Temple of Solomon

Ashlar
The rough ashlar, or masonry block, represents unformed man; the complete ashlar (opposite it), perfection itself

Checkered pavement
The black and white squares represent the struggle between good and evil

The sun, representing the day

The all-seeing eye, with rays of light, an ancient symbol of God

Moon and stars, representing night

FIRST DEGREE
TRACING BOARD

SIGN LANGUAGE
Solomon's temple is full of symbols, with winding stairs representing an internal path the individual must climb. On either side are the key to man's secrets and an ear of corn signifying plenty. The trowel "cements" brotherhood.

TROWEL

Pyramid and all-seeing eye

American eagle

ONE-DOLLAR BILL

US DOLLAR BILL
America's first president, George Washington, was a Freemason. He adopted freemasonry symbols, such as the pyramid (to denote knowledge and wisdom) and the all-seeing eye of God, as emblems of the new American nation.

SEE ALSO
SIGN LANGUAGE ☞
DOME OF THE ROCK 25
TRACING BOARD ☞
PERSONIFICATION OF
SUN AND MOON 34;
SUN KING 39;
LADDER 90; STEPS 94
US DOLLAR BILL ☞
PYRAMIDS 94

DIVINATION

TO SEE INTO THE FUTURE AND PREDICT the course of events is a desire that has preoccupied humankind from time immemorial. In some countries, animal entrails and oxen's shoulder blades are still examined for signs and answers to questions, as are the feeding habits of chickens. In the West the richly symbolic system of the Tarot, with its pictorial representations of situations or states of mind, has regained its popularity, and the medieval art of casting runes has reemerged. The ancient art of palmistry, in which the lines etched on the human palm stand for areas of human life, continues to flourish everywhere.

PENDULUM
A pendulum can be used for dowsing – discovering metal objects or water beneath the earth's surface. In especially skilled hands, a pendulum can even be suspended over a map to locate lost items.

AFRICAN DIVINING BOWL AND STICK

DIVINATION BOWL
Among the Yoruba of Nigeria, a bowl is filled with sand and then tapped with a stick. The resulting sand formation can be interpreted by a diviner to answer questions such as where to locate water or when the tribe can expect rain.

CRYSTAL BALL

CRYSTAL BALL
Crystal spheres can concentrate the rays of the sun and so have come to represent divine light and celestial powers. In Europe the crystal ball is often used in divination and is now a classic symbol of fortune telling. A medium gazes into the ball and sees "pictures," usually of the future.

OUIJA BOARD
The ouija board is a means of getting in touch with the dead and has come to represent contact with the spirit world. While many see this as a harmless pastime, others use it seriously to contact those they have lost or to ask questions about the future. A group of people sit together lightly touching a planchette and by their concentration call down a spirit that uses it to spell out particular answers.

DIVINATION USING A OUIJA BOARD

ROMAN DIVINATION DEVICE

ROMAN DIVINATION
In Roman times sacred chickens were used as messengers of the gods. They were placed in specially constructed coops and observed. The way they scratched at their food and ate was thought to show whether or not the gods approved of a particular plan. A similar form of divination is still practiced in parts of the world today.

READING HANDS

The idea that the lines of the hand reveal a person's character is very old. Different forms of palmistry appear in ancient Chinese and Jewish texts. As well as the lines, the shapes of the fingers and of the "mounts" all play a part in the diagnosis.

A developed mount of Saturn is the sign of a hardworking personality

The mount of Mercury reveals a person's ability to communicate

One of the two mounts of Mars, which denote aggressiveness

Mount of Jupiter stands for ambition and success

A developed mount of Venus indicates a kind-hearted person

Mount of the Moon relates to imagination

OIL IN HAND
In Arab countries, the traditional method of looking into the future is to "read" the formation of a pool of black ink or oil in the palm of the hand.

PALMISTRY
According to palmistry, one's character and future life is written in the lines of the hand. The palm contains numerous lines, three of which – the head line, the heart line, and the life line – are deemed particularly important. The strength and length of these major lines indicate health, relationships, and overall character, as well as destiny.

GYPSY READING TEA LEAVES

TEA LEAVES
It was once common practice in England to have one's fortune told by means of tea leaves. The tea was drunk until just one teaspoon remained in the cup. The cup would then be rotated three times before the liquid was poured into the saucer. The patterns created by the leaves that were left behind formed the basis of the "reader's" interpretation.

CHINESE THROWING STICKS
In Chinese temples it is common to see men and women shaking cylindrical pots of sticks until one stick clatters to the ground. In this type of divination, cryptic messages are attached to the sticks. The one that falls first is all-important, and books provide detailed interpretations.

DIVINATION STICKS WITH BOOK FOR TELLING FORTUNES

RUNE STONES

Casting runes for divination originated in Iceland in the Middle Ages and has recently come back into vogue. There are 24 runes, each with a symbolic meaning, plus a blank one for the unknown. The order in which the runes fall dictates their meaning.

STRENGTH

SEPARATION

PARTNERSHIP

THE SELF

PROTECTION

DEFENSE

FERTILITY

GROWTH

HARVEST

JOY

JOURNEY

FLOW

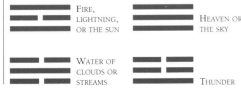

FRENCH 16TH-CENTURY TABLE

Combinations of dice can reveal the sex of a future child

DICE

Dice have been thrown in divination since ancient times and are common symbols of luck or chance. In this method of looking into the future, three dice are thrown. When they fall, the numbers that they reveal and the order in which the dice lie are checked against a table of meanings. This in turn provides answers to or interpretations of the questions raised.

I CHING

The I Ching is an ancient Chinese divinatory text in which answers to questions are set out in the form of "trigrams." Each trigram consists of three whole (male) or broken (female) lines. There are eight basic patterns that can be combined to provide a choice of 64 hexagrams of 6 lines, each giving a different meaning.

FIRE, LIGHTNING, OR THE SUN

HEAVEN OR THE SKY

WATER OF CLOUDS OR STREAMS

THUNDER

HILLS OR MOUNTAINS

WATER OF A LAKE OR MARSH

THE WIND OR WOOD

THE EARTH

THE LANGUAGE OF THE TAROT

Tarot cards probably originated in the East. They entered Europe more than 500 years ago. The cards consist of 22 major arcana, or trump cards, and 56 minor arcana, the two sets possibly originating separately. They present a picture of a personality and symbolize the soul's journey along four parallel paths toward spiritual enlightenment.

THE FOOL SYMBOLIZES NAIVE WISDOM, OR AN UNPLANNED INCIDENT OR ENDEAVOR

XIIII — TEMPERANCE
TEMPERANCE

XV — LE DIABLE.
THE DEVIL

VI — L'AMOUREUX.
THE LOVERS

XVII. — L'ÉTOILE
THE STAR

XVIII — LA LUNE
THE MOON

XX — LE JUGEMENT
JUDGMENT

XVI — LA MAISON DE DIEU
THE TOWER

PENTACLES

SWORDS

CUPS

WANDS

BACK OF I CHING CARD

FRONT OF I CHING CARD

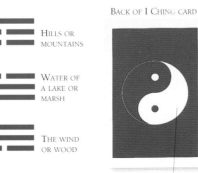
The complementary forces of yin and yang are central to the I Ching

This hexagram of the earth over the earth relates to fertility

SEE ALSO

CRYSTAL BALL ☞ CRYSTAL 39

DICE ☞ DICE 79

I CHING ☞ CROW 65; TWO 102

PALMISTRY ☞ HAND OF THE FUTURE 75; PLANETARY RULERS 113

PREDICTION ☞ SNAIL 57; NEWT 58

ROMAN DIVINATION ☞ ROOSTERS AND HENS 64

THE LANGUAGE OF THE TAROT ☞ TAROT CARD 92

ASTROLOGY

THE IDEA THAT THE MOVEMENTS of the sun, the moon, and the planets through the heavens influence our lives goes back thousands of years. As early as 3000 BC, the ancient Mesopotamian civilizations recorded the movements of these celestial bodies, and endowed their gods and goddesses with the power and attributes of the heavenly bodies. The Greeks saw them as representations of their own deities, and the Romans gave the five known planets – Mercury, Venus, Mars, Jupiter, and Saturn – the names that we still use today.

WHEEL OF FORTUNE
This astrological wheel shows 12 "houses," each representing one-twelfth of the heavens at the time of birth. The outer ring shows the signs; the inner ring shows the element assigned to each. Fire signs are energetic and forceful; water signs are emotional and intuitive; air signs are objective and logical; earth signs are practical and reliable.

ASTROLOGICAL WHEEL

EVERYTHING UNDER THE SUN

THE SUN SPENDS ONE MONTH IN EACH ZODIAC SIGN

Our Sun sign is the astrological sign of the zodiac that the powerful Sun is passing through at the time of our birth. Using symbolic language, the Sun sign in astrology describes how we express ourselves most naturally. The Moon in astrology is the feminine counterpart of the Sun. It represents our emotional responses and our links with the past.

THE MOON PASSES THROUGH EVERY SIGN EACH MONTH

 |  |  | |  |

ARIES MAR 21–APRIL 20 | TAURUS APRIL 21–MAY 21 | GEMINI MAY 22–JUN 21 | CANCER JUN 22–JUL 22 | LEO JUL 23–AUG 23 | VIRGO AUG 24–SEPT 23

ARIES
Courageous, passionate, enthusiastic, and assertive, Aries people are inclined to rush into things. This fire sign is associated with spring – a time of renewed growth and energy.

TAURUS
Those born under this earth sign are said to be practical and reliable, yet with a stubborn streak. Sensuous Taureans have a love of beauty and may have beautiful voices.

GEMINI
Versatile and quick-witted, those born under the sign of the twins can also be changeable. Geminis are communicative people and need to know what is going on around them.

CANCER
Cancerians are said to be sensitive, home-loving types who will retreat into their shell if upset. This water sign is associated with the family, and many Cancerians have very close family ties.

LEO
The typical Leo likes to be the center of attention and can have a powerful personality with a touch of the dramatic. Warm and loyal, Leos have a generous and friendly nature.

VIRGO
Cautious and quite private, the practical Virgoan pays attention to detail and likes to be well prepared. Virgoans may take a special interest in their health and diet.

 |  |  |  |  |

LIBRA SEPT 24–OCT 23 | SCORPIO OCT 24–NOV 22 | SAGITTARIUS NOV 23–DEC 21 | CAPRICORN DEC 22–JAN 20 | AQUARIUS JAN 21–FEB 19 | PISCES 20 FEB–20 MAR

LIBRA
The symbol of the scales indicates that justice and fairness are important to Librans. Charming and diplomatic, Librans need harmony and are upset by discord.

SCORPIO
Intense and passionate, with a love of mystery and secrets, Scorpios are loyal and private people. Not known for their moderation, they react strongly, especially when threatened.

SAGITTARIUS
Enthusiastic, direct, and adventurous, Sagittarians love to learn. With a great desire for freedom, Sagittarians can become restless if life becomes routine, and many enjoy traveling.

CAPRICORN
Cautious and disciplined, the earthy Capricorn is hard-working and has a marked urge to succeed. Those born under this sign can resist change or be high climbers.

AQUARIUS
Independent and with a reformist streak, Aquarians are individualists who rarely subscribe to conventional views. Champions of new causes, their opinions can appear dogmatic.

PISCES
The typical Pisces is imaginative and intuitive and has a very compassionate nature. The fish symbolism reflects the rather slippery and changeable quality of the sign.

PLANETARY RULERS

In astrology, the ten planets (the Sun and Moon are treated as planets, although technically a star and a satellite) represent basic drives or characteristics that are common to everyone. The sign the planet occupies at birth, its position, and the aspects it makes, color the expression of its energies. Below are the main symbols and associations for each planet.

 SUN
The central creative force in the zodiac, the Sun has masculine attributes and is linked with rulers and fathers. It is associated with the heart and its metal is gold. The Sun rules the sign of Leo.

MOON
Associated with mothers, the body, and childhood, the Moon is the Sun's feminine counterpart. Linked to the stomach and womb, its metal is silver. The Moon rules the sign of Cancer.

MERCURY
Fast-moving Mercury represents the mind and the urge to understand and communicate. Linked with the shoulders, arms, and nervous system, Mercury rules Virgo and Gemini.

VENUS
The planet of love, attraction, beauty, and cooperation, Venus also represents what we value in life. It is linked to the kidneys and is the natural ruler of Taurus and Libra.

MARS
Named after the god of war, Mars symbolizes direct energy and getting what we want. Ruler of Aries and Scorpio, Mars is associated with the head, and with iron and steel.

JUPITER
The largest known planet, Jupiter represents expansion, exploration, and the search for knowledge and meaning. Jupiter's associated body part is the liver, and it rules Sagittarius and Pisces.

SATURN
Once the farthest known planet, Saturn represents order, limitation, and responsibility. It is associated with the skeleton and the skin, and rules Capricorn and Aquarius.

URANUS
Discovered only in the late 18th century at a time of revolutions and social unrest, Uranus represents individual freedom, new ideas, and dramatic change. It is the ruler of Aquarius.

NEPTUNE
Neptune, discovered in the middle of the 19th century, symbolizes the intangible and the extraordinary. The planet of fantasy and dreams, Neptune rules the sign of Pisces.

PLUTO
Pluto represents powerful, hidden forces beyond our control, and is named after the Roman god of the underworld. It is associated with life, death, and renewal, and rules Scorpio.

CHINESE ASTROLOGY

THOSE BORN UNDER THE OX ARE STRONG AND STUBBORN

THE ROOSTER, DISCIPLINED BUT FUNNY

The Chinese system is based on the year of birth. Each of the 12 animal signs occurs every 12 years according to a lunar calendar that begins around January/February. The signs are further defined by 5 elements, wood, fire, air, metal, and water.

 RAT
(e.g. 1948)
The rat is ambitious, hard-working, and liable to accumulate money. Rats may be reserved and shy.

OX
(e.g. 1973)
The intelligent and hard-working ox can be stubborn. But once aroused, an ox's feelings are deep.

TIGER
(e.g. 1962)
The tiger takes risks, but is usually born lucky. Tigers have a sensual nature and often act on impulse.

RABBIT
(e.g. 1987)
The rabbit is artistic, thoughtful, intelligent, and lucky, and often pursues a comfortable lifestyle.

DRAGON
(e.g. 1940)
Dragons are strong-willed and fiery. They are usually successful, and either marry young or stay single.

NEPALESE ZODIAC, EARLY 20TH CENTURY

A WHEEL OF YEARS

This Nepalese zodiac displays the 12 images of the Chinese system in the outer circle and the 8 sacred Buddhist symbols in the central circle.

 SNAKE
(e.g. 1953)
Snakes are pleasure-loving, with a tendency to be secretive. They are as energetic and self-reliant as dragons.

 HORSE
(e.g. 1990)
Freedom-loving, good-humored, and generous, the horse is a popular and rather unpredictable character.

BOAR
(e.g. 1959)
Those born under the boar tend to be sociable, loyal, and reliable, with a passionate nature.

DOG
(e.g. 1934)
Dogs are intelligent, affectionate, honest, and loyal. They are objective, but can be inflexible.

 **ROOSTER**
(e.g. 1957)
Disciplined and good at organizing others, the rooster can be eccentric, but has a sense of humor.

MONKEY
(e.g. 1992)
The charming and conceited monkey can be promiscuous when young, but is more settled later.

SHEEP
(e.g. 1943)
Those born under this sign tend to feel easily hurt. Their compassionate nature makes them popular.

SIGNS OF THE ZODIAC FROM HARMONIA MACRO COSMICA, 1708

MAPPING THE SKIES

As men and women gazed up at the night sky, the patterns created by the stars suggested familiar objects or animals. They named the stars according to what they saw – Leo for lion and Gemini for twins – and included these images in their early maps.

HERALDIC EMBLEMS

ONE OF THE MOST COLORFUL and attractive uses of symbols is in heraldry. There is no limit to the variety of devices used – plants, animals, humans, mythical beings, geometric shapes, colors, and inscriptions are grouped in a coat of arms or as a flag to represent a family, business, or nation. The practice of heraldry began in medieval times when symbols were used to identify knights on a battlefield or jousting in tournaments. It soon became a highly complicated system that had to be strictly regulated. This was done by the king's messengers, the heralds, which is why it is called heraldry.

VIVID LANGUAGE

Heraldic devices are described in a language called "blazon." It uses terms such as "shield," "charge" (a symbol on the shield), and "supporter" (a figure on either side of a shield).

LION
The so-called king of beasts is a natural symbol of royalty.

EAGLE
The double-headed eagle is of Byzantine (late Roman) origin.

BEAR
In Central European heraldry the bear, standing for strength, often replaces the lion.

DOG
Symbol of faithfulness and loyalty, a dog may signify a Crusader.

TRAPPINGS OF CHIVALRY
Knights and their horses dressed sumptuously for battle or tournament. They wore their heraldic symbols on their shields, armor, and surcoats. A surcoat was the garment worn over the armor, and from it we get the term "coat of arms."

SPANISH PLATE, 15TH CENTURY

MIXED SIGNALS
The "charges" on this "shield" are a castle, denoting the Spanish city of Castile, and a lion, for the city of Leon. The surrounding decoration is of Islamic origin, reflecting Spain's Moorish heritage.

CRESTED EAGLE
Crests were originally heraldic symbols mounted on helmets. An eagle, symbol of German power, crowns an early 20th-century Prussian officer's helmet.

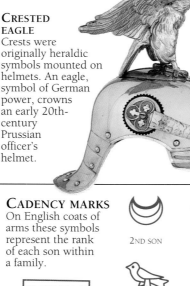

CADENCY MARKS
On English coats of arms these symbols represent the rank of each son within a family.

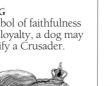

2ND SON	3RD SON
1ST SON	4TH SON	5TH SON

STATUS SYMBOLS
Since coats of arms are ultimately granted by the "fount of all honor," the Crown, they have come to represent power and authority – royal, inherited, or civic.

ARMS OF HENRY VIII
At the time of Henry VIII, the British royal coat of arms bore the English lion and the Welsh dragon. The unicorn of Scotland was not represented since Scotland was then a separate kingdom.

ARMS OF THE SWINTON FAMILY
Dating from the 12th century, the Swinton family arms have evolved from a single boar "rampant" (upright) into a herd of six, acquiring along the way the mottos "I hope" and "I think."

ARMS OF THE CITY OF LIVERPOOL
Neptune and a merman, the "supporters," refer to Liverpool's long history as a port, as does the ship. The liver bird (similar to a cormorant), is a visual pun, a device in heraldry called "canting."

ASIAN BADGES OF HONOR

Japan is the only nation that uses a similar system of heraldry to that of Europe, and it also developed in the 12th century. Japanese heraldic symbols are called "mons," and are usually circular. The red sun on the Japanese flag is the mon of the Land of the Rising Sun. Symbolic patterns were also used on Chinese court dress to denote rank.

16-PETALED CHRYSANTHEMUM

PAULOWNIA, THE NATIVE FLOWERING TREE, PRIVATE MON OF THE IMPERIAL FAMILY

IMPERIAL FLOWER
The chrysanthemum is the national flower of Japan and a symbol of long life and prosperity. The 16-petaled flower is the crest of the emperor; other imperial males use a 14-petaled mon.

OFFICIAL'S DRESS
Each round pattern on this Chinese court coat is made up of good luck symbols. The Manchurian crane was a symbol of longevity, and was supposed to carry the immortals through the air. White cranes were embroidered on the court robes of civic officials of the fourth grade. Here they are encircled by clouds and tiny bats, the bats being symbols of happiness.

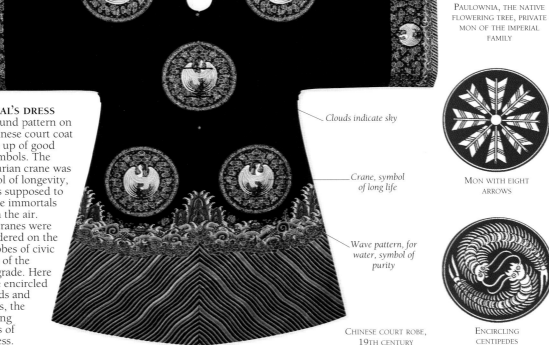

Clouds indicate sky

Crane, symbol of long life

Wave pattern, for water, symbol of purity

CHINESE COURT ROBE, 19TH CENTURY

MON WITH EIGHT ARROWS

ENCIRCLING CENTIPEDES

FIVE-SICKLED WHEEL

FLAGS

Using a range of colors, forms, emblems, and designs, flags represent a wide variety of different peoples, but probably the best-known flags are those of nation states.

PIRATE ENSIGN
A red flag meant no mercy would be shown to the victim. The winged hourglass, arm and sword, and skull-and-crossbones all signified death.

SRI LANKA
The lion emblem comes from Kandy, heart of the island's Buddhism. It is the largest animal on any national flag.

CANADA
The maple leaf, representing the local red maple, is the largest plant symbol on a national flag.

MALAWI
The sun appears on many flags, sometimes representing royalty. The rising red sun in the top band of Malawi's flag is taken from the arms of the former colony of Nyasaland.

ZAIRE
The hand holding a blazing torch is the emblem of the MPR (Movement of the Revolution). Now incorporated on the national flag, it is a symbol of the struggle for independence.

SOUTH KOREA
The "yin-yang" symbol in the center represents the two universal opposing forces of Taoism. The four trigrams of the *I Ching* represent sun, moon, earth, and heaven.

ISRAEL
The Star of David is a religious symbol. The six points represent the six days of creation; the center, the Sabbath. The blue stripes come from the prayer shawl. Blue stands for heaven; white, for purity.

BHUTAN
The dragon – similar to those that appeared on Chinese flags – is a reminder that this Himalayan kingdom's name in its own language, "Druk Yul," means "Land of the Thunder Dragon."

KENYA
The sword and crossed spears symbolize the Masai, an ancient warrior-hunter tribe. The colors are those of the main political party at the time of independence; the red is known as Kenya red.

US
The US flag is the most modified flag in the world. The 13 stripes stand for the original states of the union, but the number of stars has increased with each new state. The 50th, for Hawaii, was added in 1960.

INTERNATIONAL SIGNS

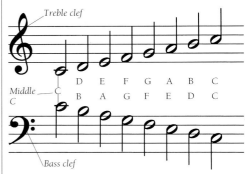

PEACE CROSS

THE NOTION OF A PICTURE BEING "worth a thousand words" is borne out by the vast number of signs and symbols that now represent words and phrases throughout the world. Take, for example, the no smoking sign. The red circle with its diagonal line over a smoldering cigarette is as instantly recognizable in New York as it would be in Kathmandu. This sign, like traffic signs or the CND peace symbol above, has been designed to communicate immediately and effectively; other signs, such as mathematical and musical notation, have evolved over centuries as virtual languages in their own right.

ORGANIZATIONS

THE RED CROSS
The International Red Cross was founded in Geneva in 1863 to provide medical relief to all during wartime. Its emblem was formed by reversing the colors and symbol of the Swiss flag.

THE OLYMPIC FLAG
The Olympic emblem of five interlocking circles was created to represent five continents – Europe, Asia, Africa, Australia, and the Americas.

THE UNITED NATIONS
The United Nations was founded in 1945 and adopted as its emblem a polar view of the world encircled by two olive branches of peace.

THE EUROPEAN FLAG
The European Union (EU) flag was formally adopted in 1986. The 12 five-pointed gold stars represent perfection according to heraldic code.

MATHEMATICAL SYMBOLS

ADD The plus sign first appeared in Germany in 1489 in *Mercantile Arithmetic* by John Widman.

SUBTRACT The symbol for the minus sign, like the plus sign, was first used in John Widman's book.

DIVIDE The division symbol was invented in 1668 by John Pell, a professor of mathematics from Cambridge, England.

MULTIPLY The symbol for multiplication first appeared in William Oughtred's *Clavis Mathematica*, published in 1631.

EQUALS The equals sign was invented by Robert Recorde, who used it in an algebraic text published in 1557.

PERCENT The percent sign derives from the formula $x/100$. The term is from the Latin, *per centum*.

INFINITY The earliest recorded use of the infinity symbol was in 1665, in *De Sectionibus Conicis*, by John Wallis.

SQUARE ROOT Coined in 1557, the square root sign is a modified form of a division sign.

MUSICAL NOTATION
The present system of representing music has evolved over hundreds of years. At the end of the Roman period a system was devised using the letters A-G to represent the 7-note scale. The standardization of the 5-line stave, used to determine pitch, came about in the 17th century.

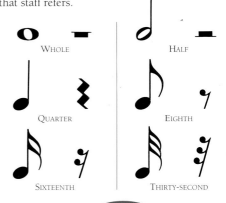

Treble clef

Middle C

Bass clef

| D | E | F | G | A | B | C |
| B | A | G | F | E | D | C |

NOTE VALUES
The duration of notes and rests – the sounds and the silences – is indicated by symbols of different shapes. These notes and rests are related to the beat of the music. A dot after a note or rest extends its value by half. The clef sign (bass or treble) determines the range of pitches to which that staff refers.

WHOLE   HALF

QUARTER   EIGHTH

SIXTEENTH   THIRTY-SECOND

QUALITY CONTROL MARKS

The system of stamping precious metals as proof of their purity came into being in the 13th century. Silver had to have at least 92.5 percent silver content in order to be considered sterling. Countries adopted different signs to denote purity, and cities also had individual stamps so that pieces could be located accurately.

SILVER MARKS·

SILVER PROOF OF 92.5 PERCENT SILVER CONTENT

SWEDEN FROM 1752 (STATE CONTROL MARK)

ITALY (PURITY OF 900/1000; BELOW STERLING)

FRANCE 1798-1809 (PURITY OF 950/1000)

LONDON LEOPARD'S HEAD, IN USE FROM 1327 (STERLING)

MUNICH GERMAN CITY MARK, C.1700

REGISTERED TRADEMARK OWNED BY IWS DENOTING PURE NEW WOOL AND QUALITY ASSURANCE

SYMBOL OF PURE COTTON   SYMBOL OF REAL LEATHER

WARNING SIGNS

International highway "sign language" has been devised for maximum visual impact. It involves a clear system of colors and shapes that can be understood instantly. Red, for example, indicates prohibition; yellow, caution; and green, safety. Similarly a triangle is a warning sign and a red circle, with or without a crossbar, is a prohibition sign.

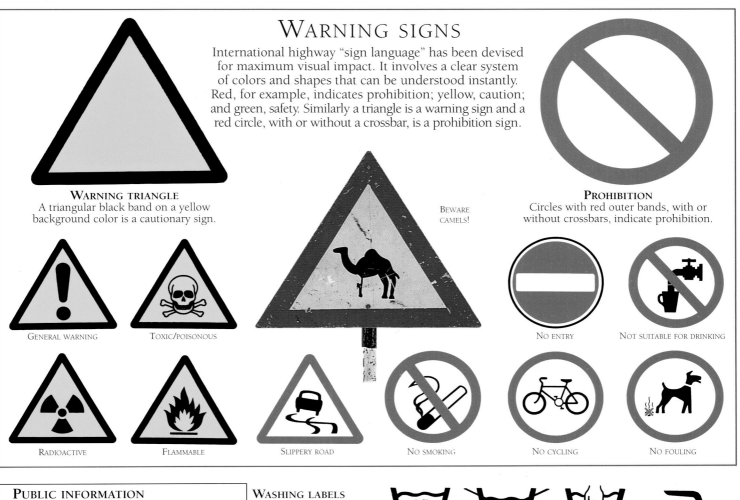

WARNING TRIANGLE
A triangular black band on a yellow background color is a cautionary sign.

GENERAL WARNING

TOXIC/POISONOUS

RADIOACTIVE

FLAMMABLE

BEWARE CAMELS!

SLIPPERY ROAD

PROHIBITION
Circles with red outer bands, with or without crossbars, indicate prohibition.

NO ENTRY

NOT SUITABLE FOR DRINKING

NO SMOKING

NO CYCLING

NO FOULING

PUBLIC INFORMATION

The standardization of public symbols has been in operation since the early 1900s, reflecting the growth of international travel. Most signs are self-explanatory.

WOMEN'S ROOM

MEN'S ROOM

DISABLED ACCESS

TELEPHONE

TOURIST INFORMATION

POST OFFICE

WASHING LABELS

An international labeling scheme exists to promote the proper care of clothes and textiles. Words are intentionally kept to a minimum. A cross through any symbol means "do not."

WASHING TEMPERATURE

DO NOT WASH

HAND WASH ONLY

REQUIRES IRONING

DO NOT IRON

DO NOT TUMBLE DRY

DO NOT BLEACH

DRY CLEAN

RECYCLE

Ever-increasing awareness of our endangered planet has prompted a return to things natural, or "eco-friendly." The recycling sign, with its constantly revolving arrows, is now a familiar sight on biodegradable products and on garbage cans where they can be disposed for further recycling.

DIRECTION

The sign indicating direction has varied over the years, from a graphic hand with outstretched finger in Victorian times to more stylized arrows used today.

SEE ALSO

DIRECTION ☞ HANDS 75
MATHEMATICAL SYMBOLS ☞ NUMBER SYSTEMS 102
ORGANIZATIONS ☞ RED FLAG 106; ISLAMIC GREEN 107; FLAGS 115
QUALITY CONTROL MARKS ☞ SILVER 39
WARNING SIGNS ☞ PIRATE ENSIGN 115

SYMBOLIC GESTURES

"ACTIONS SPEAK LOUDER THAN WORDS," and this is particularly true of gestures. The various postures that we assume, both consciously and unconsciously, are highly revealing – although just what they reveal depends on whether or not the action is intentional, and on the context in which it occurs. Some gestures, however, transcend cultures – hands clasped together and held out to another are a symbol of entreaty the world over.

THINKING
People adopt this posture unconsciously. It is a modified prayer with a reassuring touching of the lips.

TEETH FLICK
This gesture, flicking a thumb-nail against the teeth, is common in Mediterranean countries, where it denotes anger.

HANDS

FINGERS CROSSED
This widespread symbol of protection or good luck is a modified form of the Christian cross.

THUMBS UP
Meaning "okay," this stems from Roman times, when spectators would make a similar gesture covering their thumbs (symbols of swords) to spare a gladiator's life.

V FOR VICTORY
This sign is known worldwide. It was a trademark of Winston Churchill, used first to indicate victory over the Nazis. It has since been used to indicate any form of victory.

HORNS
This "horned" gesture protects against evil or bad luck and is often combined with a backward and forward rotation of the hand.

PRAYING HANDS
This familiar symbol of prayer is also one of respect and greeting in India and Southeast Asia. Originally it signified hands bound together in a symbolic offering of oneself to God.

PLEADING HANDS
This is a prayer directed at another person, usually begging for assistance.

LOOSE SCREW
This gesture indicates that someone is crazy, that he or she needs to tighten a loose screw in the head.

STUPIDITY
Common in Saudi Arabia, this implies "I can see clearly that you are a fool."

QUERY
In Italy this gesture of fingers and thumb pressed together, with the hand twitching up and down, asks "What do you want?" or "What do you mean?"

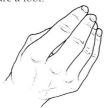

OKAY
Here the thumb and forefinger form a circle and move back and forth to indicate that something is good.

MOCKERY
Thumbing one's nose is a playful insult, familiar to all ages and all nationalities. Often the fingers are wiggled to emphasize mockery.

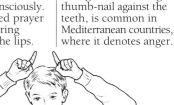

JEALOUSY
This gesture has various related meanings, and is generally an insult. In Mediterranean countries it represents the horns of a cuckold; in Japan it denotes an angry or jealous woman.

GREETINGS

WAVING
This gesture is often made on meeting or parting. The hand raised with palm upward is a classic way of drawing attention to oneself.

NOSE RUBBING
Although rare in the West, the rubbing of noses is still practiced in other cultures, notably among Polynesians.

HANDSHAKE
The clasping of hands is a common gesture both on meeting and parting. Unlike a bow or a curtsey, it signifies a certain equality of status.

JUDO CEREMONIAL BOW

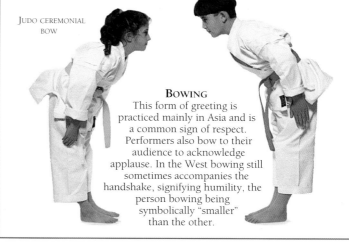

BOWING
This form of greeting is practiced mainly in Asia and is a common sign of respect. Performers also bow to their audience to acknowledge applause. In the West bowing still sometimes accompanies the handshake, signifying humility, the person bowing being symbolically "smaller" than the other.

ARMS

TRIUMPH
Arms straight in the air are a sign of success: the person feels this big.

PRAISE
In this gesture, palms, and head are turned heavenward.

HAIL
Depending on the stiffness of the arm, this is a friendly gesture or a Fascist salute. It goes back to Roman times and was adopted by Hitler in the 1930s.

SURRENDER
A recognized gesture of submission, this arms-raised posture shows that the person is not reaching for a weapon.

REJOICING
This gesture, which combines jumping in the air with the slapping of right hands, is a spontaneous display of joy. It is most common in the field of team sports.

SOCCER PLAYERS CELEBRATING A GOAL

HEAD

NO
"No" can be expressed by turning the head from side to side, or in North Africa with a single, sharp turn to one side and back.

YES
Although shaking one's head generally means "no," in India and Pakistan this wobbling from side to side means "yes."

MOUTH

CHILDHOOD INSULT
Children the world over stick their tongues out as a rude gesture – perhaps their first learned insult.

BE QUIET
An easily recognized symbol of silence, the lips are sealed.

I DON'T KNOW
This gesture involves pulling down the corners of the mouth – a facial equivalent to shrugging shoulders.

ANGER
Biting one's lower lip while shaking one's head from side to side shows barely contained anger.

EYES

EXASPERATION
A familiar sign of exasperation, the eyes are turned heavenward, as though invoking divine assistance.

WINKING
A wink has various meanings, from sexual approval by a potential partner, to collusion between two people in the know.

SKEPTICISM
Raising just one eyebrow is a common gesture of disbelief. The two sides of the face are at odds, registering a state of confusion.

ANXIETY
Eyebrows raised and furrowed is an instinctive response to extreme anxiety. It is a natural expression, common to all cultures.

KISSING

CHEEK KISS
This is a friendly gesture practiced in the West, in which both people kiss each other on one or both cheeks.

HAND KISS
This gesture is a symbol of respect, and was once commonly performed by a man greeting a woman. Usually the lips barely touch the hand.

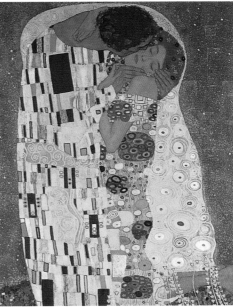

THE KISS, GUSTAV KLIMT, 1907-8

LOVERS' KISS
An erotic view of a kiss, in which two people are fused together in total intimacy.

BLOWING A KISS
A symbol of love, often from a mother to a child, or to a friend too distant to embrace.

FOOT KISS
A gesture symbolizing humility and respect, performed by the Pope during Holy Week.

SEE ALSO
ARMS ☞ DURGA, SHIVA 20; BODHISATTVA 23; ARMS 75
FINGERS CROSSED ☞ JESUS CHRIST 18
HANDS ☞ HAND OF GOD 24; HANDS 75; CLASSICAL INDIAN DANCE GESTURES 77; HENNAED HANDS 83
KISSING ☞ LIPS 82
MOUTH ☞ TONGUE 72; TEETH 73

GLOSSARY

In references to Greek and Roman mythology in the book, we have generally used the Roman names for the gods rather than their Greek counterparts, because they tend to be more familiar. The Roman gods are listed here with their Greek equivalents.

Absolute, the A term for God or the state of cosmic unity.

Adonis In Greek and Roman mythology, a beautiful youth loved by Venus. He was killed while boar hunting.

Agni Hindu fire god.

Ainu Aboriginal inhabitants of the Japanese island Hokkaido.

Aladdin The main character in *The 1,001 Nights* or *Arabian Nights*, a poor boy who has a magic lamp.

Alchemy The chemistry of medieval scientists, who tried to find a way to turn ordinary metals into gold.

Allah Islamic name for God.

allegory A story in which the characters and events are meant to be interpreted symbolically.

amulet A charm, often inscribed with a magic formula, to protect one against evil.

Annunciation The angel Gabriel's visit to the Virgin Mary to tell her that she will give birth to Jesus.

Apollo Greek and Roman sun god, and god of prophecy.

Arabian Nights A collection of Eastern folk tales, also known as the *1,001 Nights*.

Ariadne Daughter of Cretan King Minos in Greek mythology, who helped Theseus only to be later abandoned by him.

Aristotle Ancient Greek philosopher advocating reason and moderation.

Ashanti People from central Ghana.

asceticism Denying oneself physical pleasure for religious reasons.

Assyrians Ancient peoples who inhabited what is now Iraq, and who conquered a vast empire.

auspicious Bringing good luck.

avatar Incarnation; one of the Hindu god Vishnu's ten incarnations on earth.

Aztecs An American Indian people who inhabited ancient Mexico.

Babylonians Inhabitants of ancient Iraq.

Bacchus (Greek Dionysus) Roman god of fertility and wine.

Bodhisattva Future Buddha; one who postpones Nirvana in order to save others.

Brahma The four-headed god who created the universe and who, with Vishnu and Shiva, forms the Hindu trinity.

Buddha Religious leader, founder of Buddhism, who taught that enlightenment is achieved by meditation and detachment.

Cernunnos Celtic horned god, lord of nature and fertility.

Cherokee A Native American people.

Churchill, Winston British Prime Minister during World War II.

CND Campaign for Nuclear Disarmament.

Comanches A native people of North America.

cosmos, cosmology Universe; study of the universe as an ordered whole.

Crucifixion The execution of Christ by nailing him to a cross.

cuckold Man whose wife is unfaithful to him.

Cupid (Greek Eros) Roman god of earthly love, son of Venus.

David Second Hebrew king, father of Solomon.

Diana (Greek Artemis) Roman goddess of hunting, protector of women.

Donar Teutonic god of thunder.

Dreaming, the In Australian Aboriginal thought, the spiritual and natural order incorporating legends of the ancestors.

Durga A terrifying form of the Goddess in Hinduism.

elixir A liquid giving everlasting life.

erogenous zone Area of body susceptible to erotic stimulation.

Eve Biblical first woman, who lived with her husband, Adam, in the Garden of Eden.

Exodus The escape of the Jews from slavery in Egypt.

Fates Atropos, Clotho, and Lachesis, Greek goddesses controlling destiny.

Flood, the According to many religious traditions, an ancient disaster that drowned all humanity except for a chosen few.

four elements Earth, air, fire, and water, believed in medieval times to be the basic ingredients of the universe.

four humors The four fluids (blood, phlegm, yellow bile, and black bile) that, according to medieval belief, shaped the personality depending on how much of each was present in the body.

Freud, Sigmund (1856–1939) Austrian psychologist who invented psychoanalysis.

Freya In Norse mythology, Odin's wife, goddess of love, marriage, and fertility.

Furies Avenging goddesses in Greek mythology.

Gabriel Archangel in Christian and Muslim belief; God's messenger.

Gandhi, "Mahatma" (1869–1948) Indian nationalist leader, famous for heading a nonviolent freedom struggle.

Garuda Fabulous bird, mount of the Hindu god, Vishnu.

Great Goddess An embodiment of the feminine principle. May take different forms. In Hinduism, may be benign or terrifying.

griffin A mythical beast with a lion's body and eagle's beak and wings.

Hanukkah The Jewish festival of lights.

harbinger Forerunner, precursor.

Hathor Egyptian goddess of love and beauty.

Hercules (Greek Herakles) Hero of Roman mythology famous for his strength.

heresy A belief that contradicts authorized religious teaching.

Herod Herod Antipas, governor of the Jews in Jesus' time.

Hittites Inhabitants of ancient Anatolia and Syria.

Homer Blind Greek poet of the 8th century BC, author of the epics *Iliad* and *Odyssey*.

Horus Egyptian hawk-headed sun god, son of Isis and Osiris.

I Ching Ancient Chinese book of divination.

initiation ceremony A rite of admission, often marking the entry into adulthood.

Inuits Inhabitants of Greenland and the Arctic region of North America; Eskimos.

Isis Chief goddess of ancient Egypt, sister-wife of Osiris.

Israelites Descendants of the patriarch (Jacob); the Jews.

Jacob Hebrew patriarch whose twelve sons were ancestors to Israel's twelve tribes.

Jonah Biblical figure who was swallowed by a great fish.

Judas Iscariot Disciple who betrayed Christ to the Jews.

Judea Southern division of ancient Palestine.

Jung, Carl (1875–1961) Swiss psychologist and colleague of Freud who originated analytical psychology.

Juno (Greek Hera) Queen of the Roman pantheon, protector of women.

Jupiter (Greek Zeus) King of the gods in Roman mythology, god of thunder.

Koran The Muslim sacred texts as revealed to the prophet Mohammed.

Krishna Incarnation of the Hindu god Vishnu.

mandala Pictorial symbol of the universe, a Buddhist aid to meditation.

Mars (Greek Ares) Roman god of war.

martyrdom Dying for one's belief.

Mary, Virgin The mother of Jesus Christ.

Maya An ancient Indian people who lived in Central America and Southern Mexico.

Mecca The birthplace of Mohammed.

Medusa In Greek mythology, a female monster with snakes for hair whose glance turned people to stone.

Mercury (Greek Hermes) Roman messenger god, god of travelers.

Mesoamerica Central America, between Northern Mexico and Panama.

Mesopotamia The ancient name for part of modern Iraq.

microcosm The world or universe in miniature.

Minerva (Greek Athena) Roman goddess of wisdom and war.

Minoan Of prehistoric Crete.

Mithras Ancient Persian god of light, worshiped by Romans.

Moghul emperors Northern Indian Muslim dynasty rulers 1526–1857.

Mohammed (c.570–632) The prophet and founder of Islam.

monotheistic Believing in one god only.

Moses Hebrew lawgiver and judge who led his people out of Egypt.

mysticism A way of directly experiencing the Divine through ecstatic or heightened spiritual awareness.

Navajo A Native American people of North America.

Nefertem Human-headed Egyptian god of the setting sun.

Neptune (Greek Poseidon) Roman god of the sea.

Nirvana Extinction of individuality and absorption into the cosmos, never to be reborn; goal of Buddhism.

Noah Biblical character who, at God's command, built an Ark to save his family from the Flood.

Odin Chief deity of Norse mythology, sky god.

Orpheus Mythical Greek poet and musician with the power to enchant all living creatures.

Osiris Egyptian god of the dead.

Ottoman Belonging to the Ottoman Empire, ruled by the Turks AD 1300–1920.

Pan Greek god of shepherds and hunters, with a goat's horns and hoofs. His pipes had a hypnotic effect.

pantheon All the gods of a mythology collectively.

patriarchs The founding fathers of a nation or religion.

Phaeton Son of Apollo, who drove the chariot of the sun for one day, nearly set the earth on fire, and was killed by Jupiter's thunderbolt.

phoenix Fabulous Arabian bird reborn from the flames of its own destruction.

Pluto (Greek Dis) Roman god of Hades, the Underworld, kingdom of the dead.

primordial Existing from the beginning; primeval.

Promised Land Canaan (present-day Israel), which the Jews believed had been promised them by God.

Quetzalcoatl Aztec god of learning and of priestly functions, usually depicted as a feathered serpent.

Rama Vishnu's seventh incarnation, the mythical hero of India's war with Lanka.

Ramadan The ninth month of the Islamic calendar, when Muslims fast by day.

Re Egyptian sun-god, father of Osiris and Isis.

Renaissance The transitional period between the Middle Ages and modern times; literally the "rebirth" of arts and learning.

Samurai Japanese aristocratic warriors, equivalent of England's knights.

Sanskrit The ancient literary language of India.

Saturn The second largest planet. Its influence is believed by astrologers to give rise to a cold, melancholy temperament.

satyrs Half-goat and half-human woodland gods in Greek mythology.

Selket Human-headed Egyptian scorpion-goddess.

shaman Priest-doctor who works directly with the spirit world.

Shiva The Destroyer, one of the three great gods of Hinduism.

Sinai Mountain in Egypt where Moses received the Ten Commandments.

Sioux A Native American people of North America.

Solomon, King Hebrew king, son of David, famed for wisdom.

Soviet Union The former Union of Soviet Socialist Republics.

stylus Pointed implement for writing on wax tablets.

Taoism Chinese philosophical system teaching harmonious interaction with nature.

Theseus Hero of Greek mythology who killed the minotaur.

Thor Norse god of thunder.

Thoth Ibis-headed god of wisdom and learning in Egyptian mythology.

totem An object or creature regarded as sacred by a clan. Often an ancestor figure.

transcendence The surpassing of all limitations of human knowledge and experience.

tribe of Judah Descendants of Judah, son of Jewish patriarch Jacob.

Trojan War Legendary siege of the city of Troy by the Greeks.

tzars Emperors of pre-Revolutionary Russia.

Ulysses (Greek Odysseus) Hero of Roman and Greek mythology who fought the Trojans and was famous for his courage and ingenuity.

Venus (Greek Aphrodite) Roman goddess of beauty and love.

Venus, sphere of In medieval thought, the earth was encased in nine invisible rotating spheres of increasing size, each holding a planet.

Virgin Birth The birth of Jesus to the Virgin Mary after her insemination by God.

Vishnu The Preserver. With Shiva, one of the most important Hindu gods.

yin and yang Chinese opposing yet complementary principles, *yin* being negative, feminine, and dark, while *yang* is positive, masculine, and bright.

Yoruba People of southwestern Nigeria.

Zoroastrianism Pre-Islamic Persian religion.

INDEX

FURTHER READING

Ayo, Yvonne, *Africa, Eyewitness Guides*, Knopf, 1995

Baquedano, Elizabeth, *Aztec, Eyewitness Guides*, Knopf, 1993

Bechert, Heinz & Gombrich, Richard, *The World of Buddhism*, Thames and Hudson Inc., 1984

Becker, Udo, *The Continuum Encyclopedia of Symbols*, Continuum, 1994

Becket, Sister Wendy, *The Story of Painting*, DK Publishing, Inc., 1993

Black, Jeremy & Green, Anthony, *Gods, Demons & Symbols of Ancient Mesopotamia*, University of Texas Press, 1992

Blurton, Richard, *Hindu Art*, HUP, 1992

Campbell, Joseph, *The Masks of God, vol 1: Primitive Mythology; vol 2: Oriental Mythology; vol 3: Occidental Mythology; vol 4: Creative Mythology*, Viking, 1959-68

Chetwynd, Tom, *Dictionary of Symbols*, Thorsons SF, 1994

Chiron Dictionary of Greek and Roman Mythology, Chiron, 1994

Cirlot, J.E., *A Dictionary of Symbols*, Routledge, 1993

Clift, Jean & Clift, Wallace, *Symbols of Transformation in Dreams*, Crossroad NY, 1986

Cooper, J.C., *An Illustrated Encyclopedia of Traditional Symbols*, Thames and Hudson Inc., 1992

Cooper, J.C., *Symbolic & Mythological Animals*, Thorsons SF, 1992

Crossley-Holland, Kevin, *The Norse Myths, Gods of the Vikings*, Pantheon Books, 1981

De Rola, Stanislas Klossowski, *The Secret Art of Alchemy*, Thames and Hudson Inc., 1973

Dreyfuss, Henry, *Symbol Sourcebook*, McGraw-Hill, 1972

Eberard, Wolfram, *A Dictionary of Chinese Symbols, English edition*, Routledge & Kegan Paul, 1986

Farrant, Sheila, *Symbols for Women: A Matrilineal Zodiac*, Thorsons SF, 1990

Ferguson, George, *Signs & Symbols in Christian Art*, Oxford University Press, 1961

Foley, John, *The Guinness Encyclopedia of Signs & Symbols*, Guinness Publishing, 1993

Fontana, David, *The Secret Language of Symbols*, Chronicle Books, 1994

Freud, Sigmund, *The Interpretation of Dreams*, Knopf, 1994

Gordon, Matthew S., *Islam*, Facts On File, 1991

Guerber, H.A. *The Myths of Greece & Rome*, Dover, 1993

Haeffner, Mark, *Dictionary of Alchemy*, Thorsons SF, 1992

Hall, James, *Subjects & Symbols in Art*, Harper and Row, 1974

Hall, James, *The Illustrated Dictionary of Symbols in Eastern and Western Art*, HarperCollins, 1994

Hall, James, *Sangoma: An Odyssey into the Spirit World of Africa*, Putnam Pub Group, 1994

Herder Symbol Dictionary, The, Chiron Publications, 1991

Honour, Hugh & Fleming, John, *Visual Arts: A History*, Abrams, 1991

Huntingdon, Susan, *The Art of Ancient India*, Weatherhill, 1995

Hutt, Michael, *Nepal, A Guide to the Art and Architecture of the Kathmadu Valley*, Shambhala Publications, 1994

Japan, An Illustrated Encyclopedia, 2 vols., Kodansha, 1993

Jean, Georges, *Writing, the Story of Alphabets and Scripts*, Abrams 1992

Jung, Carl G., *Man and his Symbols*, Doubleday & Co. Inc., 1964

Jung, Carl G., *Psyche & Symbol: A Selection of Writings from C.G. Jung*, Princeton University Press, 1991

Kelsey, Morton, *Symbols, Dreams & Visions*, Amity House Inc., 1988

King, Francis X., *Mind, Magic & Mystery*, DK Publishing Inc., 1992

Knappert, Jan, *Aquarian Guide to African Mythology*, Thorsons SF, 1991

Knappert, Jan, *Indian Mythology, Encyclopedia of Myth and Legend*, Aquarian Press, 1991

Knappert, Jan, *The Encyclopedia of Middle Eastern Mythology and Religion*, Element, 1993

Kunz, George Frederick, *The Curious Lore of Precious Stones*, Dover Publications, 1971

Larousse Dictionary of Beliefs and Religions, Larousse, Kingfisher, Chambers, 1994

Leith, James, *Symbols in Life & Art*, University of Toronto Press, 1987

Lundquist, John M., *The Temple, Meeting Place of Heaven and Earth*, Thames and Hudson Inc., 1986

Lurker, Manfred, *The Gods and Symbols of Ancient Egypt*, Thames and Hudson Inc., 1994

Morgan, Hal, *Symbols of America*, Viking Penguin 1987

Morris, Desmond, *Bodytalk*, Crown Publishing Group, 1995

Nordon, Rudolph, *Symbols and their Meaning*, Concordia 1985

Oxford Companion to Music, Oxford University Press, 1967

Parker, Derek, *New Complete Astrology*, Random House Value, 1990

Philip, Neil, *The Illustrated Book of Myths*, DK Publishing Inc., 1995

Rawson, Philip, *Art of Tantra*, Thames and Hudson Inc., 1985

Rawson, Philip, *Sacred Tibet*, Thames and Hudson Inc., 1991

Rawson, Philip, *The Art of Southeast Asia: Cambodia, Vietnam, Thailand, Laos, Burma, Java & Bali*, Thames and Hudson Inc., 1990

Saunders, Nicholas, *Animal Spirits*, Little Brown, 1995

Saunders, Nicholas, *The Cult of the Cat*, Thames and Hudson Inc., 1991

Stutley, Margaret & James, *A Dictionary of Hinduism and its Symbols*, Routledge, Chapman & Hall, 1985

Theroux, Alexander, *The Primary Colors*, H. Holt, 1994

Thomas, Nicholas, *Oceanic Art*, Thames and Hudson Inc., 1995

Twining, Louisa, *Symbols & Emblems of Early & Medieval Christian Art*, Gordon Press, 1980

Versluis, Arthur, *Native American Traditions*, Element, 1994

Villiers, Elizabeth, *The Mascot Book: An Encyclopedia of Bringers of Good Luck Charms, Spells, Talismans, and Colors*, Gordon Press, 1991

Wangu, Madhu Bazaz, *Buddhism*, Facts On File, 1993

Wangu, Madhu Bazaz, *Hinduism*, Facts On File, 1991

Werner, E.T.C., *Myths and Legends of China*, Dover, 1984

Werner, Karel (ed.), *Symbols in Art & Religion: The Indian & the Comparative Perspectives*, Riverdale Company, 1990

Williams, C.A.S., *Outlines of Chinese Symbolism and Art Motives*, Dover, 1976

Witkower, Rudolf, *Allegory and the Migration of Symbols*, Thames and Hudson Inc., 1977

World's Religions, The, Lion USA, 1994

Yarwood, Doreen, *The Encyclopedia of World Costume*, Random House Value, 1988

Zimmer, Heinrich, *Myths and Symbols in Indian Art and Civilization*, Pantheon Books, 1946

ACKNOWLEDGMENTS

From the author:

I would like to thank the friends and colleagues who answered queries concerning the text. These include Richard Blurton, Heather Elgood, Anat Feinberg, Edward Gibbs, Meher McArthur, and John Okell and Yumiko Yamamoto. Thank you to Alison Cole, the Western Art adviser, for her many valuable comments. I owe a great debt of gratitude to those at DK: Anna Kruger, Peter Bailey, the team of Sarah Ponder, Emma Foa, Martin Wilson, Shirin Patel, Joanna Pocock, and Ali Cobb, who all worked tirelessly on this book. An especial thank you to Sarah for her calm and assured handling of the design – and her smile, and to Emma, Editor

Extraordinary, for her expertise, good advice, and good humor. Thanks also to Harriet Griffey, and to my friends at Tolli's for all their encouragement; and lastly to Robert, Jessica, and Jonathan, for their uncomplaining support through every crisis. I dedicate this book to them.

The publishers would like to thank:
Laraine Newberry, our Australian consultant; Julian Perry and John Hamill for all their help regarding Freemasonry; Hugh Myers for the loan of his precious chess set; Bentley & Co., the Bond Street Jewellers, for their advice and use of their many transparencies; Past Times for access to their historical gift collection; and Spink and Son Ltd. for all their assistance.
Special thanks to: Sue Unstead, for her continuing support and encouragement.
Additional design, editorial, and picture research: Caroline Brooke, Louise Cox, Sarah Crouch, Robert

Graham, Anderley Moore, Fergus Muir, Caroline Potts.
Specially commissioned photography: Andy Crawford, Steve Gorton, Ellen Howden at the Glasgow Museum, and Geoff Thompson at the Manchester Museum.
Specially commissioned illustrations: Peter Bull, Nick Hall, Colette Ho, Malcolm McGregor, Peter Visscher, John Woodcock.
Additional photography: Max Alexander, Peter Anderson, Geoff Brightling, Jane Burton, Peter Chadwick, Tim Daly, Geoff Dann, Philip Dowell, Andreas von Einsiedel, Neil Fletcher, Lynton Gardiner, David Garner, Philip Gatwood, Paul Goff, Christi Graham, Frank Greenaway, Peter Hayman, Stephen Hayward, John Heseltine, Alan Hills, Chas Howson, Colin Keates, Dave King, Cyril Laubscher, Richard Leeney, Liz McAulay, Andrew McRobb, Kevin Mallet, Diana Miller, Ray Moller, Nick Nicholas, Martin Norris, Stephen Oliver, Gary Ombler, Roger Philips, Martin Ploner, Laurence Pordes, Kim Sayer, Karl Shone, Steve Shott, David Spence, James Stevenson, Clive Streeter, Harry Taylor, Matthew Ward, Kate Warren, Jerry Young, Michel Zabé.
Additional illustration: Christian Hook, Danuta Mayer.

The publishers would like to thank the following for their kind permission to reproduce the photographs:

l=left, r=right, c=center, t=top, b=bottom, a=above, cb=center below, cfr=center far right, cfl=center far left, clb=center left below, crb=center right below, bcl=bottom center left, bcr=bottom center right, bfl=bottom far left, bfr=bottom far right, tfl=top far left, tfr=top far right.

AKG 17tl, 19tl, 34-35, 53cr, 81tr, 94br; /Erich Lessing 15cra, bl, 19cb, 38bl, bc, 89cr, 91cr; Staatliche Antikensammlungen und Glyptothek 54tr; **Reproduced by permission of The American Museum in Britain, Bath** 70bl; **American Museum of Natural History** 63cra, 77cra, cbr, 78br, 86c; **Ancient Art & Architecture/Ronald Sheridan** back jacket, 16tl, 20cr, 96cra; **Heather Angel** 21cla; **The College of Arms** 114tr; **Ashmolean Museum, Oxford** 18tr, 20tr, 25tc, 29tl, 52cr, 103tcl, 105tc; **The Australian Museum/Nature Focus Library** 26br; **Bentley & Co.** 86tl, br, bcr, 87tl, cb, cr, cfr, bla, bl, br; **Bibliothèque Nationale** (01FR 143 fol 198v) 42tr; **Birmingham Museum** 49bl; **BLC** 116bfr; **The Bridgeman Art Library** 8br, 26cr, 27tr, 34ca, 42br; / Archeological Museum, Naples 15cl; Musée des Beaux-Arts, Le Havre 36b; Bibliothèque Nationale, Paris 8b, 16tr, 27bc; Bonhams, London 2tr, 34b, 40cl; Brancacci Chapel, Santa Maria del Carmine, Florence 59br; © Brewster Arts Ltd., New York, *Tuesday*, Leonora Carrington 9cr; British Library 24c, 34l, 46c, 75bl, 98-99, 113br; Schloss Charlottenburg, Berlin 89cfr; Christies, London 29bc; Musée Cluny, Paris 3b, 28cl; De Morgan Foundation, London 78c, bc; © Fondation P. Delvaux-St. Idesbald, Belgium/DACS 1996, *The Temple 1949*, Paul Delvaux 6-7; Ferens Art Gallery, Hull 29cr; Giraudon 43tr /Musée des Beaux-Arts, Nantes 8t; / Musée Condé, Chantilly 103tl; /Musée Municipal, Laon, France 81tl; Index/Museo Diocesano de Solsona, Lerida 44cl; Kremlin Museum, Moscow 89trb; Museum of Mankind 26bc, 40br; National Gallery, London 73bl; Oriental Museum, Durham University 58c; Österriches Gallery, Vienna 119cr; Prado, Madrid 10tl, 42bl, cl, Preweat Neate Fine Art Auctioneers, Newbury 45crb; Reims Cathedral 51c, St. Peters, Leuven 49cr; Santa Maria delle Grazie, Milan 103tr; Scrovegni (Arena) Chapel, Padua 107tfl; Tate Gallery 50br, 106bl/©ADAGP, Paris and DACS, London 1996, *The Reckless Sleeper* René Magritte 10b; Galleria degli Uffizi, Florence 48bl; Courtesy of the Board of Trustees of the V & A 29tr, 60bl, 71bc, 82br (detail), 89tl; Walker Art Gallery, Liverpool 53t; Wallace Collection 96bl; Westminster Abbey, London 88tr; Woburn Abbey (detail) 88cl; **The British Hedgehog Preservation Society** tr; **The British Library, London** 19br, 22c, 31tr, 60tl, 61tl, 62tc (Or Ms. 2748 f. 208b),

21bc (Or 11387 f.10b); **The British Museum, London** 9tl, 14tr, c, bc, cl, cfl, cfr, 15tc, tr, cr, bc, 25cl, 27tl, cl, 39cfl ,41tr, 48tr, 52cla,54br, 55bla, tc, 57br (obj no. 1900.4-7.48), 59bla, 60tr, 61bl, tl, br (obj no.1936.4-11.023), 62cl, tr (obj no. 19102-12-464), 63b, 64-65, 65tr, 66cl, 70cl, 71br, 78cra, cr,79cl, 86bcl, 93tcl, 96cr, 105bc; **Duncan Brown** 28c, 39cr, 75tcl, 93cb, 107br; **J.Allan Cash** 77c, 93crb, 94tr, bl; **Lester Cheeseman** 21bl, 72cl, 73br; **Christie's Images** 32-33, 47tr; **Cinema Bookshop, London** 11br; **Bruce Coleman Ltd.**/Christer Fredriksson 106tl; Carol Hughes 37bc; Luiz Claudio Marigo 36tr; Hans Reinhard 26bc; **Cotton Technology International** 116br; **National Museum of Denmark, Copenhagen** 4clb, 18bl, 30tr, 90cla; **James Davis Photography** 16bc; **C.M.Dixon** 35tr, 74bl, 75tl; **Museum of English Rural Life, University of Reading, Leeds** 90cfr; **ET Archive** 1, 2cl, 20l, 22tr, 31tl, 62bl, 66tr, 71cra, 72bc, 74cl, 81tc, 89tc, 101tr, 103bl; **Mary Evans Picture Library** 4b, 4cra, 9bl, 9tr, 28cfr, 31br, 37c, 45tr, 65br, 72tr, 73tr, 74tl, 75br, 79tr, 80tl, 81cfr, 84bra, 89cl, 90cl, 90bl, 92c, 95tcl, 102bl, 110crb, clb; **Eye Ubiquitous** 43c; /David Cumming 21cr; Frank Leather 27cr; **Exeter Museum** 86cl; **Chris Fairclough Colour Library** 18br, 95bl; **Forest Light/Alan Watson** 95cl; **Werner Forman Archive** 23cb/British Museum, London inside jacket, 4cla, 28tr; Philip Goldman Collection 52bl; Musée National du Bardo, Tunis 63tl; National Museum of Man, Ottawa, Ontario 63clb; Statens Historiska Museum, Stockholm 15br; University of Philadelphia, U.S. 39br; **The Garden Picture Library** 42cb./John Bethell 73cr; Bridgitte Thomas 43clb; **Garrard, London** 39cl; **Glasgow Museums** 4crb, 5cra, 16cla, cb, br, clb, 20br, 21cra, tfr, tc, 22bc, 23tr, 25cfl, cr, tl, 26tfr, tr, tc, 59c, 64bla, 76-77cs,79tc, crb, 81bra, 82tr, cr, 89clb; **Golders Green Old Synagogue** 16cr; **Ronald Grant Archive** 54bl; **Greenjackets Museum, Winchester** 80cfl; **Greenpeace**/Dorreboom 65cra; **Sonia Halliday and Laura Lushington Photographs** 19bc 37crb, 90bc, 106crb; /Barry Searle 16crb; **Robert Harding Picture Library** inside jacket, 14bl, 39c, 73bra; British Library 95cr; Alain Evrard 83tl; Paolo Koch 106ca; Kodak Ltd. 83c; T.J. Larse-Collingen 27bl; Jenny Pate 25bl; John Ross 88bl; J.H.C.Wilson 20c, 104crb; Adam Woolfitt 6tr; **Hodder & Stoughton** 89bc; **Michael Holford** 10tr, 30cl, 72br; **HMSO Crown Copyright** 89bc; **Hulton Getty Picture Collection** 77br, 89crb; **The Hutchison Library**/Sarah Errington 93cl, Goy Coolea 21c; **Ikona**/Galleria Borghese 15cla; **The Image Bank**/Andrea Pistolesi 12-13; Guido Alberto Rossi 36c; F. Reginato 34c; **Images Colour Library** 77tc, 95c; /The Dawes Collection 106cra; /Charles Walker Collection front jacket, 4clb, 5t, 6tl, 7b, 23tc, 28bl, 72cb, 74tr, 79bl,

92tr, 102c, 103clb, br, 107c, 108tl, c, b, 110c, 111cl, 113tr; **Impact Photos** Christopher Bluntzer 25br; Colin Jones 21br; Rachel Morton 84cl; Homer Sykes 83tr; Rajesh Vora 107bl; **Imperial War Museum** 114bc; **Japan Archive** 63tr; **Michael Jenner** 18bc; **The Jewish Museum** 16bl, 17tr, c; **JNTO** 23cb; **Joods Historich Museum, Amsterdam** 17br; **Kobal Collection** 11tr, 73tfr; **Anna Kruger** 18c; **Museum of London** 91br; **Manchester Museum** back jacket, 4cl, 14cfl, cr, bcr, 15clb, 20tc, 28br, 29bl, 31c, 55tr, 56cl, 61cl, 62cr, 75cr, 93cra, 100cl, bc; **Mansell Collection** 47cl, 85br; **Arxiu Mas** 41bl; **Museum of Mankind** 55bl, 66bl; **Miranda Bruce-Mitford** 23cl, bc; **Museum of the Moving Image** 76bl; **NASA** 11tl, 34cr; /JPL 36tl; **National Army Museum** 66c; **The National Gallery, London** 19tc, 30br, bl, 57tl, cb; **National Maritime Museum, London** 2crb, 29br, 59bc, 72bl, cr; **National Museum of Scotland** 31tc, 93tr; **National Trust Photographic Library**/Nick Meers 43tl; **National Trust for Scotland**/Harvey Wood 48br; **Natural History Museum, London** 38br, 39tl, tr, bl, 40tl, bcl, 40bcr, c, cr, 55cr, 56cr, 79cra; **Past Times, Witney, Oxfordshire** 43cla, 79cr; **Peter Newark's Western Americana** 61tr, 76tr; **Photostage**/Donald Cooper 77tl; **Pictor** 76c; **Pitt Rivers Museum** back jacket, 18cl, 41tcr, 47tcl, 54cr, 58tr, 62br, cla, crb, 70tr, 75tr, 77cb, 78tr, 86tr, 86cr, clb, 87cl, 91tl, tr; **Sarah Ponder** 93 tfl, bc; **Powell Cotton Museum** 23c, br, 70cra, 80cl; **Retna Pictures**/A&M Records 11bl; **Rex Features Ltd** 76bc, 80tr; /Tim Rooke 85bl; Simmons 106tr; **Royal Mail** 65cl; **Peter Sanders** 24bc; **Scala** 19bl, 105bl; **Sir John Soane's Museum** 46tr; **Sotheby's, London** 21tcl, 22br, 24tr, bl, 25tr, 37tl; **Spink & Son Ltd.** 30c, 37cra, 107clb, 115tc; **Frank Spooner Pictures**/Jane Taylor 91c; **Sporting Pictures (U.K.) Ltd.** 39tc, 119cl; **Statens Historiska Museum** 28cr, 93tc; **Tony Stone**/Christopher Arnesen 68-69; Kevin Miller 26br; Tate Gallery 51br; **Thames & Hudson Ltd**/Jeff Teasdale (from *Tantra* by Philip Rawson) 74cr; / John Webb 104cl, tl, bc, bl; **Trip**/H. Rogers 20bc, 21clb; **United Grand Lodge of England** 35tl, 109tr, tc, cr, bl; **US Postal Service** 70crb, bca; **V & A Museum, London** 56br; **The Vegetarian Society** 107bc; **The Wallace Collection, London** 63c, 66tl, tc, 73tl, 114bl; **Rodney Wilson** 35tc; **Westminster Cathedral** 106cb; **Elizabeth Whiting Associates** 95bcl; **Robin Wigington, Arbour Antiques** 91tfl, bc; **Wimbledon Buddhist Temple** 23tl; **International Wool Secretariat** 116bra; **Michel Zabé** 66cb; **Zefa Pictures Ltd.** 95tr; /Taner 24cr.

Every effort has been made to trace the copyright holders. DK apologizes for any unintentional omissions and would be pleased, in such cases, to add an acknowledgment in future editions.